D1535455

THEY ALSO SPOKE

An Essay on Negro Literature in America, 1787–1930

THEY ALSO SPOKE:

An Essay on Negro Literature in America, 1787-1930

by

<u>Kenny J. Williams</u>

Chicago, Illinois

TOWNSEND PRESS

Nashville, Tennessee

Acknowledgments

For permission to quote copyrighted materials, the author is indeed grateful.

"O Black and Unknown Bards" and excerpts from *"Fifty Years"* from SAINT PETER RELATES AN INCIDENT by James Weldon Johnson. Copyright 1917 by James Weldon Johnson. All rights reserved.
Reprinted by permission of The Viking Press, Inc.

From the SELECTED POEMS OF CLAUDE McKAY by permission of Twayne Publishers, Inc.

The poems of Paul Laurence Dunbar reprinted by permission of DODD, MEAD, & COMPANY, INC. from THE COMPLETE POEMS OF PAUL LAURENCE DUNBAR

"The Lynching of Jude Benson" reprinted by permission of DODD, MEAD, & COMPANY, INC. from THE BEST STORIES OF PAUL LAURENCE DUNBAR, edited by Benjamin Brawley

"The Negro Speaks of Rivers" copyright 1926 and renewed 1954 by Langston Hughes. Reprinted from SELECTED POEMS, by Langston Hughes, by permission of Alfred A. Knopf, Inc.

First Printing 1970

Townsend Press
Nashville, Tennessee

Library of Congress Catalog Card Number: 78-125314

Printed in the United States of America

Dedication

For the two people . . .

Who first told me the story of the Africans who started the long journey to America in the slave ships, a journey which frequently ended in despair and death . . .

Who helped me understand the significance of the bondsmen who sang at dusk "Nobody Knows De Trouble I've Seen" in front on weather-beaten cabins . . .

Who emphasized the heritage which the freedmen—while groping for life in this their country—bequeathed to me and to future generations . . .

Who have demonstrated by their own lives the need for a commitment to the responsibilities of human existence and for the necessity of believing in the goodness of life . . .

Who through their singular devotion to the past of their ancestors have been able to cope with the present and look toward the future . . .

Who through their love and faith have taught me the meaning of love and faith . . .

For these two people, my mother and father,

MAUDE THELMA AND JOSEPH HARRISON JACKSON

They Also Spoke is dedicated.

Table of Contents

Preface

ONE OF THE serious problems facing twentieth-century scholarship is the determination of the significance of the past. In an attempt to make all of life "relevant" the study of literature in America has often ignored the literary movements of a past age and has concentrated its attention on the efforts of the present. This is especially true of the study of Negro literature in America which has suddenly—for the most part—dismissed the writers of the eighteenth and nineteenth centuries because they did not subscribe to the currently-held doctrines of the mid-years of the twentieth century.

They Also Spoke is an attempt to re-tell the story of Negro literature in America by focusing on some of the dominant motifs of our national literature. For obvious reasons every Negro writer who ever lived is not included nor are there complete analyses of the work of those who are. This book purports to be nothing more than an "essay in American literature." The writers who are included are representative of trends and motifs present in a segment of American literature. After all, Negro literature is really American literature—nothing more nor nothing less. The faults of it are inherent in our national literature. To continue to look at Negro literature as a separate phenomenon is to miss the totality of American literature itself, a literature which necessarily is a result of the multitude of national and racial strains which constitute the nation.

This does not mean that the Negro experience in the United States has been—or is—the same as that of other groups. Nor does it mean to suggest that our literature has been unaffected by our peculiar status in America. But these differences and peculiarities must ultimately be considered as a part of American literature rather than as a separate literature with its own rationale. Thus to view nineteenth-century American literature means to include both the spiritual and the slave narrative, two distinct forms which were created by Negroes to give voice to their experiences in America. A study of American literature which omits these two forms excludes the two purely "American" literary techniques devised in this country. The other genres used were types used in other places and were not indicative of the creative powers of the writers themselves. From a pragmatic view these forms are no less valid than the novels of Cooper or the short stories of Irving or Poe or the poetry of Bryant. Neither are the spirituals and slave narratives any less a result of the American experience than the works of the giants of the American Renaissance: Emerson, Thoreau, Hawthorne, Melville, and Whitman. The anonymous writer of "Nobody Knows De Trouble I've Seen" was giving poetic voice to his life in American democracy just as much as Whitman who chanted, "I celebrate myself, and sing myself/ And what I assume you shall assume/ For every atom belonging to me as good belongs to you." The various writers of the slave narratives, and there were a host of them, fulfilled much the same desire for adventure stories which had been initiated on a popular level by Cooper in the early years of the nineteenth century.

There has been a circulated myth—perhaps more current today than ever—that there is (or ought to be) a single theme in the works of Negro Americans. In part this is true. The desire for freedom does comprise an oft-repeated theme, but it is not the only one. No single writer can speak for the total Negro experience in America, and no one work can synthesize all of the operative forces which affect the creative artist. The most that any writer can do is to give form at a specific moment to his own singular reactions to a multiplicity of influences. And sometimes by so doing he captures the mood of a people. But this is not necessarily his goal. A Phillis Wheatley can survive as a neoclassicist because at her given moment in American culture neoclassicism was more than a literary theory it was a way of life. And she became—as is true of the writer—merely a product of her environment. She is condemned by some critics today because she did not openly advocate an overthrow of slavery; yet with the restraint of the neoclassicist she too wrote of liberty. To assume that she should have done more is to imply that she should have had greater insights than the neoclassical poets who were her contemporaries. She lived in an age when the funeral elegy and similar other poetic efforts were the vogue. These she wrote with dispatch and with skill.

A study of Negro literature, if it is to be separated from American literature, ought to be a study of the types of diversity which have existed and which exist today in Negro life. To contend that there is a single reaction is to ignore those other forces which at certain points in history have been significant. From the eighteenth century when Negro writers began to react to the American experience to the Harlem Renaissance of the 1920's a variety of patterns are discernible. In each instance these patterns were guides or complements to the existing mood of American literature. By the end of the nineteenth century it became apparent that the Negro writer was expected to be *different;* hence, there occurred "the masking" of the writer which was in direct response to prevailing conditions of American society. By the opening years of the twentieth century American fiction was beginning to assume a great social thrust, and the novels of economic and social protest fit very well into the dominant mood of the Negro novelist who wished to react to the virulent anti-Negro attacks of these years. By the time of the Harlem Renaissance American literature was emphasizing the primitive and the exotic, and there was the "rediscovery" of the Negro segment of the population. But perhaps more important, the Renaissance was able to draw together the various strands which had been part of its literary heritage and out of this weave a cultural declaration of independence which was partially a restatement of the affirmation of faith to which Negroes had subscribed since the beginning of their years in America. *They Also Spoke* ends with the years of the Renaissance not because of a lack of significant literary events since that time but because this is simply a partial story of a people at one time in one place.

There are those among us now who insist that Negro literature belongs to some other national literature. For them the past has no meaning. They would silence the voices of those men and women of the eighteenth and nineteenth centuries who created and wrote out of the belief that they too were Americans. They would scoff at a Jupiter Hammon or a Lucy Terry, eighteenth-century slave poets. They sneer at what is now called the "other-worldliness" of the spirituals without always realizing that these are also great songs of freedom. They decry the role of the church without considering that in one of the blackest hours of human history it was the church which sustained a people. They scorn those writers who came to look upon America as their country, a country which though imperfect was their home. And they would reject the creations of these writers who collectively form meaningful chapters in American literature. Perhaps our knowledge of American literature will become more perceptive when we realize that there have been other voices in the land, voices which have not been stilled. As the men and women of the eighteenth and nineteenth centuries reacted to the American experience, their reactions have become a part of America's total literary heritage. To attempt to silence them is to deny that *they also spoke*.

Chicago, Illinois
November, 1969

THEY ALSO SPOKE

An Essay on Negro Literature in America, 1787–1930

CHAPTER I

A New Home in a New Land

WHEN TWENTY NEGROES were landed on the shores of Virginia in 1619, no one was especially concerned about their cultural heritage—least of all the shipmaster who saw in his human cargo only the possibility of great riches. The fact that some of these people had been tradesmen and farmers, artists and artisans, was not completely lost on those who made the first bids for slave labor; however, there was little general interest in these people aside from their potentials as laborers. No one particularly cared to be reminded that these Negroes were the spiritual descendants of a mighty race, a race which had created the highly developed civilizations of Egypt, Ethiopia, and Ghana as well as the lesser known states of Songhay and Hausa. Neither was there undue interest in the progress of Negro slavery in Europe and in South America. Even a casual perusal of the course of slavery in these two regions might have served as an immediate deterrent to the American colonies. Those who saw the Negro as a slave in the New World were completely oblivious to the fact that Negro explorers had accompanied the Spanish and French adventurers in their quests for land and riches in North America. These Negro explorers had been among the trailblazers of the very land which was to enslave them. But in 1619 (as in the remainder of the seventeenth century) there was not a great deal of curiosity concerning these black men. And so began the history of Negro servitude in the territory which was to become the United States of America.

By 1807, the year in which the law abolishing the slave trade was passed, more than a million Africans had been herded into the slave ships which were bound for the New World. These captive passengers were a highly heterogeneous group. In Africa they had followed different avocations and trades and had occupied different positions in society although the slave traders tried to bargain for the "very best" of any community. Within their states and tribes some were of royal birth, some were warriors, some were the official poets and musicians, and some were the reprobates of the group. Yet the chains which physically bound them on the long sea voyage did much to eradicate the differences between them. By the time this profitable human cargo landed in the New World, stunned and bewildered by the strangeness of their surroundings, the traders were able to make much of their apparently uniform docility. But the traders forgot—indeed if they had ever remembered—that many of these people were physically incapable of withstanding the expected hard labor; and, perhaps more important, they were psychologically incapable of being bound in slavery forever.

Two fallacies have hindered the study of Negro literature of the United States. One is based upon the assumption that liberty, freedom, and leisure are necessary before any cultural progress can be made. The second asserts that with the exception of Phillis Wheatley (and possibly Jupiter Hammon) the literary production of Negroes in America prior to the end of the nineteenth century was minimal. This has resulted in the tendency to regard the literature of American Negroes as more or less sporadic efforts which do not have a direct relationship to the national literature; yet, the patterns of Negro literature closely parallel those of American literature in general. In the beginning colonial writers were concerned with religious and philosophical works at the same time there were some attempts made to record their history in the new land. Soon there followed various imitations of existing European models. In the years preceding the Revolutionary War the colonial writers busied themselves with the analysis of the problems of political and civil liberty, and finally there was the search for new forms which would best portray the new country. Throughout all of these stages there was also the search for identity. The history of Negro literature in the United States shows a similar development. Religious, philosophical, and historical works preceded imitative writings. There then followed a large body of writing devoted not only to civil liberty but also to freedom for all. Out of the slave experience there did develop two new literary forms, the spiritual and the slave narrative, the only distinctively different forms produced in America. As seen in their American counterparts, Negro writers have also concerned themselves with the search for identity.

The history of the development of colonial writing in this country during the seventeenth and eighteenth centuries certainly attests to the fact that extensive writing can take place in the absence of either liberty or freedom or leisure. Furthermore, many classics of world literature have been produced under adverse circumstances thereby denying the need of any absolute prerequisite for creativity, but perhaps no group overcame more obstacles than Negroes in America. From the landing of that first band of twenty slaves in 1619 to the Emancipation Proclamation of 1863 most of them were enslaved. Not only did the enforced servitude severely handicap any artistic production which might have been forthcoming but also the cultural background of the African heritage was not similar to that in America. In addition to the general differences between the African and American environments, the first kidnapped immigrants were faced with a distinctly different language and an entirely new set of social customs. Yet, in spite of these barriers, a considerable body of literature was written before the end of the Civil War in 1865. And this literature was initially produced not by the use of their native languages as a means of communication but in an alien land with strange customs, through the medium of a foreign language, and with the serious disadvantage of slavery as their way of life. When one considers the types of writing produced in colonial America and the advent of a national literature after the Revolutionary War and when one considers the paucity of *belles-lettres* in America at this time, then one can see that the slaves were faced with a formidable task.

During the seventeenth century Negroes were brought into the country in relatively small numbers. Customarily it was the practice to separate not only kinsmen but also those who could communicate with each other. This meant that the slaves were faced with masters with whom they could not talk as well as with fellow countrymen from different states and tribes. The inability to communicate successfully led to complete bewilderment which in turn created a certain degree of lethargy or docility. At the same time many of the slaves entertained vague hopes of "returning home." The oral tradition of literature, so prevalent in Africa at this time, was not particularly suited to the American experience; however, there are still extant some folk tales which may well have been produced during the seventeenth century.

With the beginning of the eighteenth century there were increases in the slave traffic and in slave trading. Bewilderment on the part of the slaves gave way to a resolve to adjust to the new environment because it became increasingly clear that the journey home was in the far distant future if such a trip were to be possible at all. Snatched from their homes, they were forced to make a home in an environment which was essentially hostile. Aiding in this period of adjustment was the early presentation of Christianity to them. If the slaves were to benefit from the sermons and if they were to understand the Bible, then it was necessary for them to know the English language. Consequently, very early religion and education became the tools by which the ultimate salvation of the slaves was to be achieved, for one of the first justifications of slavery was reported as its being a means to give the Negro an opportunity to receive the means of salvation. Ministers, masters, and missionaries frequently combined the teaching of Christian principles as they interpreted them with instruction in the basic forms of written and spoken English.

Soon there were developments which were to mark the beginning of a strongly religiously oriented people. At first Anglican missionaries worked with the Negroes of the South, and Puritan missionaries worked with them in New England. One of the first attempts at an independent religious organization was aided by Cotton Mather in 1693. Shortly thereafter Samuel Sewall sounded the note, at least in New England, for abolition in the first anti-slavery tract *The Selling of Joseph* (1700). Both Mather and Sewall, staunch Puritans, recognized the incompatibility of the Christian doctrines with human slavery.

With the prominence of the Great Awakening in the opening years of the eighteenth century and with its emphasis upon the evangelical message of Christianity, the Methodist and Baptist churches soon became popular and were the first to have all Negro congregations. For example, Baptist churches were organized in South Carolina at Silver Bluff and in Virginia at Petersburg and at Williamsburg during the 1770's, and the First Baptist Church in Savannah, Georgia, was established in 1788. While major Negro congregations were being formed in the South, a great deal of Methodist activity was taking place in the North, especially in Philadelphia. It was here that Richard Allen and Absalom Jones convinced the Negro membership of St. George's Methodist Episcopal Church to form the Free African Society. In time there was an amiable parting between Allen and Jones as the Free African Society split with Jones becoming the first rector of the Episcopalian group and with Allen as the founder and organizer of Bethel Church, the Methodist segment. While he was not primarily concerned with a religious organization, Prince Hall made a significant contribution to social organizations when he obtained a charter from England and set up the first Negro lodge of Masons in 1787.

The church assumed the role of ministering not only to religious needs but also to social and educational needs as well. Through the church, and augmented by the lodge, there was the development of a new culture which appealed to Negroes both in the North and in the South. Once these organizations took root, it was impossible to halt their influence, and one can not ignore their great effect on the progress which was made by Negroes during this period. Consequently, by the beginning of the nineteenth century many churches had been organized by free Negroes in both the North and in the South (which resulted in an increase of Negro preachers and teachers), and on many plantations the slaves were permitted to hold regular services with their own preachers. Thus, the church served not only as a means of conversion and as an educational institution but also as the primary—if not only—social outlet.

In addition to the emphasis upon religion and education, the ideas of the eighteenth century benefited Negroes in still another way and aided in the assimilation of new cultural concepts. This was the period which included the American Revolution. As the Declaration of Independence with its assertion of "life, liberty, and the pursuit of happiness" proclaimed the doctrines of equality, men such as Jefferson were forced to consider the incongruity of the idealistic doctrine upon which the American nation was to be built with the very realistic fact of the existence of the institution of human slavery. Some slaveholders, either because of idealism or because of the unprofitable nature of slaveholding, freed their slaves and gave them a start in the world. Other slaves gained their freedom after their partipation in the Revolutionary War.

While these seventeenth- and eighteenth-century beginnings may seem meager at best and while the great majority of Negroes lived a primitive existence on the plantation with only the merest rudiments of education, by the end of the eighteenth century there were Negroes who were not only free but also productive. Though they represented a minority, to be sure, they laid the foundation for the cultural contributions of the next century. When one considers the initial language barrier, the phenomenon is not that there was a literature being produced by Negroes but that they should have written at all. It is further significant that the man who is considered to be the first Negro poet in America, Jupiter Hammon, was writing at the same time as were Timothy Dwight, John Trumbull, and Joel Barlow, three of the more important Hartford Wits, who consciously attempted after the Revolutionary

War to create a native American literature. It is also an interesting coincidence of history that Hammon published some of his work in Hartford when that city was thought of as the literary capital of the United States in part because of the work of the Hartford Wits. Consequently, the span of American literature, that literature which was produced after the United States became an independent nation, covers the same period as a native Negro literature in the country.

I

Jupiter Hammon was born about 1720 and lived through the years of the development of the Negro church, through the period of the idealism of the American Revolution, and on until the establishment of the United States as a nation dedicated to the principles of equality and liberty. He probably died in 1806. His first publication was a poem of eighty-eight lines entitled "An Evening Thought; Salvation by Christ, With Penitential Cries." The title page carries his name and asserts that he is a slave "belonging to Mr. Lloyd, of Queen's Village, on Long Island," and the poem is dated December 25, 1760. As the title pages of his publications indicate, Hammon belonged to three different members of the Lloyd family of Long Island. During the Revolutionary War when the British were occupying Long Island, the Lloyds and their slaves lived in Hartford, Connecticut. After the War Hammon probably returned with the Lloyds to their estate on Long Island. Apparently the Lloyds were considerate masters who allowed Hammon a great deal of freedom of movement, for he wrote in *An Address to the Negroes in the State of New York* in 1787: "I have good reason to be thankful that my lot is so much better than most slaves have had. I suppose I have had more advantages than most of you who are slaves have ever known, and I believe more than many white people have enjoyed (p. 6)." Among the advantages to which he referred was the granting of the opportunity, elementary though the results might have been, to receive instruction in reading and writing and to attend church freely, where he probably absorbed the doctrines of Calvinism which are an integral part of his poetry.

Stimulated by his religion, Hammon read not only the Bible and the hymn books of his day but also such pious poems as Wigglesworth's then popular *The Day of Doom*. In fact Hammon's "A Poem for Children with Thoughts on Death" seems to paraphrase that section of Wigglesworth's poem which describes the fate of children who die in infancy without the benefits of church membership. Hammon's knowledge of both prose and poetic style was probably greatly influenced by his reading. Although it is difficult to determine the extent of Hammon's popularity in his own day, there was a considerable market in America for didactic poetry. Hammon himself said in his *An Address to the Negroes in the State of New York:* "When I was at Hartford, in Connecticut, where I lived during the War, I published several pieces which were well received, not only by those of my own colour, but by a number of white people, who thought they might do good among the servants (p. 4)."

Although most of his poetry was published at Hartford at a time when the Hartford Wits were attempting to aid in the creation of a national literature, there is a great deal of difference between any of their works and the existing poems by Hammon. His poetry was not hampered by the rules of neoclassicism as was the work of the Hartford Wits, neither was his poetry pallid imitations of current English modes. Rather, his poetry is closer in spirit and technique to the poetry of the earlier century of New England, the poetry produced by the New England Puritans of the seventeenth century. Much of this poetry is buried in the annals of New England, but there does exist a tremendous body of it which grew out of the religious fervor of the period. There is in Hammon's poetry a religious feeling which resulted in an intensity which he apparently achieved without conscious effort. From hearing evangelical sermons and from reading the Bible according to his own interpretations, he adapted his ideas regarding salvation, penitence, redeeming grace, God's mercy, death, and judgment

day to his poems. He recorded his ideas and impressions in a
poetic meter which is designed to be heard. A word which appealed
to him is repeated until the very word itself seems to cast a spell.
In "An Evening Thought . . ." the word *salvation* appears so often
that the sound of the word becomes far more important than the
message of the poem.

> Salvation comes by Christ alone,
> The only Son of God;
> Redemption now to everyone,
> That love his holy Word.
> Dear Jesus we would fly to Thee,
> And leave off every Sin,
> Thy tender Mercy well agree;
> Salvation from our King;
> Salvation comes now from the Lord,
> Our Victorious King.
> His holy name be well ador'd,
> Salvation surely bring.
> Dear Jesus give thy Spirit now,
> Thy Grace to every Nation,
> That han't the Lord to whom we bow,
> The Author of Salvation.
> Dear Jesus unto Thee we cry,
> Give us the Preparation;
> Turn not away thy tender Eye;
> We see thy true Salvation.
> Salvation comes from God we know,
> The true and only One;
> It's well agreed and certain true,
> He gave his only Son.
> Lord hear our penitential Cry:
> Salvation from above;
> It is the Lord that doth supply,
> With his redeeming Love.
> Dear Jesus by thy precious Blood,
> The World Redemption have:

Salvation now comes from the Lord,
He being thy captive.
Dear Jesus let the Nations cry,
And all the People say,
Salvation comes from Christ on high,
Haste on Tribunal Day.
We cry as Sinners to the Lord,
Salvation to obtain;
It is firmly fixt his holy Word,
Ye shall not cry in vain.
Dear Jesus unto Thee we cry,
And make our Lamentation:
O let our Prayers ascend on High;
We felt thy Salvation.
Lord turn our dark benighted Souls;
Give us a true Motion,
And let the Hearts of all the World,
Make Christ their Salvation.
Ten Thousand Angels cry to Thee,
Yea louder than the Ocean.
Thou are the Lord, we plainly see;
Thou art the true Salvation.
Now is the Day, excepted Time;
The Day of Salvation;
Increase your Faith, do not repine:
Awake ye every Nation.
Lord unto whom now shall we go,
Or see a safe Abode;
Thou hast the Word Salvation too
The only Son of God.
Ho! everyone that hunger hath,
Or pinest after me,
Salvation be thy leading Staff,
To set the Sinner free.
Dear Jesus unto Thee we fly;
Depart, depart from Sin,
Salvation doth at length supply,
The Glory of our King.

Come ye Blessed of the Lord,
Salvation greatly given;
O turn your Hearts, accept the Word,
Your souls are fit for Heaven.
Dear Jesus we now turn to Thee,—
Salvation to obtain;
Our Hearts and Souls do meet again,
To magnify thy Name.
Come holy Spirit, Heavenly Dove,
The Object of our Care;
Salvation doth increase our Love;
Our hearts hath felt thy fear.
Now Glory be to God on High,
Salvation high and low;
And thus the Soul on Christ rely,
To Heaven surely go.
Come Blessed Jesus, Heavenly Dove,
Accept Repentance here;
Salvation give, with tender Love;
Let us with Angels share.   Finis.

Originally the poem was printed without a break between any of the lines; however, Hammon used a variation of the ballad stanza, a verse form which is often found in Methodist and in Baptist hymnals and which is the basic pattern of *The Day of Doom.* This pattern consists of quatrains whose first and third lines are iambic tetrameter and whose second and fourth lines are iambic trimeter; the four-line stanza has a usual rhyme scheme of abcd. Although Hammon followed this pattern in most of his poems, there are instances of irregularities which can be seen in "An Evening Thought. . . ." In addition to his adaptation of the ballad rhyme pattern to abab, there are examples of distorted accents as well as of syncopation which occur most frequently in the iambic trimeter lines. To the twentieth-century reader, Hammon's poetry seems similar to so much of eighteenth-century poetry for his work tends to employ unusual rhyming patterns and com-

binations, such as: sin/king, ocean/salvation, abode/God, given/
heaven, obtain/name, care/fear, here/share. When odd uses of
poetic diction occur, they often result because his choice of language is an immediate outgrowth of an apparent need for rhyming
patterns.

"The Kind Master and the Dutiful Servant" was published in
Hartford apparently during the Revolutionary War. It is a dialogue
between a master and his servant on such matters as salvation,
grace, Heaven, and other subjects bordering on religion. Interestingly enough, the two poetic characters do not mention the
inconsistency of the principles of Christianity with the belief in
human slavery. Throughout the entire dialogue the two participants manage to keep the affairs of earth and heaven separate.
The poem's concluding ideas seem to justify the poet's own belief
that both slaveholder and slave can be practicing Christians and
both can be considered the children of God. The poem appeared
at the end of a sermon by Hammon entitled *An Evening's Improvement* which was issued as a pamphlet, and it was an attempt to
summarize the essential meaning of the sermon.

It is apparent that most of Hammon's religious poetry is characterized by a certain naivete, and his art of versification seems
little more than spontaneously rhymed doggerel; but this is the
same charge which is frequently hurled at Michael Wigglesworth
who also used poetry as a means of instruction and as a means of
simply stating basic religious concepts. The difference between
these two poets, however, rests in the difference between the complexity of the religious dogma of Puritanism which is explained by
Wigglesworth and the simplicity of the more primitive forms of
Protestantism. In the eighteenth century complexity of dogma and
creed was not a characteristic of the Methodist and Baptist movements which appealed to those who wanted their religion unen-
cumbered by the perplexity of an involved or a complicated
philosophical system. These more primitive groups stressed "religion by faith" as opposed to the Puritan emphasis on "religion by
reason." Wigglesworth—for example—in attempting to simplify

Puritanism made its doctrines appear harsh and terrible when he placed them into ballad form; while Hammon, on the other hand, in attempting to capture the tone of primitive Christianity, seems extremely childlike in his wonder and in his awe.

In "A Poem for Children With Thoughts of Death" Hammon visualizes the horrors of judgment day very much as Wigglesworth had done in *The Day of Doom*. While he includes words of warning to sinful children, Hammon approaches his subject with a lightness of feeling, unlike the tone of *The Day of Doom,* which pervades the poem. The last line of the following two quatrains illustrates Hammon's technique for making an unpleasant subject at least palatable.

> Then shall ye hear the trumpet sound,
>   The graves give up their dead,
> Those blessed saints shall quick awake,
>   And leave their dusty beds.

> Then shall ye hear the trumpet sound,
>   And rend the native sky,
> Those bodies starting from the ground,
>   In the twinkling of an eye.

One of Hammon's more polished poems was addressed to Phillis Wheatley in 1778. Five years before this poem Wheatley had written "On Being Brought From Africa to America," in which she claims that "mercy" had brought her to this country and had introduced her to the redemptive powers of Christianity. Hammon repeats the same motif by asserting:

> God's tender mercy brought thee here;
>   Tost o'er the raging main;
> In Christian faith thou hast a share,
>   Worth all of the gold in Spain.

Hammon concludes his poem by praising divine providence for bringing Phillis Wheatley from Africa to a place where she could not only know the true religion but also instruct others in its beneficent ways.

Hammon's two sermons appeared as pamphlets. *A Winter Piece* was published in Hartford in 1782 and *An Evening's Improvement* is an undated Hartford publication. Both works illustrate rather erratic organization and structure. In each one, however, he did include a poem. "A Poem for Children With Thoughts On Death" appeared in the former sermon, and "The Kind Master and the Dutiful Servant" appeared in the latter. Both sermons include admonitions to the unconverted to accept the ways of Christianity, and both praise the practicing Christian. Hammon completely minimizes the present in favor of a future where all shall receive their "just rewards" for life on earth.

Of all of Hammon's known prose compositions "An Address to the Negroes in the State of New York" demonstrates greater coherence. It begins with a series of autobiographical details which are important for they have furnished most of the known information about the poet. This information is followed by a veritable list of "do's and don't's" addressed to his race. He advocates faithfulness, honesty, diligence, and obedience to both earthly masters and to God. He chastises those who would be disloyal, dishonest, and disobedient. And he concludes the work with a discussion on liberty and freedom which, to him, were ideals which he did not associate with earthly life. He then dismisses slavery in a passage which has become famous or infamous (depending upon the interpreter):

Now I acknowledge that liberty is a great thing, and worth seeking for, if we can get it honestly; and by our good conduct prevail on our masters to set us free: though for my own part I do not wish to be free; for many of us who are grown up slaves, and have always had masters to take care of us, should hardly know how to take care of themselves; and it may be for our own comfort to remain as we are (p. 9).

Hammon has been condemned because of his acceptance of the

institution of slavery; yet, it must be remembered that he was in no position to understand it in its fullest impact. With his limited experiences in Long Island and in Hartford and with his own lot being much better than that of the average workingman of the period, it is no wonder that he tended to place all of his attention on matters of religion. While his poems are far superior to his prose works, his poetry is, after all, eighteenth-century religious poetry and does not differ too greatly from other such works of the period. His infrequent references to slavery and to his race are the only distinguishing marks of his work. The chaos of the rhythmic structure and the distortions of rhyme which appear, the sudden bursts of religious fervor, the sometimes strained poetic diction coupled with apparent sincerity are characteristics of religious poetry in America during the seventeenth and eighteenth centuries.

Far more is known about the life of Phillis Wheatley than about that of Jupiter Hammon because, until the twentieth century, she was considered as having been America's first Negro poet and because she was apparently far more prolific than Hammon. Furthermore, she was a considerably popular poet in New England as might be discerned from the extent of critical comment which survives from her own day concerning her work and from the fact that she was a member of the Old South Meeting House in Boston at a time when that church did not extend its membership to slaves. That she was known to the famous men of her day is attested by the fact that in her first published volume of poetry in 1773 there appeared the following notice:

We whose names are underwritten, do assure the World, that the Poems specified in the following [pages], were (as we verily believe) written by Phillis, a young Negro Girl, who was but a few Years since, brought an uncultivated Barbarian from Africa, and has ever since been, and now is, under the Disadvantage of serving as a Slave in a

Family in this Town. She has been examined by some of the best judges, and is thought qualified to write them.

His Excellency Thomas Hutchinson, Governor

The Hon. Andrew Oliver, Lieutenant-Governor

The Hon. Thomas Hubbard	The Rev. Charles Chauncey, D.D.
The Hon. John Erving	The Rev. Mather Byles, D.D.
The Hon. James Pitts	The Rev. Ed. Pemberton, D.D.
The Hon. Harrison Gray	The Rev. Andrew Eliot, D.D.
The Hon. James Bowdoin	The Rev. Samuel Cooper, D.D.
John Hancock, Esq.	The Rev. Mr. Samuel Mather
Joseph Green, Esq.	The Rev. Mr. John Moorhead
Richard Carey, Esq.	Mr. John Wheatley, her master

The purpose of the notice is clearly a testimony to the authenticity of her work; however, from the first appearance of her poetry there really was no great doubt concerning her authorship although people continued to be amazed by her apparent facility with the language.

While her former home is not certain, it has been assumed that she came from Senegal. Phillis Wheatley was brought to America in 1761 when she was seven or eight years of age and purchased by John Wheatley of Boston as a maid for his wife, Susannah, who became extremely fond of the sickly child. She early demonstrated an interest in language which was immediately supported by the Wheatleys who put numerous books at her disposal. Throughout her early years, Mary Wheatley, her owner's daughter, served as her tutor, and Phillis' aptitude for the classics became a point of great discussion in the rather restricted social and intellectual circles of Boston. According to Rufus Griswold in *The Female Poets of America* (New York, 1877), "she became acquainted with grammar, history, ancient and modern geography, and studied Latin so as to read Horace . . . (p. 30)." Benjamin Brawley notes in *The Negro in Literature and Art in the United States* (New York, 1934), that she had "a thoroughly appreciative acquaintance with the most important Latin classics, especially the works of

Virgil and Ovid (p. 18)." Her accomplishments were outstanding for in a day when women were not integral parts of the cultural life of their communities, Phillis Wheatley was a renowned poet and classical scholar.

In 1772 John Wheatley wrote a letter which was affixed to the 1773 volume in which he attempted to explain her development. The letter read in part:

. . . Without any assistance from school education, and by what she was taught in the family, she, in sixteen months' time from her arrival [in 1761], attained the English language, to which she was an utter stranger before, to such a degree, as to read any, the most difficult parts of the Sacred Writings, to the great astonishment of all who heard her.

As to her writing, her own curiosity led her to it; and this she learnt in so short a Time, that in the year 1765, she wrote a letter to the Rev. Mr. Occum, the Indian Minister, while in England.

She has a great inclination to learn the Latin tongue, and has made some progress in it. This relation is given by her master who bought her, and with whom she now lives.

Her first published poem appeared in 1770 and followed the tradition of using a long explanatory title: "AN ELEGAIC POEM, On the DEATH of that celebrated Divine, and eminent Servant of JESUS CHRIST, the late Reverend, and pious GEORGE WHITE-FIELD, Chaplain to the Right Honourable the Countess of Huntington . . . , Who made his Exit from this transitory State, to dwell in the celestial Realms of Bliss, on LORD'S-DAY, 30th of September, 1770, when he was seiz'd with a Fit of the Asthma, at NEWBURYPORT, near BOSTON, in NEW-ENGLAND. In which is a Condolatory Address to His truly noble Benefactress the worthy and pious Lady HUNTINGTON,—and the Orphan-Children in GEORGIA; who, with many Thousands, are left, by the Death of this great man, to Lament the Loss of a Father, Friend, and Benefactor. By PHILLIS, a Servant Girl of 17 Years of Age, Belonging to Mr. J. WHEATLEY, of Boston:—And has

been but 9 Years in this Country from Africa." The following
version of the poem is the one which appeared in her 1773 collection of poems:

ON THE DEATH OF
THE REV. MR. GEORGE WHITEFIELD. *1770*

HAIL, happy saint, on thine immortal throne,
Possest of glory, life, and bliss unknown;
We hear no more the music of thy tongue,
Thy wonted auditories cease to throng.
Thy sermons in unequall'd accents flow'd,
And ev'ry bosom with devotion glow'd;
Thou didst in strains of eloquence refin'd
Inflame the heart, and captivate the mind.
Unhappy we the setting sun deplore,
So glorious once, but ah! it shines no more.

Behold the prophet in his tow'ring flight!
He leaves the earth for heav'n's unmeasur'd height,
And worlds unknown receive him from our sight.
There *Whitefield* wings with rapid course his way,
And sails to *Zion* through vast seas of day.
Thy pray'rs, great saint, and thine incessant cries
Have pierc'd the bosom of thy native skies.
Thou moon hast seen, and all the stars of light,
How he has wrestled with his God by night.
He pray'd that grace in ev'ry heart might dwell,
He long'd to see *America* excel;
He charg'd its youth that ev'ry grace divine
Should with full lustre in their conduct shine;
That Saviour, which his soul did first receive,
The greatest gift that ev'n a God can give,
He freely offer'd to the num'rous throng,
That on his lips with list'ning pleasure hung.

"Take him, ye wretched, for your only good,
"Take him ye starving sinners, for your food;
"Ye thirsty, come to this life-giving stream,

"Ye preachers, take him for your joyful theme;
"Take him my dear *Americans, he said,
"Be your complaints on his kind bosom laid:
"Take him, ye *Africans,* he longs for you,
"*Impartial Saviour* is his title due:
"Wash'd in the fountain of redeeming blood,
"You shall be sons, and kings, and priests to God."

Great Countess, we *Americans* revere
Thy name, and mingle in thy grief sincere;
New England deeply feels, the *Orphans* mourn,
Their more than father will no more return.

But, though arrested by the hand of death,
Whitefield no more exerts his lab'ring breath,
Yet let us view him in th' eternal skies,
Let ev'ry heart to this bright vision rise;
While the tomb safe retains its sacred trust,
Till life divine re-animates his dust.

The poem was immediately popular. Having been published as a broadside in Boston, it was subsequently reprinted in the same form in New York, Philadelphia, Newport, and on four different occasions in Boston. It frequently appeared at the end of the many funeral sermons which were delivered in memory of Whitefield. Not only did Phillis Wheatley extensively revise the poem, but also she published American and English versions of it. It is difficult to determine now whether the popularity of the elegy was due to the popularity of Whitefield, who was an outstanding Methodist evangelist in America and in England or to the fact that Phillis Wheatley was a slave or to her fidelity to the neoclassical principles of Alexander Pope. At any rate, her fame went beyond the confines of New England. When she was sent to England in 1773 for her health, she was feted by the Countess of Huntington to whom she had addressed her first published poem and to whom the 1773 volume of poems was to be dedicated. The poet was lionized by English society, and her brilliance as a conversationalist made her a welcomed addition to any gathering. The grave illness of Mrs. Wheatley cut short her visit as she hurriedly returned to Boston.

While in England Miss Wheatley apparently submitted a group of her poems to a publisher there, and these appeared, in 1773, as *Poems on Various Subjects, Religious and Moral.* The title page identifies the author, Phillis Wheatley, as "Negro Servant to Mr. John Wheatley, of Boston, in New England." The volume contained thirty-nine poems some few of which had appeared in earlier versions. A number of her poems deal with nature but always with the restraint associated with neoclassicism. Both "An Hymn to the Morning" and "An Hymn to the Evening" demonstrates the extent to which she had absorbed the neoclassical approach to the subject of nature. One cannot read these companion poems without at least thinking of "L'Allegro" and "Il Penseroso" by John Milton. Although her two poems do not have the rolling sonorous lines of Milton, she has included some good poetic lines.

AN HYMN TO THE MORNING

ATTEND my lays, ye ever honour'd nine,
Assist my labours, and my strains refine;
In smoothest numbers pour the notes along,
For bright *Aurora* now demands my song.

Aurora hail, and all the thousand dies,
Which deck thy progress through the vaulted skies:
The morn awakes, and wide extends her rays,
On ev'ry leaf the gentle zephyr plays;
Harmonious lays the feather'd race resume,
Dart the bright eye, and shake the painred plume.

Ye shady groves, your verdant gloom display
To shield your poet from the burning day:
Calliope awake the sacred lyre,
While thy fair sisters from the pleasing fire:
The bow'rs, the gales, the variegated skies
In all their Pleasures in my bosom rise.

See in the east th' illustrious king of day!
His rising radiance drives the shades away—
But Oh! I feel his fervid beams too strong,
And scarce begun, concludes th' abortive song.

AN HYMN TO THE EVENING
SOON as the sun forsook the eastern main
The pealing thunder shook the heav'nly plain;
Majestic grandeur! From the zephyr's wing,
Exhales the incense of the blooming spring.
Soft purl the streams, the birds renew their notes,
And through the air their mingled music floats.

Through all the heav'ns what beauteous dies are spread!
But the west glories in the deepest red:
So may our breasts with ev'ry virtue glow,
The living temples of our God below!

Fill'd with the praise of him who gives the light;
And draws the sable curtains of the night,
Let placid slumbers sooth each weary mind,
At mourn to wake more heav'nly, more refin'd;
So shall the labours of the day begin
More pure, more guarded from the snares of sin.

Night's leaden sceptre seals my drousy eyes,
Then cease, my song, till fair *Aurora* rise.

Of the thirty-eight poems in *Poems on Various Subjects, Religious and Moral* fourteen of them are elegies. The fact that more than a third of the poems were occasioned by the death of someone whom the poet knew was in keeping with a New England tradition which emphasized the funeral elegy as a means of consolation for a bereaved family. The annals of Puritan literature are filled with poems of this genre, and Wheatley's are far better examples of this poetic form than are most of the elegies of New England for many of them are simply rhymed doggerel. Among the specific families addressed by Wheatley were some of the elite of the

Boston area. For example, one poem is addressed to the Sewall family on the death of the Rev. Dr. Joseph Sewall who was the pastor of the Old South Meeting House at the time when Phillis Wheatley became a communicant and who was the son of the famous Puritan diarist and jurist, Samuel Sewall. Another is addressed to Thomas Hubbard on the death of his wife. Hubbard, a distinguished citizen of Boston who was associated with Harvard College during most of his public life, was one of the signers of the testimony at the beginning of the 1773 volume. Earlier Wheatley had written an elegy "To A Lady On the Death of Her Husband" which was occasioned by the death of the husband of Hubbard's daughter and which is included in *Poems on Various Subjects, Religious and Moral.* The death of Boston's eminent physician, Dr. Samuel Marshall in 1771, motivated still another funeral poem. The wife of Andrew Oliver, the lieutenant-governor of Massachusetts who signed the notice attesting to the creativity of Phillis, died in 1773 and included among these poems is "To His Honour the Lieutenant-Governor, On the Death of His Lady. March 24, 1773." Of all the elegies, however, none contains such simple dialogue as "A Funeral Poem On the Death of C.E. An Infant of Twelve Months" in spite of the restrictions of the heroic couplet.

> Through airy roads he wings his instant flight
> To purer regions of celestial light;
> Enlarg'd he sees unnumber'd systems roll,
> Beneath him sees the universal whole,
> Planets on planets run their destin'd round,
> And circling wonders fill the vast profound.
> Th' ethereal now, and now th' empyreal skies
> With growing splendors strike his wond'ring eyes:
> The angels view him with delight unknown,
> Press his soft hand, and seat him on his throne;
> Then smiling thus. "To this divine abode,
> "The seat of saints, of seraphs, and of God,
> "Thrice welcome thou." The raptur'd babe replies,

"Thanks to my God, who snatch'd me to the skies,
"E'er vice triumphant had possess'd my heart,
"E'er yet the tempter had beguil'd my heart,
"E'er yet on sin's base actions I was bent,
"E'er yet I knew temptation's dire intent;
"E'er yet the lash for horrid crimes I felt,
"E'er vanity had led my way to guilt,
"But, soon arriv'd at my celestial goal,
"Full glories rush on my expanding soul."
Joyful he spoke: exulting cherubs round
Clapt their glad wings, the heav'nly vaults resound.

Say, parents, why this unavailing moan?
Why heave your pensive bosoms with the groan?
To *Charles,* the happy subject of my song,
A brighter world, and nobler strains belong.
Say would you tear him from the realms above
By thoughtless wishes, and prepost'rous love?
Doth his felicity increase your pain?
Or could you welcome to this world again
The heir of Bliss? with a superior air
Methinks he answers with a smile severe,
"Thrones and dominions cannot tempt me there."
But still you cry, "Can we the sigh forbear,
"And still and still must we not pour the tear?
"Our only hope, more dear than vital breath,
"Twelve moons revolv'd, becomes the prey of death;
"Delightful infant, nightly visions give
"Thee to our arms, and we with joy receive,
"We fain would clasp the *Phantom* to our breast,
"The *Phantom* flies, and leaves the soul unblest."

To yon bright regions let your faith ascend,
Prepare to join your dearest infant friend
In pleasures without measure, without end.

During the Revolutionary War Phillis Wheatley lived in Providence, Rhode Island, where she sent the following letter (dated October 26, 1775) and poem to George Washington:

Sir,

I have taken the freedom to address your Excellency in the enclosed poem, and entreat your acceptance, though I am not insensible of its inaccuracies. Your being appointed by the Grand Continental Congress to be Generalissimo of the armies of North America, together with the fame of your virtues, excite sensations not easy to suppress. Your generosity, therefore, I presume, will pardon the attempt. Wishing your Excellency all possible success in the great cause you are so generously engaged in, I am,

> Your Excellency's most obedient
> humble servant,
> **PHILLIS WHEATLEY**

Celestial choir! enthron'd in realms of light,
    Columbia's scenes of glorious toils I write.
While freedom's cause her anxious breast alarms,
She flashes dreadful in refulgent arms.
See mother earth her offspring's fate bemoan,
And nations gaze at scenes before unknown!
See the bright beams of heaven's revolving light
Involved in sorrows and the veil of night!
    The goddess comes, she moves divinely fair,
Olive and laurel binds her golden hair:
Wherever shines this native of the skies,
Unnumber'd charms and recent graces rise.
    Muse! bow propitious while my pen relates
How pour her armies through a thousand gates,
As when Eolus heaven's fair face deforms,
Enwrapp'd in tempest and a night of storms;
Astonish'd ocean feels the wild uproar,
The refluent surges beat the sounding shore;
Or thick as leaves in Autumn's golden reign,
Such, and so many, moves the warrior's train.
In bright array they seek the work of war,
Where high unfurl'd the ensign waves in air.
Shall I to Washington their praise recite?
Enough thou know'st them in the fields of fight.

Thee, first in peace and honours,—we demand
The grace and glory of thy martial band.
Fam'd for thy valour, for thy virtues more,
Hear every tongue thy guardian aid implore!
One century scarce perform'd its destined round,
When Gallic powers Columbia's fury found;
And so many you, whoever dares disgrace
The land of freedom's heaven-defended race!
Fix'd are the eyes of nations on the scales,
For in their hopes Columbia's arm prevails.
Anon Britannia droops the pensive head,
While round increase the rising hills of dead.
Ah! cruel blindness to Columbia's state!
Lament thy thirst of boundless power too late.
    Proceed, great chief, with virtue on thy side,
Thy ev'ry action let the goddess guide.
A crown, a mansion, and a throne that shine,
With gold unfading, WASHINGTON! be thine.

According to Jared Sparks, the editor of *The Writings of George Washington* (1834), the following letter was sent to Phillis Wheatley in response to her letter and poem:

Miss Phillis,

Your favor of the 26th of October did not reach my hands, till the middle of December. Time enough, you will say, to have given an answer ere now. Granted. But a variety of important occurrences, continually interposing to distract the mind and withdraw the attention, I hope will apologize for the delay, and plead my excuse for the seeming but not real neglect. I thank you most sincerely for your polite notice of me, in the elegant lines you enclosed; and however undeserving I may be of such encomium and panegyric, the style and manner exhibit a striking proof of your poetical talents; in honor of which, and as a tribute justly due to you, I would have published the poem, had I not been apprehensive, that, while I only meant to give the world this new instance of your genius, I might have incurred

the imputation of vanity. This, and nothing else, determined me not
to give it place in the public prints.

If you should ever come to Cambridge, or near headquarters, I shall
be happy to see a person so favored by the Muses, and to whom
nature has been so liberal and beneficent in her dispensations. I am,
with great respect,

Your obedient servant,

GEO. WASHINGTON

Later that same year (1776) Phillis Wheatley did indeed visit
George Washington at his Cambridge headquarters.

While it may be true that Phillis Wheatley's poetry has little or
no interest for the reader who finds eighteenth-century poetry
irrelevant for the twentieth century, her work is characteristic of
her age and ultimately she must be judged on its terms with its
restrictions. Although she used other verse forms at times, she was
extremely faithful to the use of the heroic couplet after the manner
of Alexander Pope, and the faults of Pope became her own. One,
for example, finds little evidence of emotional outpourings; all
such outbursts were sifted through a neoclassical philosophy which
did not permit the poet the luxury of a display of great personal
feeling. Even her many funeral elegies are stilted and sophisticated
which are peculiarities of that form. She seldom explored her own
thoughts, and—as a result—her poetry is quite impersonal even
though her subjects were well known to her. Her letters, however,
demonstrate that she was capable of strong emotion. Unlike Anne
Bradstreet, the early Puritan poet, who used the poetic form to
examine her relationship to life and to her family, Phillis Wheatley
seldom even included a reference to herself. And it is interesting to
note that she did not write elegies after the deaths of Mrs. Wheatley
in 1774, Mr. Wheatley and his daughter (who was Phillis' first
teacher) in 1778. These three were members of the only family
she knew until her marriage to John Peters in 1778. Did she fear
her inability to maintain the neoclassical detachment had she
attempted poems on these three occasions? Her poetry is, of course,

more "religious" than that of the average neoclassicist. There are constant references to divine Providence, mercy, and grace; but the religion of Wheatley—in spite of her interest in Whitefield's Methodism—was strongly conditioned by the Puritanism of Boston and by her membership in the Old South Meeting House. Furthermore, there are echoes of Milton which permeate her work, and this may be an outgrowth of her intense reading of *Paradise Lost*, a copy of which was presented to her in England by Brook Watson who became in later years the Lord Mayor of London.

Much of her poetry appears to have been composed in response to certain events; consequently, the occasional nature of many of her poems tends to date her work as does its poetic form. Yet, once again, when one considers the type of poetry being produced in America in the latter part of the eighteenth century, one can see that her poetry does exemplify some of the best, as well as the worst, features of that period's poetry. And the literary critics from the nineteenth century (such as Rufus Griswold, Clarence Stedman, Charles Richardson, Evert and George Duyckinck) tended to rank her as one of the best of the American poets. Certainly she was able to produce the rhythmic structure of Pope with greater fidelity than Trumbull, Dwight, and Barlow (the Hartford Wits) who also relied heavily upon the neoclassical approach to poetry. At the same time, one cannot accuse her of mere imitation for her ability to use both biblical and classical allusions correctly and her many creative lines indicate that she did have the imaginative faculties to produce good—if not great—poetry. Neither was she a mere slave to the heroic couplet for she did experiment with other verse patterns. On at least two occasions she tried a stanza of six lines. In "Ode to Neptune" the six lines are composed of a quatrain of iambic tetrameter and the heroic couplet. In "An Hymn to Humanity" she attempted a rather difficult structure. The six-lined stanza is composed of two tercets each one of which consists of an iambic tetrameter couplet and an iambic trimeter line. The iambic trimeter lines (the third and sixth of each stanza) rhyme. It may well be that she was one of the first

practitioners of free verse in American poetry. "On Virtue" consists of free verse with a concluding heroic couplet. "To the University of Cambridge, In New England" is basically in blank verse,
and "A Farewell to America" employs the ballad stanza. Most of
her poems are restrained lyrics, but she did attempt two long narrative poems: "Goliath of Gath" and "Niobe in Distress for Her
Children Slain by Apollo, from Ovid's *Metamorphoses,* Book VI,
and from a View of the Painting of Mr. Richard Wilson."

Phillis Wheatley has been accused of being oblivious to the
conditions of slavery, and there are those who assert that she would
have had far more value had she spent her time in the cause of
abolition. Her subjects, however, were circumscribed by her life
in Boston. On the whole, she tended to write about people whom
she knew and about places and things which either interested her
or held especial significance for those around her. She did write
in more general terms, but these works—while more meaningful
to the modern reader—are few. Her work does demonstrate her
broad reading background. Speaking of her educational achievements, Benjamin Brawley aptly notes in *The Negro in Literature
and Art* (New York, 1934) that in addition to her proficiency in
biblical literature, she was familiar with Homer, Horace, Ovid,
Virgil, and Terence. He continues:

If in the light of twentieth century opportunity and methods these
attainments seem in no wise remarkable, one must remember the dis-
advantages under which not only Phillis Wheatley, but all the women
of her time, labored; and recall that in any case her attainment would
have marked her as one of the most highly educated young women in
Boston (p. 16).

Her slave status was similar to that of Jupiter Hammon but because of her achievements she was even farther removed from the
actuality of bondage than Hammon himself. Taken into a family
whose members practically put themselves at her disposal, Phillis
Wheatley moved in the best social circles of Boston and of England.

Hardship as such was not hers until 1778 (after the deaths of three members of the Wheatley family) when she married Peters who apparently did much to alienate her former friends. While she did spend some time as a scrub woman in a Bostonian lodging house in order to support herself and her small children, her death in 1784 cut short this life of suffering and of poverty. Had she lived longer it may well be that she would have been forced to consider her station in life. But within her short life, she did consider matters of immediate concern to her. Her poem "To the Right Honourable William, Earl of Dartmouth, His Majesty's Principal Secretary of State for North America, Etc." was addressed to its subject on October 10, 1772, with the hope that he would contemplate the possibility of freedom for New England as well as for the remainder of the colonies. After her traditional opening invocation and a discussion of freedom, she continues with perhaps some of her most personal lines:

> Should you, my lord, while you peruse my song,
> Wonder from whence my love of *Freedom* sprung,
> Whence flow these wishes for the common good,
> By feeling hearts alone best understood,
> I, young in life, by seeming cruel fate
> Was snatch'd from *Afric's* fancy'd happy seat:
> What pangs excruciating must molest,
> What sorrows labour in my parent's breast?
> Steel'd was that soul and by no misery mov'd
> That from a father seiz'd his babe belov'd:
> Such, such my case. And can I then but pray
> Others may never feel tyrannic sway?

The poem concludes with a complimentary passage to the Earl whom she probably met in 1773 during her sojourn in England.

No discussion of Phillis Wheatley can end without the inclusion of what was probably one of her first poetic exercises. Written when she was apparently no more than thirteen, "On Being Brought From Africa to America" demonstrates her early belief in divine

Providence. While the poem certainly does not compare favorably with either the structure, style, or development of thought in her later works, it is another of the few examples of the personal element which sometimes found its way into her poetry. It was in response to the publication of this poem in the 1773 volume that inspired Hammon's long laudatory poem to her in 1778.

> 'Twas mercy brought me from my *Pagan* land,
> Taught my benighted soul to understand
> That there's a God, that there's a *Saviour* too:
> Once I redemption neither sought nor knew.
> Some view our sable race with scornful eye,
> "Their colour is a diabolic die."
> Remember, *Christians, Negroes,* black as *Cain,*
> May be refin'd, and join th' angelic train.

Hammon and Wheatley offer an interesting study in contrasts. Where Hammon's poetry exhibits the simplicity and exhuberance of his religious fervor, Wheatley's work demonstrates the complexity and the sophistication of neoclassicism. The warmth of Hammon's poetry is lost in the precision of Wheatley's verse which, after opening with an invocation (either religious or classical), uses elegant and stately language as she presents her thoughts in a controlled and balanced manner.

In addition to the poetic endeavors of Jupiter Hammon and Phillis Wheatley, the eighteenth century saw the development of Negro prose writers. As the authors of single works, many of them can not occupy a place of major literary importance; however, these prose writers frequently laid the foundation for the trends followed by nineteenth-century writers. For example, the autobiography eventually became a distinctive literary type known as the *slave narrative,* and among the early writers of such narratives Briton Hammon, John Marrant, and Gustavus Vassa made noteworthy contributions. These autobiographies were marked by no specific patterns aside from the assertion, usually in the opening pages of the story, that the writers were slaves who purported to relate a segment of their lives. These works, as we shall see later, extended from a rather loosely constructed reports of slave life to the well-organized chronicles which can be compared—rightly or wrongly—with the effective adventure stories of American literature. Not only are the works of Briton Hammon, John Marrant, and Gustavus Vassa among the first examples of the slave narrative but also they represent the wide possible range of this type of prose.

It is rather interesting that the earliest known American Negro poet should have shared the same surname with the first published prose writer. In 1760, the year of Jupiter Hammon's first published work, Briton Hammon published a pamphlet in Boston whose complete title also presents a summary of the story: *A Narrative of the Uncommon Sufferings, and Surprising Deliverance of Briton Hammon, A Negro Man,—Servant to General Winslow, of Marshfield, in New England; Who Returned to Boston, After Having Been Absent Almost Thirteen Years. Containing an Account of the Many Hardships He Underwent From the Time He Left His Master's House, in the Year 1747, to the Time of His Return to Boston.—How He Was Cast Away in the Capes of Florida;—the Horrid Cruelty and Inhuman Barbarity of the Indians in Murdering the Whole Ship's Crew;—the Manner of His Being Carry'd by Them into Captivity. Also an Account of His Being Confined Four Years and Seven Months in a Close Dungeon,—and the Remarkable Manner in Which He Met His Good Master in London; Who Returned to New England, a Passenger, in the Same Ship.* The "uncommon sufferings and surprising deliverance" recounted by Hammon make it clear, even to the modern reader, that the author was not only concerned with presenting a series of "hair-raising" episodes and adventures but also was convinced that divine providence continually saved him from a fate even worse that that which actually befell him. The story, which is loosely constructed, is nonetheless simply told. The prevailing mood is essentially religious as Hammon ends his narrative with a hymn of thanksgiving in which he praises God for bringing him out of captivity.

John Marrant's story, *A Narrative of the Lord's Wonderful
Dealings with J. Marrant, A Black . . . Taken from His Own
Relation,* is similar to Briton Hammon's in that the author is
highly selective in presenting his details. The reader learns little
of the life of Marrant other than that which pertains to his conversion to Christianity and to his religious life. Furthermore, the
work, like Hammon's, emphasizes the importance of divine providence in saving the author from a series of rather unbelievable
adventures. Yet, the story is well-told and was extremely popular
after its publication in London in 1785. Part of its popularity
may certainly have been due to the patronage of the Countess of
Huntington who convinced him to publish his adventures and to
become a minister. But the work was also probably popular because Marrant included a long section dealing with his capture by
the Cherokees and his miraculous escape after he began to pray
in their language which was unknown to him. His use of their
language so shocked the Indians that they, too, became converted.
Stories of pursuit and capture by Indians were popular during the
later part of the eighteenth century, and Marrant's story appealed
to a vast reading audience.

In 1789 the *Journal of John Marrant* was also published in
London probably as a result of the interest which Whitefield and
the Countess of Huntington had manifested in him. The *Journal,*
however, is simply a restatement of the facts and incidents of the
Narrative . . ., and Marrant still does not share with his readers
too much of his life's story. Neither was he especially concerned
in either work with the plight of his people; consequently, both
works become interesting examples of a type of detachment which
became increasingly more rare as one moves toward the nineteenth
century.

It is difficult to determine how much of Marrant's work was
true and how much of it sheer fabrication. That he did become a
minister, one of the first Negro preachers in North America, is
attested by the fact that in 1787, as the chaplain of the African
Lodge of Masons in Boston, he delivered a sermon on the building

of Solomon's Temple. The very vivid and symbolic work was subsequently published. In the editions of his *Narrative* which appeared after 1790, sermons—reportedly by Marrant—were appended.

While both Hammon's story and that of Marrant emphasized Indian captivity and the redeeming features of Christianity, one of the best stories concerning the bewildernment of the slaves in America appeared in 1791 with the publication of *The Interesting Narrative of the Life of Olaudah Equiano, or Gustavus Vassa the African, Written by Himself.* According to his story, he had been born in Benin in 1745, and by 1756 he had been kidnapped from his family and sold into African slavery. A short while thereafter he had been sold to the slave traders who constantly raided the west coat of Africa. Thus began his long harassing trip to America, the terror of which Vassa describes in detail. He makes it clear that much of the horror of the voyage was based not only upon his inability to communicate with the other slaves and with the crew but also upon his fear concerning what his life was to be once all of them arrived at their destination. During his journey across the Atlantic he made a vow to himself to learn the language as quickly as possible. He was first sold to a Virginia planter. The planter sold him to a British naval officer who took him to England for a short stay. He was next sold to a Quaker merchant in Philadelphia who permitted him to buy his freedom. Although he had been spared the worst physical distress of slavery, Vassa—once free—worked incessantly for anti-slavery legislation. The three owners of Vassa had been extremely sympathetic and had aided him in the securing of a much-desired education, and ultimately his last owner had helped him purchase his freedom. Because of the simplicity and the directness of Vassa's autobiography there was an immediate appeal made to the consciences of all of those who had supported slavery either through actual participation or through silence.

With the autobiography of Vassa a new strain entered American Negro writing. Prior to Vassa, the significant writers (Jupiter

Hammon, Phillis Wheatley, Briton Hammon, and John Marrant) had been so content within their own little worlds that they had neither the inclination nor the need to look beyond their limited experiences. In each case religion was used as a panacea for whatever was amiss in their lives. Because they lived in circumstances which placed them above the average person of the period, the horrors of slavery were frequently removed from their communities and they saw no need to treat extensively the subject. However, Vassa who began his life in America as a slave like Hammon and Wheatley used his preoccupation with religion to support his antislavery doctrines. He felt that Christianity was incompatible with human slavery, and he wasted no time in pointing this out. For the first time the element of protest was not veiled in obscure language neither was it hidden within the confines of provincialism.

One of the most effective cases against slavery was penned not by a literary artist but rather by a mathematician. Benjamin Banneker, a free Negro, was born near Baltimore and early demonstrated his great intellectual curiosity. As a youngster he became familiar enough with Latin, Greek, German, French, Astronomy, and Mathematics to be considered one of the most distinguished scholars in Maryland. He was aided in his quest for knowledge by George Ellicott who put his vast library at young Banneker's disposal. In the early 1790's Benjamin Banneker decided to take advantage of the prevailing interest in almanacs by issuing a series of them until 1797. The eighteenth-century almanac was designed not only for the farmer who was concerned about the dates for planting but also for those in urban areas for whom the almanacs supplied the year's reading material. Banneker's almanacs, as befitted works of this type, included material which dealt with astronomical matters, and frequently Banneker was more correct than the other almanac-makers who had not had the benefits of extensive training in mathematics and astronomy. He also included the usual medical advice, excerpts from popular books and magazines of the period, as well as other useful or informational material.

Feeling that his work could do much toward dispelling the usual charge of "innate inferiority" which frequently accompanied the work of Negroes, Banneker sent a copy of his first almanac to Thomas Jefferson with a letter. The letter should take its place as one of the most eloquent pleas for the abolition of slavery. Although Banneker pointed out that he had never been a slave, he was aware of the fact that one man's enslavement negated the freedom of all men. His plea against slavery was developed by commending Jefferson for including in the Declaration of Independence worthy sentiments on freedom. For fear that Jefferson, who was at this time Secretary of State, might not have remembered the words which Banneker felt ought to be "remembered in all succeeding ages," he quoted the statement: "We hold these truths to be self-evident, that all men are created equal; that they are endowed by their Creator with certain unalienable rights, and that among these are life, liberty, and the pursuit of happiness." He then suggests to Jefferson that slaveholding does not appear to be in harmony with the ideas of that great document of freedom which had been written only a few years before. The letter ends with Banneker offering himself as proof against the charge of "innate inferiority." While there can be no doubt concerning the message of Banneker, his writing style does much to eradicate the hostility that might have resulted.

Jefferson not only answered Banneker immediately but also forwarded a copy to Condorecet, who was the secretary of the Academy of Sciences in Paris, with the hope of dispelling some of the myths which circulated about Negroes. The two letters were first published in 1792; later editions were used by the anti-slavery forces. Subsequently Banneker served, upon the recommendation of Jefferson, as a member of the team designated to survey the land which was to become Washington, D.C.

II

As the nineteenth century opened, a number of new elements which were to affect American slavery became apparent. Of all of them the invention of the cotton gin, the abolition of the slave trade, and the fear of slave rebellions were probably most significant. The gin, for example, made cotton far more important and demanded agricultural expansions which in turn required more slave labor in order to make the cotton kingdom a profitable one. Those sections of the country which could not benefit from the actual production of cotton took advantage of the situation by "raising" and furnishing slaves for the market. Emancipation became less frequent for individuals as the chains of slavery were bound more tightly than ever. The increase of any slave's value was further intensified by the abolition of the slave trade in 1807. Of course, it was many years before this law became effective because the law was not enforced. Yet, with the source of original supply practically cut off, greater care had to be taken in order to mutiply the existing slave population. This matter was further complicated by the successful slave rebellion which had occurred in Santo Domingo during the closing years of the eighteenth century, for many of the whites escaped to the United States where they spared no detail in describing the terror of the revolt. The "it-can-happen-here" approach instilled an apprehension in the minds of many slaveholders, an apprehension which often turned to panic. As a result, more stringent regulations were put into operation as more and more slaveholders tried to alleviate the reality of their fears. Thus the slaves' bid for freedom and their advances toward liberty were seriously curtailed.

During this same period David Walker played a significant role. He was born free in North Carolina, but his hatred for slavery as it existed around him finally compelled him to flee the South. Arriving in Boston, he worked at odd jobs until 1829 when he published a message to the slaves entitled: *Walker's Appeal in Four Articles: Together with a Preamble, to the Coloured Citizens of the World, but in Particular, and Very Expressly, to those of the United States of America, Written in Boston, State of Massachusetts, September 28, 1829*. The *Appeal* was the most severe

indictment of slavery which had appeared up to this time. The "Preamble" sets the tone for the entire work.

My dearly beloved Brethren and Fellow Citizens.

Having travelled over a considerable portion of these United States, and having, in the course of my travels, taken the most accurate observations of things as they exist—the result of my observations has warranted the full and unshaken conviction, that we, (coloured people of these United States,) are the most degraded, wretched, and abject set of beings that ever lived since the world began; and I pray God that none like us ever may live again until time shall be no more. They tell us of the Israelites in Egypt, the Helots in Sparta, and of the Roman slaves, which last were made up from almost every nation under heaven, whose sufferings under those ancient and heathen nations, were, in comparison to ours, under this enlightened and Christian nation, no more than a sypher—or, in other words, those heathen nations of antiquity, had but little more among them than the name and form of slavery; while wretchedness and endless miseries were reserved, apparently in a phial, to be poured out upon our fathers, ourselves and our children, by *Christian* Americans!

These positions I shall endeavour, by the help of the Lord, to demonstrate in the course of this *Appeal,* to the satisfaction of the most incredulous mind—and may God Almighty, who is the Father of our Lord Jesus Christ, open your hearts to understand and believe the truth.

The *causes,* my brethren, which produce our wretchedness and miseries, are so very numerous and aggravating, that I believe the pen only of a Josephus or a Plutarch, can well enumerate and explain them. Upon subjects, then, of such incomprehensible magnitude, so impenetrable, and so notorious, I shall be obliged to omit a large class of, and content myself with giving you an exposition of a few of those, which do indeed rage to such an alarming pitch, that they cannot but be a perpetual source of terror and dismay to every reflecting mind.

I am fully aware, in making this appeal to my much afflicted and suffering brethren, that I shall not only be assailed by those whose greatest earthly desires are, to keep us in abject ignorance and wretchedness, and who are of the firm conviction that Heaven has designed us and our children to be slaves and *beasts of burden* to them and their children. I say, I do not only expect to be held up to the public as an ignorant, impudent and restless disturber of the public peace, by such avaricious creatures, as well as a mover of insubordination—and perhaps put in prison or to death, for giving a superficial exposition of our miseries, and exposing tyrants. But I am persuaded, that many of my brethren, particularly those who are ignorantly in league with slaveholders or tyrants, who acquire their daily bread by the blood and sweat of their more ignorant brethren—and not a few of those too, who are too ignorant to see an inch beyond their noses, will rise up and call me cursed—Yea, the jealous ones among us will perhaps use more abject subtlety, by affirming that this work is not worth perusing, that we are well situated, and there is no use in trying to better our condition, for we cannot. I will ask one question here.—Can our condition be any worse?—Can it be more mean and abject? If there are any changes, will they not be for the better, though they may appear for the worst at first? Can they get us any lower? Where can they get us? They are afraid to treat us worse, for they know well, the day they do it they are gone. But against all accusations which may or can be preferred against me, I appeal to Heaven for my motive in writing—who knows that my object is, if possible, to awaken in the breasts of my afflicted, degraded and slumbering brethren, a spirit of inquiry and investigation respecting our miseries and wretchedness in this *Republican Land of Liberty! ! ! ! ! !*

The sources from which our miseries are derived, and on which I shall comment, I shall not combine in one, but shall put them under distinct heads and expose them in their turn; in doing which, keeping truth on my side, and not departing from the strictest rules of morality, I shall endeavor to penetrate, search out, and lay them open for your inspection. If you cannot or will not profit by them, I shall have done *my* duty to you, my country and my God.

And as the inhuman system of *slavery,* is the *source* from which most of our miseries proceed, I shall begin with that *curse to nations,* which has spread terror and devastation through so many nations of antiquity, and which is raging to such a pitch at the present day in Spain and in Portugal. It had one tug in England, in France, and in the United States of America; yet the inhabitants thereof, do not learn wisdom, and erase it entirely from their dwellings and from all with whom they have to do. The fact is, the labour of slaves comes so cheap to the avaricious usurpers, and is (as they think) of such great utility to the country where it exists, that those who are actuated by sordid avarice only, overlook the evils, which will as sure as the Lord lives, follow after the good. In fact, they are so happy to keep in ignorance and degradation, and to receive the homage and the labour of slaves, they forget that God rules in the armies of heaven and among the inhabitants of the earth, having his ears continually open to the cries, tears and groans of his oppressed people; and being s just and holy Being will at one day appear fully in behalf of the oppressed, and arrest the progress of the avaricious oppressors; for although the destruction of the oppressors God may not effect by the oppressed, yet the Lord our God will bring other destructions upon them—for not unfrequently will he cause them to rise up one against another, to be split and divided, and to oppress each other, and sometimes to open hostilities with sword in hand. Some may ask, what is the matter with this united and happy people? —Some say it is the cause of political usurpers, tyrants, oppressors, &c. But has not the Lord an oppressed and suffering people among them? Does the Lord condescend to hear their cries and see their tears in consequence of oppression? Will he let the oppressors rest comfortably and happy always? Will he not cause the very children of the oppressors to rise up against them, and oftimes put them to death? "God works in many ways his wonders to perform."

I will not here speak of the destructions which the Lord brought upon Egypt, in consequence of the oppression and consequent groans of the oppressed—of the hundreds and thousands of Egyptians whom God hurled into the Red Sea for afflicting his people in their land— of the Lord's suffering people in Sparta or Lacedaemon, the land of the truly famous Lycurgus—nor have I time to comment upon the cause which produced the fierceness with which Sylla usurped the title, and absolutely acted as dictator of the Roman people—the conspiracy of Cataline—the conspiracy against, and murder of Caesar in the Senate house—the spirit with which Marc Antony made himself master of the commonwealth—his associating Octavius and Lipidus with himself in power—their dividing the provinces of Rome among themselves—their attack and defeat, on the plains of Phillippi, of the last defenders of their liberty, (Brutus and Cassius)—the tyranny of Tiberius, and from him to the final overthrow of Constantinople by the Turkish Sultan, Mahomed II. A.D. 1453. I say, I shall not take up time to speak of the *causes* which produced so much wretchedness and massacred among those heathen nations, for I am aware that you know too well, that God is just, as well as merciful!— I shall call your attention a few moments to that *Christian* nation, the Spaniards—while I shall leave almost unnoticed, that avaricious and cruel people, the Portuguese, among whom all true hearted Christians and lovers of Jesus Christ, must evidently see the judgments of God displayed. To show the judgments of God upon the Spaniards, I shall occupy but a little time, leaving a plenty of room for the candid and unprejudiced to reflect.

All persons who are acquainted with history, and particularly the Bible, who are not blinded by the God of this world, and are not actuated solely by avarice—who are able to lay aside prejudice long enough to view candidly and impartially, things as they were, are, and probably will be—who are willing to admit that God made man to serve *Him* alone, and that man should have no other Lord or Lords but Himself—that God Almighty is the *sole proprietor* or *master* of the WHOLE human family, and will not on any consideration admit of a colleague, being unwilling to divide his glory with another— and who can dispense with prejudice long enough to admit that we are *men,* notwithstanding our *improminent noses* and *woolly heads,* and believe that we feel for our fathers, mothers, wives, and children, as well as the whites do for theirs.—I say, all who are permitted to see and believe these things, can easily recognize the judgments of God among the Spaniards. Though others may lay the cause of the fierceness with which they cut each other's throats, to some other circumstance, yet they who believe that God is a God of justice, will believe that SLAVERY *is the principal cause.*

While the Spaniards are running about upon the field of battle cutting each other's throats, has not the Lord an afflicted and suffering people in the midst of them, whose cries and groans in consequence of oppression are continually pouring into the ears of the God of justice? Would they not cease to cut each other's throats, if they could? But how can they? The very support which they draw from the government to aid them in perpetrating such enormities, does it not arise in a great degree from the wretched victims of oppression among them? And yet they are calling for *Peace! Peace!!* Will any peace be given unto them? Their destruction may indeed be procrastinated awhile, but can it continue long, while they are oppressing the Lord's people? Has he not the hearts of all men in His hand? Will he suffer one part of his creatures to go on oppressing another like brutes always, with impunity? And yet, those avaricious wretches are calling for *Peace! ! ! !* I declare, it does appear to me, as some nations think God is asleep, or that he made the Africans for nothing else but to dig their mines and work their farms, or they cannot believe history, sacred or profane. I ask every man who has a heart, and is blessed with the privilege of believing—Is not God a God of justice to *all* his creatures? Do you say he is? Then if he gives peace and tranquility to tyrants, and permits them to keep our fathers, our mothers, ourselves and our children in eternal ignorance and wretchedness, to support them and their families, would he be to us a God of *justice?* I ask, *O ye Christians! ! ! !* who hold us and our children in the most abject ignorance and degradation, that ever a people were afflicted with since the world began—I say, if God gives you peace and tranquility, and suffers you thus to go on afflicting us, and our children, who have never given you the least provocation—would he be to us *a God of justice?* If you will allow that we are MEN, who feel for each other, does not the blood of our fathers and of us their children, cry aloud to the Lord of Sabaoth against you, for the cruelties and murders with which you have, and do continue to afflict us. But it is time for me to close my remarks on the suburbs, just to enter more fully into the interior of this system of cruelty and oppression.

Walker then proceeds in Article I, "Our Wretchedness in Consequence of Slavery," to point out the brutality of American Christians toward the slaves. He also attacks Jefferson's *Notes on Virginia* in which Jefferson asserted the basic inferiority of Negroes. Article II, "Our Wretchedness in Consequence of Ignorance," examines the need for education. At the same time Walker emphasizes the various ways white America has of keeping the slaves "ignorant." One of the most effective ways, against which Walker warns, is the tendency to make the slaves lose respect for themselves and for their people. In the third Article, "Our Wretchedness in Consequence of the Preachers of the Religion of Jesus Christ," attacks the type of misinformation which is distributed about the slaves in the name of religion. Soon these Christians who have been responsible for the state of affairs in America will be destroyed unless, according to Walker, there is widespread repentance. The aura of doom hangs over this section as Walker proceeds to the fourth and last article: "Our Wretchedness in Consequence of the Colonizing Plan." He attacks the various schemes of colonization as an effort of white Americans to get rid of those Negroes who are most independent in order to secure their own hold on the more docile slaves. However, Walker asserts: "This country is as much our as it is the whites, whether they will admit it now or not, they will see and believe it by and by." Walker concludes by quoting extensively from the Declaration of Independence and by affirming his commitment to the principles stated within the document. At the same time he cautions Americans to remember that their sufferings under Great Britain were not "one hundredth part as cruel and tyrannical as you have rendered [to us]." And just as Americans broke the yoke which bound them to England, so it can be expected that in the not too distant future, Negroes will rise in revolt.

Throughout the entire work Walker makes it clear that he believes "God is on our side" and claims God is eventually going to avenge those who have been subjected by white Christians who have forsaken all principles of religion. He further announces that "woe . . . will be to you if we have to obtain our freedom by fighting." The work is further marked by extensive quotations from the Scriptures and from history including the contemporary history of his day. While the *Appeal* is extremely emotional and caused men to suppress it out of fear, it is clearly written and demonstrates the scholarship of its author.

The work was immediately popular. Three editions were issued within three years, each one more popular than the preceding edition. The South was terrified. All efforts were made not only to suppress the document but also to capture the author "dead or alive." Georgia, for example, offered a reward of $10,000 to anyone who could present a live Walker in the state capitol and $1,000 for a dead Walker. Even reading the *Appeal* was considered a crime in the South, and the records are full of cases of slaves being beaten and tortured because a copy of the pamphlet was found in the slaves' quarters. Many of the regulations designed to curtail the education of Negroes followed quickly in the wake of this work because it was believed that the possible effect of the document would be seriously hampered if the slaves were unable to get its message. Although Walker disappeared mysteriously, his *Appeal* remained one of the oustanding protest documents of the nineteenth century, and unwittingly he set the stage for the host of abolitionist tracts which followed.

The severity of nineteenth-century conditions gave rise to a number of situations: education was forced underground, escape routes were seriously considered, rebellions were viewed as possible means for ending slavery, and an aggressive abolition movement was organized. Although the slaves were more restricted, the free Negroes—in spite of their own peculiar problems—were becoming more and more articulate. David Walker's publication of his *Appeal* in 1829 and Nat Turner's revolt of 1831 aggravated the fears of the South, but with William Lloyd Garrison's active participation in the cause of abolition, it was apparent that the North was becoming increasingly repelled by the idea of human slavery. At the same time that the ideas concerning slavery were being polarized in the South and in the North, the Negroes themselves, in an demonstration of great ingenuity, founded the Underground Railroad, an arrangement by which escaping slaves were protected and escorted to free territories. The free Negro population in 1790 was 59,557, but by 1860 it had reached 488,070 comprising eleven per cent of the Negroes in this country. And this eleven per cent was not silent neither was it a homogeneous group. It was extremely diversified and included Negro slave holders in both the North and the South as well as laborers who searched daily for a different means of earning their wages. Some of these men were highly skilled artisans who were constantly in demand. Some few were tradesmen. And even fewer entered the professions in spite of the restrictions against the education of Negroes which existed throughout the country. Thus while the conditions of slavery tended to equalize all Negroes under its system, the reality of freedom indicated that the type of heterogeneity which one easily finds in other races existed among Negroes as well. The single point on which the freemen agreed was the necessity for purging slavery from American society. For some this was to be achieved by elevating the status of Negroes in this country; othere were dedicated to colonization efforts as the effective means of combating slavery.

Although he became active in the movement to colonize Africa with American Negroes (an involvement which he later regretted), Paul Cuffee served a noble purpose by establishing a school on his own property which was open to all. Cuffee's decision was his answer to the denial of the selectmen of Dartmouth, Massachusetts, that Negro children had a right to attend the public school. Whenever he heard of an organization devoted to the suppression of the slave trade or to the education of Negroes, he willingly donated money. Born in New Bedford, Massachusetts, Cuffee was largely self-taught, but he became a prosperous shipowner who used his fortune to provide aid for his race. His only publication, *A Brief Account of the Settlement and Present Situation of the Colony of Sierra Leone in Africa . . .*, appeared in 1812 and was designed to present his views on the possibility of Negroes establishing societies in Africa where they would have a greater opportunity for growth and development.

Prince Saunders also saw in the movements to re-locate either in Africa or in the West Indies a feasible solution to the problem of Negro life in America. Born in Thetford, Vermont, he had had the benefits of excellent schools. For a while he taught in New England;

' eventually he took the first of many trips to Haiti. Once there he became involved in developing an educational system and was sent to England by King Henri Christophe to study England's forms of education and to purchase supplies. While he was in England, so goes a popular story, his first name was assumed to be an indication of royalty, and he did nothing to clarify the error. Many homes were opened to him because of his supposed title, and he took full advantage of the misconception. His writings today are little more than historic curiosities, but he did provide in *Haytian Papers: A Collection of the Very Interesting Proclamations, and Other Official Documents; Together with Some Account of the Rise, Progress and Present State of the Kingdom of Hayti* one of the most valuable studies of Haiti; at the same time he used Haiti as an example of what could be achieved in this country. The work first appeared in London in 1816.

Among the foes of colonization enterprises were James Forten, Richard Allen, and Absalom Jones. Of the three, Forten was the only one who came from a long line of freemen. Born and educated in Philadelphia, he became one of the wealthiest men of his community. As the owner of a shipping supply company which provided employment for both Negro and white workers, Forten was highly respected in Philadelphia. Although he had not been personally affected by slavery, he worked hard in the cause of abolition and was instrumental in convening the first national convention of free Negroes in 1830 to consider the role which had to be assumed by free men. Earlier, however, he had been the presiding officer of an anti-colonization society which also included Allen and Jones. The proceedings of these meetings contain some of the most lucid explanations against slavery. While the immediacy of the essays written for the meetings and the orations delivered there had passed, the essays and speeches are excellent examples of the discussion of Negro welfare and advances *within* the structure of the United States. The doctrine of self-help was a prevailing theme as these men denied the efficacy of returning to Africa or escaping to Canada or to one of the islands.

Just as individuals and singly published works aided the cause of abolition so also did the advent of newspapers. By 1827 there appeared the first Negro newspaper, *Freedom's Journal,* edited by John B. Russwurm who received his A.B. from Bowdoin College and who has the distinction of being the first Negro college graduate from a school within the United States. (Earlier James McCune Smith, M.D. had returned to the United States to practice, but he had received his degrees in Scotland.) Russwurm's paper appeared from March 16, 1827 to March 28, 1829, and it published material designed to develop not only a desire for educational advancement but also a recognition of racial pride. It contained numerous sermons, orations, essays, and poems by early Negro writers. Russwurm was aided in his enterprise by Samuel E. Cornish who remained in journalism years after Russwurm departed the United States in 1829 for Africa. After *Freedom's Journal* a number of short-lived newspapers and journals appeared but none quite so popular as Frederick Douglass' *North Star* which began publication in 1847. Douglass had escaped from slavery in 1838 the same year in which David Ruggles, a Negro physician who had conducted over 600 people on the Underground Railroad, founded *The Mirror of Liberty* which was the first Negro magazine and which was also dedicated to the rights of Negroes. *North Star* was well-known in part because of Douglass' activities both in this country and in Europe, but it also represented one of the most influential specimens of Negro journalism.

Less than one hundred years had passed since Jupiter Hammon's first poem had been published, but during that time there had arisen a group of spokesmen who were dedicated to the principle of liberty for all. Many of them wrote with facility and lectured with dignity. Much of their work is occasional in that the prose writers were impelled to write because of the urgency of the situation, but the sheer emotionalism so common in the propaganda of the abolition movement is strangely absent from the bulk of these works as men logically and coherently analyzed the relationship of slavery to the spirit and to the ideals of American democracy.

During the same period that the small articulate band of freemen were devoting their energies toward the abolition of slavery, there developed among the host of silent slaves two literary forms, the spiritual and the slave narrative, that were destined to become perhaps the only distinctively American contributions to the world of literature. Both forms owe a great deal to the American experience, and both forms are essentially products of the nineteenth century. Although it is possible to trace the development of Negro prose writers from Jupiter Hammon to Frederick Douglass, the spiritual (which is a poetic form as well as a musical one) owes nothing to the poetic efforts of Jupiter Hammon and Phillis Wheatley. Thus, as far as Negro poetry in America is concerned, the nineteenth century saw a new beginning.

CHAPTER II

Faith of Our Fathers:
The Spiritual and
Its Poetic Tradition

SINCE THERE IS a tendency to focus attention on the small, but articulate, group of free Negroes because most of them were active in the anti-slavery movement and because their prose was relatively well-known, the work of another productive group frequently goes unnoticed. During the nineteenth century when Negro prose writers were gaining popularity in the North and notoriety in the South, from the host of silent slaves there developed an oral poetic and musical tradition which led to the creation of the jubilees, blues, work songs, and spirituals. The unknown composers of the spirituals who emerged from a depressed people ultimately were to furnish America with its first truly native music. The poets of these *songs of sorrow* had not had the benefits of a neoclassical education nor had they engaged in extensive reading programs, but they managed to create poems—simple though they were—which followed as many conventions as those produced by the neoclassicist. But poetic technique was not their major concern. These poets emphasized a religious element which was to become, in later years, one of the dominant motifs of Negro poetry in America. Thus, while the more literate Negroes were writing prose of an argumentative nature and while their works were being published in the North and often in London, the spiritual evolved as a literary development primarily of the South.

The spiritual was essentially the result of two dominant influences. The first was the tightening of control on matters of education. With the law designed to abolish the slave trade and with the constant fear of possible insurrections, it was generally conceded in the South that the merest rudiments of education should be withheld. In the period which followed the American Revolution when there was so much talk about liberty and freedom and in the subsequent period of the French and Haitian Revolutions with emphasis upon equality, liberty, and fraternity, there was a need—so it was believed—to close the outside world to the slaves. Banning reading materials was attempted as in the case of the suppression of David Walker's *Appeal* of 1829, but the surest way to keep the documents of freedom out of the grasp of the slaves was to prohibit education. Where once even the most cruel masters felt a responsibility to see to it that their charges learned to read the Bible, if nothing else; there was now a concerted effort made to restrict all such activities. The fears of rebellion grew, but it was believed that peace rested in maintaining the illiteracy of the slaves. Consequently, legal restrictions were soon introduced making it a crime to teach a slave to read. As a result of these laws, education was forced underground, and creative expression itself turned toward an oral tradition. For those who remembered the African experience, the oral transmission of literature was not strange because the oral literature of Africa was far more extensive than its written literature.

The second dominant influence upon the creation of the spirituals was a Christianity superimposed upon the American slave experience. To a people oppressed by slavery, the subjugations of the early Christians and the crucifixion of Jesus Christ were understandable. When Christianity was introduced into the slave camps, it was not as a vague theological philosophy but rather as a tender and interesting story. From the poverty of Jesus Christ, from His life of goodness and service, from His death, and from the establishment of His church on earth, the slaves were able to draw significant parallels and were able to deduce essential meanings.

Therefore, in spite of the discrepancy between the Christianity which they heard and that which they saw, the early slaves did not seriously question the validity of the Christian concepts. They already knew much about earthly suffering. Furthermore, the prospect of heaven as the place where one would receive his payment and reward for all work done on earth appealed to those who had little hope of remuneration in this world. The rejection of material things in order to obtain the heavenly crown was not difficult for them because they were automatically denied earthly goods. Of course, the idea of looking toward heaven as a solution to the problems of life was not peculiar to the slaves. Among the poor and downtrodden of the country, especially among those who were also oppressed by the great economic system of a slave-holding society, religion was fundamentally otherworldly. The speculations which characterized Puritanism or the formalism of the Anglican church had little value as a folk religion. Rather it was toward the Methodist and Baptist churches that the disfranchised both white and black in America turned. Here were approaches to religion which were extremely personal and which emphasized the concepts of present-day suffering in order to be rewarded in an after-life. While many of the poor of the nation were in a comparable spiritual, economic, and social condition as the slaves, religion for the slaves presented not only a means of escape from the trials of daily living but also the opportunity to assert themselves as human beings. Even though there was much in both the Old and New Testaments with which they could identify, the slaves brought to their religion a fervor which defies complete explanation.

The spirituals, the first direct evidence that distinguishes the religious beliefs of the race from others in America, obviously resulted from the merging of various remembered African beliefs, superstitions, and traditions with the ideas of Christianity which were prevalent at that time. The songs that the slaves composed and sang are not inherent in the brand of Methodism which swept the South. These songs ran the gamut from great militancy to a rather pathetic acceptance of the conditions of servitude. But whether they were being militant in "Go Down, Moses" or pathetic in "Were You There," the spirituals actually voiced a significant appeal for a redeeming religion. As any folk literature of any other era, the spirituals sprang from the people; hence, from the hearts of a people tormented by the anguish of slavery arose a form of poetry which is essentially a *song of sorrow*. These poems generally refrained from bitterly accusing their captors neither did they make a conscious search for earthly or heavenly revenge. It is impossible to determine how many of these songs existed during slavery, but from the surviving examples it can be noted that there is a strong unwavering note of hope in all of them as well as a belief in final recompense and the assurance of the perfection of another life to come. The ability to give meaning to their religious experience through the spirituals very likely served as a safety valve for the pent-up emotions of the slaves and thereby probably saved the country from an even greater tragedy than the Civil War and saved the Negro from a still greater disaster.

Originally the spirituals were not well-known outside of the South although ex-slaves in the North spoke often of their music. Former slaves would sometimes, once they had escaped to other sections of the country, mention the slave songs; but the world really knew little about these songs. Colonel Thomas Wentworth Higginson, who had led a Negro regiment during the Civil War, wrote an article for the June, 1867, issue of *The Atlantic Monthly* in which he likened the spirituals which he had heard in the camp to Scottish ballads. After asserting that he had always been "a faithful student of [these ballads] and had always envied Sir Walter Scott the delight of tracing them out amid their own heather, and of writing them down piecemeal from the lips of aged crones," he continued:

It was a strange enjoyment, therefore, to be suddenly brought into the midst of a kindred world of unwritten songs, as simple and indigenous as the Border Minstrelsy, more uniformly plaintive, almost always more quaint, and often essentially poetic (p. 685).

Earlier in 1864 Charlottle Forten, the granddaughter of James Forten, had published an article in *The Atlantic Monthly,* "Life on the Sea Islands," in which she described her life as a teacher in the South and for which she had collected a few spirituals. Sporadically other articles and notices had appeared, but Higginson's article, "Negro Spirituals," was the first to deal exclusively with the songs. In 1871 the Jubilee Singers of Fisk University took the songs to the North and then to Europe. By the conclusion of the tour the world had literally been introduced to this soulful music, to these songs which came out of the slave experience.

Although the Jubilee Singers, and later the Quartets of Hampton Institute, did much to resurrect the charm of these songs and poems, an intangible feeling of hostility existed toward them for many years. In fact, for a period after the Civil War the spirituals were held in disrepute. Many Negroes refused to admit that these works even were products of former years. Understandably the ex-slaves wanted nothing which would remind them of bygone days. Freedom, for some, meant the breaking of all old ties; yet many of them had no idea of what to do nor where to go. Obviously they had to get away from memories, and in so doing they left their music. But the Reconstruction proved almost useless to a people thrown into freedom without a clear knowledge of what freedom actually meant. Try as they might, the widespread lack of education made it impossible for many of them to cope with the political maneuverings of white southerners and northerners. Some ex-slaves were misled into believing that freedom meant putting into practice their ideas of heaven, and these sat down and sang because heaven on earth had certainly come, so they reasoned, from Abraham Lincoln in Washington, D.C. The disillusionment which came so suddenly was much more than many could bear. They turned back to life as it had existed, and the older folks returned to the music from which they had never really departed.

It was these people who had spent their yesterdays preparing land they could never reap who preserved for the race the poetic tradition which had sprung from slavery. It was these people who in the twilight of life viewed the first ray of a new dawn.

The criticisms levied against the spirituals included the charge that they were too otherworldly. It is true, of course, that many of the spirituals do deal with what is to happen in heaven. As a result, death or "crossing the river Jordan," the repeated image, is viewed as a pleasurable experience because it serves as a passport to everlasting happiness and rest. Another objection to the spirituals cites them as being in a tradition which is exemplified by excessive submission and humility. This often resulted in a "do-nothing" attitude. The idea of the following couplet from a spiritual does express a common idea:

> You may talk about me as much as you please;
> I'll talk about you down on my knees.

But the submission, humility, "do-nothingness," or whatever else this complacency may be called, did not exist in a vacuum for its sake alone. It was a means to an end. The earthly denials were important for the life in the kingdom to come. More than anything, the songs gave to the people who sang them not only a sense of belonging but also a much-needed faith in a better day, a faith which is still discernible in so much of Negro poetry. Perhaps the certainty of that faith is portrayed by the following stanza from a popular spiritual:

> Oh, stand the storm, it won't be long,
> We'll anchor by and by;
> Stand the storm, it won't be long,
> We'll anchor by and by.

I

It has generally been believed that the great force of the spirituals is a result of the music; yet, the words can be isolated as examples of a primitive poetry. When this is done, the child-like quality of the language does not stand as a barrier to poetic beauty. The spirituals do contain an enormous amount of repetition, many inaccurate images, and often the language seems to be used incorrectly; however, all of these apparent faults actually serve to create a unique example of poetic charm, and the poetic form serves to intensify the strong feeling which is being conveyed. "Jesus Walked This Lonesome Valley" does not contain intricate poetic imagery; yet one cannot forget that in its simple language it contains an idea and a single image which supported a people who vainly battled against a hot sun with bared backs, who tramped the endless rows of cotton, who waited—and waited patiently—for the midnight of their existence to be broken by the first rays of the morning sun. For them the knowledge that Jesus also walked alone created the emotional experience necessary for any poem.

> Jesus walked this lonesome valley,
> He had to walk it by himself,
> Nobody else could walk it for him,
> He had to walk it by himself.

This early folk poetry dealt with various aspects of religion. Not only were the unknown poets concerned about God in a general way but also were they concerned about man's relationship to God and to man. Furthermore, they were attracted to portions of the life of Jesus Christ and to death with all of its implications. Usually one tends to think of the image of God as being divided into three rather basic relationships: man to God, to other men, and to himself. The Negro religious poet, in many instances, extends these fundamental relationships into four major categories: man to God, to men of other races, to men of his own race, and to himself. When the Negro poet discusses man's relationship to man, he is primarily interested in the Negro's status in a so-called white world, and his work tends to be characterized by social protest and condemnation. When the same poet deals with men of his own race, he tends to do it sympathetically. In addition to poetic renditions of these relationships, religious poetry does tend to deal with the accepted leader of that faith; therefore, the literature of Christianity reveals numerous efforts by writers to explore the life of Jesus on earth in terms of racial life in America; thus some Negro poets present in addition to social protest an interesting and revealing concept of Christ. Frequently, Christ is used as a pattern for obedience and humility but at the same time His royalty, or kinship with God, and his strength in the midst of adversity are emphasized. The poems which deal with death almost always extend the meaning of man's relationship to God, for these poems express not only man's attitude toward God but also toward life itself. The concept of immortality is extremely important in poems of this nature.

The great force of religion is evident in Negro poetry, and in spite of all attempts to prove otherwise, that force has been one of the most influential single elements in the lives of American Negroes. And the spirituals represent the early folk attempt to render meaning for this very real relationship between the American Negro and the matters of the spirit. Consequently many of these poems represent simple utterances designed to illustrate one facet of the Negro's relationship to God or to Jesus Christ or to death. While in an elementary form they cover the general basic relationships between mortals and the immortal spirit, the spirituals tend to translate these ideas into concrete terms and to deal specifically with deliverance from worldly sorrows often through death, the majesty of God, and the trials of Jesus on earth. And these works are presented through an extensive use of figurative language. Although there have been some efforts to prove that the spirituals were actually coded messages, these songs are strangely lacking in the expression of discontent merely for the sake of protest.

Most of the poems of the spirituals carry a minor narrative thread. In "Nobody Knows De Trouble I've Seen" the poet tells how earthly trouble can be mitigated through conversion to Christianity. The poem also indicates a pattern which is rather common.

First of all, the poet employs the subjective pronoun; and the experience which he attributes to himself is completely personal; however, it is one which is applicable to others. Furthermore, the poet uses the quatrain, the most popular stanza pattern. The first stanza structurally differs from the others. The first and third lines of it are the same with some very minor variation. The rhyme, when it appears, is maintained only through the repeated first and third lines. Beginning with the second stanza the pattern is the same throughout the remainder of the poem. The second and fourth lines are repeated while the first and third lines, metrically longer, contain the rhyme. When these poems are sung, the first stanza, or the refrain, is sung in unison by a group; then the first and third rhyming lines of succeeding stanzas are sung by a leader who is supported in the second and fourth lines by the group answer. As choral poetry the spirituals are very similar to the choral poetry of ancient Greece; however, the major difference is that after each stanza of a spiritual it is customary to return to the introductory quatrain. Therefore, every spiritual in effect is much longer than the present-day efforts to record them would appear.

> Oh, nobody knows de trouble I've seen
> Nobody knows but Jesus.
> Nobody knows de trouble I've seen
> Glory Hallelujah.

>> Sometimes I'm up, sometimes I'm down,
>> O yes Lord.
>> Sometimes I'm almost to de ground,
>> O yes Lord.

>> Although you see me goin' 'long so,
>> O yes Lord.
>> I have my trials here below,
>> O yes Lord.

>> One day when I was walkin' 'long,
>> O yes Lord.

> De el'ment open'd an' Love came down,
>   O yes Lord.
>
> I never shall forget that day,
>   O yes Lord.
> When Jesus washed my sins away,
>   O yes Lord.

A different method of treating the subject of conversion occurs in "I Know the Lord's Laid His Hands On Me" the refrain of which consists of only two lines.

> O, I know the Lord, I know the Lord,
> I know the Lord's laid his hands on me.
>
> Did ever you see the like before
>   I know the Lord's laid His hands on me,
> King Jesus preaching to the poor?
>   I know the Lord's laid His hands on me.
>
> O wasn't that a happy day
>   I know the Lord's laid His hands on me,
> When Jesus washed my sins away?
>   I know the Lord's laid His hands on me.
>
> Some seek the Lord and don't seek Him right,
>   I know the Lord's laid His hands on me,
> They fool all day and pray at night.
>   I know the Lord's laid His hands on me.
>
> My Lord's done just what He said,
>   I know the Lord's laid His hands on me,
> He's healed the sick and raised the dead.
>   I know the Lord's laid His hands on me.

Once an individual had become converted, his next step was to interest others by proselytizing. Both "Git on Board, Little Children" and "Come Down, Sinner" are poems of this nature. In the former there is an elaborate use of a train image to explain the idea. No doubt this image evolved out of the experiences which

were common to the speaker. The second poem is structurally
unique because the refrain, or the repeated stanza, contains far
more variation than is customary.

Git on board, little children,
Git on board, little children,
Git on board, little children,
There's room for many a more.

De Gospel train's a-comin',
    I hear it just at hand
I hear de car wheels rumblin',
    And rollin' through de land.

I hear de train a-comin',
    She's comin' round de curve,
She's loosened all her steam and brakes,
    And strainin' every nerve.

De fare is cheap and all can go,
    De rich and poor are there,
No second class a-board this train,
    No diff'rence in de fare.

Come down, come down,
Come down, sinner, yo' none too late;
Come down, come down,
O come down, sinner, yo' none too late.

Some seek the Lord, but don't seek Him right,
    Come down, sinner, yo' none too late;
Lil' at the day and none at night;
    Come down, sinner, yo' none too late.

Pray hard, pray hard,
Pray hard, sinner, yo' none too late;
Pray hard, pray hard,
O pray hard, sinner, yo' none too late.

Times ain't like they used to be,
    Come down, sinner, yo' none too late;

I for yo' and yo' for me;
Come down, sinner, yo' none too late.

Bow low, bow low,
Bow low, sinner, yo' none too late;
Bow low, bow low,
Bow low, sinner, yo' none too late.

Went down de hill t' say my prayer,
Come down, sinner, yo' none too late;
When I go there, ole Satan was there,
Come down, sinner, yo' none too late.

Seek hard, seek hard,
Seek hard, sinner, yo' none too late;
Seek hard, seek hard,
Seek hard, sinner, yo' none too late.

What do yo' think ole Satan say?
Come down, sinner, yo' none too late;
"Jesus dead, and God gone away,"
Come down, sinner, yo' none too late.

Shout hard, shout hard,
Shout hard, sinner, yo' none too late;
Shout hard, shout hard,
Shout hard, sinner, yo' none too late.

What t' do, I did not know,
Come down, sinner, yo' none too late;
Right back home I had to go,
Come down, sinner, yo' none too late.

Mourn hard, mourn hard,
Mourn hard, sinner, yo' none too late;
Mourn hard, mourn hard,
Mourn hard, sinner, yo' none too late.

Something spoke unto my soul,
Come down, sinner, yo' none too late;
"Go in peace, and sin no more,"
Come down, sinner, yo' none too late.

The poetry of the spirituals is peculiarly free from anger, bitterness, or reproach. Yet the misconception that they were products of contentment prevailed for a long time. People who really heard these works and people who sang them recognized that the spirituals were essentially sad songs. Only the most callous could interpret the words and the mournful minor key as emanating from earthly happiness or satisfaction. There is, however, a jubilation which is sometimes expressed in such terms as "glory hallelujah" and which tends to increase the pathos of the simple message of faith. The comic spirit, often present in folk poetry, is totally absent from the spiritual.

The symbolism used in these early poems is neither complicated nor intricate. As many other unlettered people in other lands, the authors of the spirituals tended to use the simple things of life which they knew to explain religious experiences and the unknown. Since the idea of heaven was a dominant one, many of the symbols tend to deal with this concept. Heaven itself is variously referred to as "home," "the promised land," "Paradise," "Jerusalem," "Canaan," "Zion," or "upper bright world." However, there are very few spirituals which do not at some point include the term *heaven* which is usually described as a place of security, beauty, happiness, complete freedom and equality; it is further emphasized that in heaven reunion of families will take place. Reaching heaven, as the poets interpret it, means the victory of man over the trials and temptations of life. Once in heaven life there is in direct contrast to that on earth; yet the imagined beauty of heaven is sometimes compared with the ugliness of hell. The following spirituals illustrate how simply, yet directly, these ideas were incorporated.

IN THAT BEAUTIFUL WORLD ON HIGH
Oh, I will be there, I will be there,
With the palms of victory
Crowns of glory you shall wear
In that beautiful world on high.

I hope my mother will be there,
  In that beautiful world on high,
That used to join with me in prayer,
  In that beautiful world on high.

I hope my sister will be there,
  In that beautiful world on high,
I hope my sister will be there,
  In that beautiful world on high.

I hope my brother will be there,
  In that beautiful world on high,
I hope my brother will be there,
  In that beautiful world on high.

I hope my Saviour will be there,
  In that beautiful world on high,
I hope my Saviour will be there,
  In that beautiful world on high.

GOING TO SHOUT ALL OVER GOD'S HEAVEN

Heav'n, Heav'n,
Everybody talkin' 'boun heav'n ain't goin' there
Heav'n, Heav'n,
Goin' to shout all over God's heav'n.

  I've got a robe, you've got a robe,
    All God's children got a robe.
  When I get to heav'n goin' to put on my robe
    Goin' to shout all over God's heav'n.

  I've got a crown, you've got a crown,
    All of God's children got a crown.
  When I get to heav'n goin' to put on my crown
    Goin' to shout all over God's heav'n.

  I've got a-shoes, you've got a-shoes,
    All of God's children got a-shoes.
  When I get to heav'n goin' to put on my shoes
    Goin to walk all over God's heav'n.

I've got a harp, you've got a harp,
  All of God's children got a harp.
When I get to heav'n goin' to play on my harp
  Goin' to play all over God's heav'n.

I've got a song, you've got a song,
  All of God's children got a song.
When I get to heav'n goin' to sing a new song
  Goin' to sing all over God's heav'n.

BY AND BY

O' by and by, by and by,
I'm going to lay down this heavy load.
By and by, by and by,
I'm going to lay down this heavy load.

  I know my robe's going to fit me well,
    I'm going to lay down this heavy load.
  For I tried it on at the gates of hell,
    I'm going to lay down this heavy load.

  O, hell is a deep and dark despair,
    I'm going to lay down this heavy load.
  So stop, poor sinner, and don't go there,
    I'm going to lay down this heavy load.

  O, when I get to heaven going to sing and shout,
    I'm going to lay down this heavy load,
  For there's no one there to turn me out,
    I'm going to lay down this heavy load.

  O, Christians can't you rise and tell,
    I'm going to lay down this heavy load,
  That Jesus hath done all things well,
    I'm going to lay down this heavy load.

The apparent preoccupation with death which occurs in these poems is a concern which uses death as a means to get to heaven. Invariably the spirituals which are concerned with "crossing over the River Jordan," the most popular death image, are also intent upon describing—usually in the last stanza—what is to happen or what can be expected in heaven. The rewards are often the same: white robe, starry crown, golden shoes, golden harp, with all relatives assembled for an eternity of resting, singing, or just playing around the throne of God. Occasionally, the joy of getting to heaven is replaced by a concentration upon death itself. Perhaps nowhere in this folk literature is death more fervently desired than in "I Know Moon Rise."

> I know moon rise, I know star rise,
>   Lay this body down.
> I walk in the moonlight, I walk in the starlight,
>   To lay this body down.
>
> I'll walk in the graveyard, I'll walk through the graveyard,
>   To lay this body down.
> I'll lie in the grave and stretch out my arms;
>   Lay this body down.
>
> I go to the judgment in the evening of the day,
>   When I lay this body down;
> And my soul and your soul will meet in the day
>   When I lay this body down.

During the Civil War there is a strong indication that some of the spirituals were interpreted purely on their symbolic levels by listeners. Consequently, heaven became an equivalent of the north, freedom was thought of only in terms of earthly freedoms, and traveling was interpreted as either escape or more specifically as the Underground Railroad. Higginson records in his article on the Negro spiritual that people were jailed in Georgetown, South Carolina, for singing "We'll Soon Be Free." The central idea, however, of the song is a recurring one, but apparently it was considered far more risky than the others. The last stanza does, however, seem peculiarly out of place and must have been a later addition.

We'll soon be free,
We'll soon be free,
We'll soon be free,
  When the Lord will call us home.

My brother, how long,
My brother, how long,
My brother, how long,
  'Fore we done suffering here?

It won't be long,
It won't be long,
It won't be long,
  'Fore the Lord will call us home.

We'll walk the miry road,
We'll walk the miry road,
We'll walk the miry road,
  Where pleasure never dies.

We'll walk the golden street,
We'll walk the golden street,
We'll walk the golden street,
  Where pleasure never dies.

My brother, how long,
My brother, how long,
My brother, how long,
  'Fore we done suffering here?

We'll soon be free,
We'll soon be free,
We'll soon be free,
  When Jesus sets me free.

We'll fight for liberty,
We'll fight for liberty,
We'll fight for liberty,
  When the Lord will call us home.

It is true that the spirituals which are concerned with freedom from earthly woes are not always subtle. Frequently, of course, the attitude expressed in "Steal Away" does seem to prevail, but "Oh, Freedom" and "Slav'ry Chain" are clearly results of contemporary conditions although the latter uses the concept of slavery in a more ambiguous way.

STEAL AWAY

Steal away, steal away,
Steal away to Jesus;
Steal away, steal away home,
I ain't got long to stay here.

My Lord calls me,
    He calls me by the thunder;
The trumpet sounds within-a my soul,
    I ain't got long to stay here.

Green trees are bending,
    Poor sinner stands a-trembling;
The trumpet sounds within-a my soul,
    I ain't got long to stay here.

Tombstones are bursting,
    Poor sinner stands a-trembling;
The trumpet sounds within-a my soul,
    I ain't got long to stay here.

My Lord calls me,
    He calls me by the lightning;
The trumpet sounds within-a my soul,
    I ain't got long to stay here.

OH, FREEDOM

Oh, freedom over me,
    And before I'd be a slave,
    I'll be buried in my grave,
And go home to my Lord and be free.

No more moaning over me!
    And before I'd be a slave,

I'll be buried in my grave,
And go home to my Lord and be free.

No more weeping over me,
    And before I'd be a slave,
    I'll be buried in my grave,
And go home to my Lord and be free.

There'll be singing over me,
    And before I'd be a slave,
    I'll be buried in my grave,
And go home to my Lord and be free.

There'll be shouting over me,
    And before I'd be a slave,
    I'll be buried in my grave,
And go home to my Lord and be free.

There'll be praying over me,
    And before I'd be a slave,
    I'll be buried in my grave,
And go home to my Lord and be free.

SLAV'RY CHAIN

Slav'ry chain done broke at las',
Broke at las', broke at las',
Slav'ry chain done broke at las',
Goin' to praise God 'til I die.

Way up in-a dat valley,
Prayin' on my knees;
Tellin' God about my troubles,
An' to he'p me ef-a He please.

I did tell Him how I suffer
In de dungeon an' de chain;
An' de days I went wif head bowed down,
An' my broken flesh an' pain.

I did know my Jesus heard me,
'Cause de spirit spoke to me

An' said "Rise my chile, your chillun
An' you too shall be free."

I done 'p'int one mighty captain
For to marshall all my hosts;
An' to bring my bleeding ones to me
An' not one shall be lost.

Now no more weary trav'lin'
'Cause my Jesus set-a me free
An' dere's no more auction block for me
Since He gave me liberty.

The symbolism of heaven and the emphasis upon freedom remain important ideas in Negro poetry. During the great migration of the 1920's there were additional references in literature to the North as being the epitome of heaven. Needless to say, it was not long before this dream was completely shattered for the migrants, and in its place two other approaches were substituted. One attitude simply intensified the idea of a "real" heaven existing somewhere beyond the realm of human life; and the second attitude began to doubt the existence of a heaven at all. The first attitude produced optimistic poetry, for the poets repeated the concept of the spirituals, a concept which defined heaven as a place of eternal rest, a land of plenty, and a land of peace. Out of the second attitude there developed an interest in hell. Initially in the poetry of the spirituals hell was merely the antithesis of heaven, a place to which all sinners were to be confined. In some of the early slave sermons there was a great deal of time spent in describing hell as a place of intense heat, of dark crevices and caverns, and of torment. As time passed, hell ceased to be used as a theological concept and became a geographical one. At first it was located "somewhere in the southern part of the United States" and later was expanded to include any place where the denial of freedom for all still occurred. In the early poetic references to hell there was a belief that eternal torture could be avoided by a conscientious dedication to Christian principles. Later it became an unavoidable destiny of all black men.

The poetry of the spirituals implicitly supports the idea which was frequently prevalent among the slaves that the race was in actuality God's chosen people. This meant that the people had to be subjected to trials in order to prove worthy. The slaves constantly compared themselves to the Hebrews who were led out of Egypt and of out bondage by Moses, and there were—as there still are—references to any leader as being a "Moses." They further emphasized the fact that God led the Jews out of their captivity only when He was ready to do so and only when He thought they were prepared; the slaves reasoned that at the appropriate time they, too, would be led out of their bondage. Out of these beliefs has emerged the insistence upon believing in God's plan. "Waiting for the Lord" to act came as a direct result of believing that God had so planned His universe that He—and He alone—could cause events to occur. This attitude has had various poetic consequences. On the one hand, it produced the interest in heaven as a place of refuge. Still further, it produced a type of complacency which ultimately resulted in great faith. This was a faith that made the present bearable, but—perhaps more important —it made the future believable.

Faith, of course, is not peculiar to any one ethnic group; yet, it can frequently be found in a concentrated form among those who feel unnecessarily oppressed. To some, the faith of the Negro may appear simply as an escape mechanism depriving him of an ability to face immediate reality. However, one must remember that faith plays an integral part in any religious concept, and it cannot be divorced from its body of literature. As these early poets looked optimistically to the world beyond this one, they also believed that as God's chosen people they could not forever be suppressed by man. Out of the pride of knowing their relationship with God developed their pride in their ability to adjust to life on earth. As pilgrims in this world they could sing with conviction:

I'm a poor wayfarin' stranger
 While journeyin' through this world of woe,
Yet there's no sickness, toil, and danger,
 In that bright world to which I go.

I'm goin' there to see my father,
 I'm goin' there no more to roam,
I'm just a-goin' over Jordan,
 I'm just a-goin' over home.

I know dark clouds will gather round me,
 I know my way is rough and steep,
Yet bright fields lie just before me,
 Where God's redeemed their vigil's keep.

I'm goin' there to see my mother,
 She said she'd meet me when I come,
I'm just a-goin' over Jordan,
 I'm just a-goin' over home.

I'll soon be free from ev'ry trial,
 My body will sleep in the ole churchyard,
I'll drop the cross of self-denial,
 And enter on my great reward.

I'm goin' there to see my Saviour,
 To sing His praise in heaven's dome,
I'm just a-goin' over Jordan,
 I'm just a-goin' over home.

II

There have been many attempts to explain the creation of the spirituals; these attempts range from assertions of total African influences to endeavors to prove that they were coded messages. While there are some indications of African influence, most notably in the oral nature of the literary tradition, the spiritual was a product of the American experience and the American environment. Any cursory perusal of the bulk of spirituals will reveal the extent to which they are direct results of what the slaves thought and felt, what they saw and heard. It may be asserted that the excessive repetition was an attempt to cast some sort of magical spell, but the repetition was also a means to establish rhythm in a poetry which did not rely heavily upon pre-determined metrical patterns. "I Want To Go Home" is a good example not only of the frequent ambiguity to be found in these poems, but also of the use of a repeated line to establish rhythm and the complete absence of rhyme.

> There's no rain to wet you,
>   O, yes, I want to go home.
> There's no sun to burn you,
>   O, yes, I want to go home;
> O, push along, believers
>   O, yes, I want to go home.
> There's no hard trials,
>   O, yes, I want to go home.
> There's no whips a-crackin'
>   O, yes, I want to go home.
> My brother on the wayside,
>   O, yes, I want to go home;
> O, push along, my brother,
>   O, yes, I want to go home.
> Where there's no stormy weather,
>   O, yes, I want to go home.
> There's no tribulations,
>   O, yes, I want to go home.

The importance of the spirituals as a type of secret language has been seriously over-emphasized. To view them in this manner minimizes the religious aspect which is far too dominant to be overlooked. That some of them, however, were used for specific purposes is made clear by the language. At the same time that ex-slaves have recorded the significance of such songs as "Many Thousand Gone," often the need for secrecy had less to do with the implied code than with the fact that slaves were frequently forbidden to gather in large groups. When they met for religious purposes, it was necessary to do so in secret; or when whites were present, it was necessary to veil ideas in such a way that the ideas would appear acceptable. Needless to say, many of the spirituals which mention the need to avoid being caught while "praising the Lord" had reference to these types of restrictive measures. On the whole, these poems are examples of the need of a people for expression, and what better subject could they use than the religion which had created in them a sense of dignity and worth?

After his association with the Negro soldiers who had introduced him to the spiritual, Higginson concludes his article in the June, 1867, issue of *The Atlantic Monthly:*

By these [the spirituals] they could sing themselves, as had their fathers before them, out of the contemplation of their own low estates, into the sublime scenery of the Apocalypse. I remember that this minor-keyed pathos used to seem to me almost too sad to dwell upon, while slavery seemed destined to last for generations; but now that their patience has had its perfect work, history cannot afford to lose this portion of its record. There is no parallel instance of an oppressed race thus sustained by the religious sentiment alone. These songs are but the vocal expression of the simplicity of their faith and the sublimity of their long resignation (pp. 693-694).

But perhaps nowhere in American literature has there been a greater tribute to the creators of the spirituals than in "O Black and Unknown Bards" by James Weldon Johnson, who has been referred to as the "dean of Negro poets":

> O black and unknown bards of long ago,
> How came your lips to touch the sacred fire?
> How, in your darkness, did you come to know
> The power and the beauty of the minstrel's lyre?
> Who first from midst his bonds lifted his eyes?
> Who first from out the still watch, lone and long,
> Feeling the ancient faith of prophets rise
> Within his dark-kept soul, burst into song?

Heart of what slave poured out such melody
As "Steal away to Jesus"? On its strains
His spirit must have nightly floated free,
Though still about his hands he felt his chains.
Who heard great "Jordan roll"? Whose starward eye
Saw chariot "swing low"? And who was he
That breathed that comforting, melodic sigh,
"Nobody knows de trouble I see"?

What merely living clod, what captive thing,
Could up toward God through all its darkness grope,
And find within its deadened heart to sing
These songs of sorrow, love and faith, and hope?
How did it catch that subtle undertone,
That note in music heard not with the ears?
How sound the elusive reed so seldom blown,
Which stirs the soul or melts the heart to tears.

Not that great German master in his dream
Of harmonies that thundered amongst the stars
At the creation, ever heard a theme
Nobler than "Go down, Moses." Mark its bars
How like a mighty trumpet-call they stir
The blood. Such are the notes that men have sung
Going to valorous deeds; such tones they were
That helped make history when Time was young.

There is a wide, wide wonder in it all,
That from degraded rest and servile toil
The fiery spirit of the seer should call
These simple children of the sun and soil.
O black slave singers, gone, forgot, unfamed,
You—you alone, of all the long, long line
Of those who've sung untaught, unknown, unnamed,
Have stretched out upward, seeking the divine.

You sang not deeds of heroes or of kings;
No chant of bloody war, no exulting paean
Of arms-won triumphs; but your humble strings
You touched in chord with music empyrean.

> You sang far better than you knew; the songs
> That for your listeners' hungry hearts sufficed
> Still live,—but more than this to you belongs:
> You sang a race from wood and stone to Christ.

As time progressed, the primitive technique of the spiritual was supplanted by more experimentation in poetic form and diction. Later poets tended to use the current popular forms for their work; however, many of the attitudes found in the spirituals have been maintained in religious poetry. The element of faith, for example, which is prevalent in the spiritual has been manifested in later poetic developments, and the belief in a tomorrow which will be better than today has been expressed by numerous Negro poets from the close of the Civil War to the present. "Supplication" by Joseph Seamon Cotter, Jr. is a typical illustration of the way in which the mood of the old spiritual has been captured.

> I am so tired and weary,
>   So tired of the endless fight,
> So weary of waiting the dawn
>   And finding endless night.
>
> That I ask but rest and quiet—
>   Rest for days that are gone,
> And quiet for the little space
>   That I must journey on.

For a period after the Civil War Negro poets were just as interested in analyzing the Negro's relationship to God as had been the earlier unknown poets. Generally these analyses can be divided into two dominant approaches. One idea explains the plight of the race in terms of God, acting as the supreme judge, meting out punishment for some unnamed crime. The other idea emphasizes the concept of Negroes as being God's chosen people. As the elect of God, Negroes are forced to be subjected to earthly inconveniences in order to justify their selection by God. This point of view concludes with the belief that at the appointed time God will formally acknowledge His people before the entire universe. With this belief firmly established, a people can endure the many stumbling blocks thrust before them.

James Madison Bell views the Negro's situation in America as being a result of sin; however, Leslie Pinckney Hill does not. Hill maintains that the race has been chosen by God. In "God Sends the Negro on a Special Errand" he pleads for an awareness of the basic worth of the Negro as a human being. The Negro's job, as he sees it, is to create in the world the true spirit of brotherhood. And as was later implied by the noted English historian Arnold Toynbee, Hill claims that as creators of a faith-oriented culture, Negroes are destined to become leaders in any social reorganization which takes place in the world. Referring to him as an Ishmael "of an unchosen land," Hill then attempts to characterize the role of the Negro in America and to list his gifts to America including the spiritual. He concludes with the religious mission of the race in America.

The idea of a God-chosen people is not new. The spirituals had sung of the relationships between God and the Negro. But the interpretation which Hill places upon the idea is adapted to suit the modern scene. It has great racial and social implications. The idea is developed to help foster a saner psychological adjustment to the world and to aid Negroes in maintaining a belief in their intrinsic worth. According to Hill, the race—with the help of God—is to lead the world into a new social structure. Because the poet maintains that Negroes have a higher status in the eyes of God than those who oppress them, Hill insists that pride should evolve out of this special mission.

In still another way Claude McKay in "To the White Fiends" supports Hill's thesis regarding the special mission of the race. McKay's poem is bitter at the outset, but in the latter part there is the contention that God has set the Negro in America to be a light to burn upon a "benighted earth." He expresses the view that the world will be swallowed up in darkness; nevertheless,

God has put the Negro here to prove himself of greatest value before this darkness comes.

> Think you I am not fiend and savage too?
> Think you I could not arm me with a gun
> And shoot down ten of you for every one
> Of my black brothers murdered, burnt by you?
> Be not deceived, for every deed you do
> I could match—outmatch: am I not Africa's son,
> Black of that black land where black deeds are done?
> But the Almighty from the darkness drew
> My soul and said: "Even thou shall be a light
> Awhile to burn on the benighted earth,
> The dusky face I set among the white
> For thee to prove thyself of highest worth;
> Before the world is swallowed up in night,
> To show thy little lamp: go forth, go forth!"

Once again there is the emphasis, like that of Hill's poem, of the Negro's intrinsic value as being part of some plan. Denied proper recognition and status by men, he receives a higher position with God.

James Weldon Johnson in his poem "Fifty Years," written fifty years after the Emancipation Proclamation, expresses the belief that God has some great plan for the Negro. It is clear that God will not let the good "come to naught." It is implied in the poem that God sent out Garrison, Phillips, John Brown, and Lincoln to do what they did in behalf of freeing the Negro. God, then, continues to protect the work of these men. He cannot allow His work to fail. Being thus convinced, Johnson admonishes the Negro to have faith in his "God-known destiny."

> . . . .
> Courage! Look out, beyond, and see
> the far horizon's beckoning span!
> Faith in your God-known destiny!
> We are part of some great plan.

> Because the tongues of Garrison
> And Phillips now are cold in death,
> Think you their work can be undone?
> Or quenched the fires lit by their breath?
>
> Think you that John Brown's spirit stops?
> That Lovejoy was but idly slain?
> Or do you think those precious drops
> From Lincoln's heart were shed in vain?
>
> That for which millions prayed and sighed,
> That for which tens of thousands fought
> For which so many freely died
> God cannot let it come to naught.

Among the older writers who were influenced by the entire religious tradition of the spirituals patience was considered to be the answer to all problems. Consequently, they could—with varying degrees of eloquence—avow with Theodore Shackelford that "God Will Make It Right." "Long, Black Line" by L. Zack Gilbert, a more recent poem, does not emphasize the necessity for waiting until heaven in order to achieve freedom, but in the struggle to create a heaven on earth the quality of patience is still important.

The poetry of the spirituals and the religious poetry which developed from the songs tend to emphasize the Christian concept of suffering as a means of salvation. The end, therefore, was in a sense good and justified the means. The resignation which is a dominant motif in this poetry seldom is completely pessimistic. Melancholic though many of these lyrics are, they are essentially optimistic. As one moves into the poetry of the mid-twentieth century, one discovers a darker view of life. There is a rejection on the part of many poets of those religious patterns which had been such an integral part of a religiously oriented culture. The tragic sense of life is replaced by a condemnation of the whole process of human life, a condemnation which regards life as essentially evil both in its nature and in its end. While there has not been a total poetic rejection of Christianity, it is interesting to note that the artistic expression of the 1960's might well be summarized in Don L. Lee's "In the Interest of Black Salvation." From the intensity of the religious fervor of the unknown poets of the spirituals through the Harlem Renaissance and to the despair which frequently reverberates in present-day poetry, one can trace the significance of religion in Negro culture. The despair, however, evident in the published poetry of the 1960's is in a large measure an attempt to deliberately reject the prominent influence of the church and of religion without substituting another comparable power. For many of the younger poets, the significance of the church is well known for many of them are rejecting the religion of their immediate kin, their parents. Yet, even though Lee can end his poem by saying: "Jesus saves—S. and H. Green Stamps," the overwhelming evidence is that for the first time in Negro history the poets are not mirroring the dominant idea of a large segment of the people who still find in religion and in the church that type of sustaining solace that has been extremely effective in the past. Those who would dismiss the spirituals and the later poetic tradition which derived from them merely as a submissive surrender to prevailing conditions must remember that these works contain powerful statements on the need for freedom. Poignant though they are, the songs of sorrow are also songs of freedom.

CHAPTER III

"We Hold These Truths To Be Self-Evident . . .": The Slave Narrative and The Prose of Freedom

THE SLAVE NARRATIVE is one of the little investigated types of American literature; yet, it forms a large body of nineteenth-century literature. Just as the spiritual evolved to meet certain conditions so the slave narrative is an absolutely American document born out of the needs of ex-slaves to communicate their experiences to others and created to tell the age-old story of man's quest for freedom and human dignity. As a literary type the slave narrative became so popular that white abolitionists began to use the genre in hopes of "cashing in" on the commercial success of them. Unfortunately the world today knows of these works almost solely from the point of view of the white writers who simply adopted the form after its success was assured and after the larger publishing houses, to which they had access, were willing to issue these pseudo-slave narratives. It must be admitted, however, that some of these writers were anxious to see the end of slavery and were doing all within their power to speed its demise. Yet, there was a time in the nineteenth century when the black authors of the slave narratives were hailed as the new American writers. Because of the ease with which the form was copied, it became increasingly difficult as the nineteenth century progressed to distinguish between an authentic slave narrative and a spurious one which was simply a story about an ex-slave.

The slave narrative was extremely popular between 1830 and 1860 although there are examples of them before and after these years. One of the central characteristics of an authentic slave narrative is that it is autobiographical rather than biographical for the writer recounts his own experiences which led him from slavery to freedom. In his story he usually places great emphasis upon the adventures which befell him, the providential nature of God, and upon his own belief in the American Dream. Hence these works were nationalistic in the sense that they expressed a belief in the optimism which pervaded the period concerning the destiny of the country. Never did a single body of literature more clearly demonstrate the efficacy of the principles of the Declaration of Independence. The optimism was further heightened by the element of protest which was nearly always present. The protest ranged from a direct attack on slavery to the more subtle attack on it through a discussion of man's inhumanity to man. But like other protest writing, the slave narratives assumed that changes were possible once people recognized the problem.

Thus for the first time in American literature there was the merger of democratic ideals with protest elements into a distinct literary pattern, and this pattern was to become important in our national literature. These early slave writers—as later writers were to do—used the ideal of the American dream to explain the reality of the system itself. But seldom is there the total rejection of the ideal. It was the institution of slavery which they repudiated. In dealing with their subject the authors of the slave narratives emphasized the toll taken upon the human mind and human spirit by this peculiar social structure. The use of psychology, elementary though that use may have been, was to become an integral part of American literature as the major writers of the nineteenth century—Hawthorne, Thoreau, Melville, Twain, James—were to explore the psychological ambiguities of human existence. Thus a pattern which was to become popular in American literature was

developed not by professional writers but rather by a group of
ex-slaves whose only immediate concern was to tell their stories
to anyone who would listen.

I

The slave narratives became an immediate success among the
American reading public especially in the North. For one reason,
these works appeared at a time when on the popular level of reading there was a great deal of interest in adventure stories and in
those stories which emphasized the melodramatic as well as the
sentimental. The American reading public had been saturated
with the Cooper novels which dealt with the sea, the forest, and
the conquest of the West. With the intention of creating adventure
Cooper had recounted in an often-repeated formula the escape-
pursuit-capture theme which we today associate with modern
"westerns." But even Cooper had dealt with the woods, the sea,
and Indians—subjects which were not always emotionally appealing but which provided a basis for the American myth. While
they did not feel the urgency of the adventurous situations recounted by Cooper, all readers could not but feel the urgency of
the story of the ex-slave who in his search for freedom of body
and freedom of mind had started the long journey to the North.
Readers thrilled as the hero eluded the patrols and hounds and as
he eventually fell exhaustedly into the land of freedom. Readers
wept as the slave mother begged to keep her children and often
killed them to prevent their sale. Not only was the escape-pursuit-
capture motif given new dimension, but also the recital of the
horrors of slavery provided additional thrills for an audience which
enjoyed reading stories that were concerned with the difficulties
which a hero was forced to overcome. Excessive floggings, the
disruption of family life, the violations of body and spirit were
just a few of the horrendous experiences with which the narratives
dealt as the authors demonstrated the strength of the hero who
could survive. The recital of horrors, both physical and mental,

provided ammunition for the anti-slavery. forces and served as a persuasive device for those who had not fully decided what position to take on the matter of slavery. Even the most conservative reader could hardly justify the physical and spiritual degradation to which slavery subjected a man.

There were those, of course, who used the slave narratives as presenting an authentic view of slavery. Certainly the stories stressed the terror of human slavery and in this respect were highly reliable. Since the dreadful nature of human servitude had already been established, the writers of the slave narratives employed information which was faily well-known, and it may well be that incidents and episodes were used at times not so much because they had occurred in the life of the particular writer but rather because they had occurred to someone and were consequently a part of the common storehouse of knowledge.

The uniqueness of the slave narrative is to be found in its ability to combine various motifs of American literature and American ideology into a new and different form. Much of the prose in the America of the seventeenth and eighteenth centuries as well as that of the early years of the nineteenth century had emphasized not only religious but also political freedom. The concern for personal liberty is certainly present in the slave narrative, and they contain an appeal for adherence to religious principles. These concepts were combined with the elements of the sentimental and adventure stories to provide an admirable link between the popular adventure stories of the early years of the nineteenth century and the melodramatic works of the latter part of the century. Hence the link between the two periods is found not in the work of Emerson, Thoreau, Hawthorne, or Melville but rather in the work of a group of Negro writers the names of whom are little more than historic curiosities today. Thus a survey of nineteenth-century American literature which begins and ends with the popular adventure stories and sentimental novels must take into account the slave narrative.

To view these works individually is to wonder at the popularity of them. All of the faults associated with popular nineteenth-century fiction (stilted language, impossible events, one-dimensional characters, forced endings) are present, but to view them as a body of literature is to note at least some of the reasons for success. They reached their heyday during the so-called sentimental period of American life, a period when readers enjoyed reading of the misfortunes and hardships of characters, when readers enjoyed crying as the hero was apparently caught in a situation which provided no solution. Just as modern audiences thrill today with the adventures of the characters of some current soap opera or best seller so some nineteenth-century audiences felt the same urge for adventure. Coupled very closely with the sentimentalism of these stories is the larger philosophy of Romanticism into which these stories also fit. The romantic tradition in America had placed great emphasis upon the need for personal freedom and liberty as well as upon adventure. The humanitarian emphasis of Transcendentalism was more than satisfied in these works which appeared during the height of the American romantic philosophy of Transcendentalism. The self-reliance of Emerson, the concept of marching to the drummer which one hears promulgated by Thoreau, and the power of man's heart so ably described by Hawthorne were more than amply demonstrated by this body of literature. The popularity of these works is further testimony that romanticism and sentimentalism were dominant strains in American literature before 1860.

The slave narratives appealed to a wide audience and won its approval in that audience. The abolitionist, of course, took these stories as absolutely reliable records of slavery and used them in much of the anti-slavery activities of the period. Here the concern was not so much upon the fact that these stories were cast in a popular mode, although the emphasis upon the sensationalism of the narratives was not lost upon audiences, but rather that these works presented views of slavery which no white man could ever see. And at least if he saw it, he would not be able to comprehend it fully. Therefore, the narratives served as the necessary eyewitness accounts to illustrate the philosophical reasons against slavery as used by the abolitionists. Had it not been for the early slave narratives and their influence, Harriet Beecher Stowe would not have had a ready-made audience for *Uncle Tom's Cabin*.

While the slave narrative, as a popular form of literature, was substantially a product of the mid-years of the nineteenth century, there were forerunners of it which demonstrated the techniques and subjects which were later to be popularized and reduced to a formula. The three authors already mentioned in Chapter I— Vassa, Briton Hammon, and John Marrant—executed the themes which were to be more subtly integrated in later works. In the work of Hammon and Marrant the dominant idea is one which deals with the varied adventures of the escaping slave as well as with the providential nature of God. Since the religious experience is paramount in both works, they are essentially spiritual auto-biographies recounting the road which led the authors to a knowl-edge of God and to a commitment to His work. Slavery, while morally wrong, becomes in this context simply one of the earthly evils to be endured as one is being "tested" for God's work. The Vassa autobiography, on the other hand, deals specifically with matters of this world as it registers a clear protest against the injustices of slavery. In order to present the dilemma of his slave experience, Vassa recounts his early life in Africa and contrasts his life of freedom there with his enforced servitude here. The Vassa narrative deviates from most of them because it is one of the few to mention the writer's earlier life in Africa. Underlying all of the narratives is the unanswerable question, the same ques-tion which Frederick Douglass was later to articulate as "why am I a slave?" Thus these works represent more than records of escapes from slavery to freedom, they also represent varying attempts to answer the question of the role of a human being in human society.

Just as the slave narratives are philosophically similar, they are also structurally similar. The repeated formula varies only in the specifics of the escape-pursuit-capture theme and in place names. They are very simply written with little or no allusion to complicated images or symbols. The central symbol, and frequently the only one, deals with the *journey* itself as the hero travels not only from one place to another but as he travels from one position in life to another. In his journey the narrator makes it clear that his friend has been the "cover of night" with its guidance of the stars, most especially the North Star. Significantly, however, the darkness of night befriends the traveler only when he goes beyond the surrounding darkness and looks heavenward toward the direction of the North Star. When the escaping slave, the narratives recount, gazed only at the immediate encompassing darkness, he became hopelessly lost. The message of what Henry Bibb in his narrative was to call "the unchangeable North Star" became clear. It was nature's symbol of liberty.

The narratives are highly subjective as each author recounts his particular experiences. Seldom does he include the experiences of others except in a very general way. He becomes almost the sole actor in a drama played against the backdrop of American slavery. People with whom he has contact in his journey do obviously play a role in a successful escape, but this is minimized in order to focus upon the narrator-hero. These subjective accounts are most frequently treated chronologically, and in this way the reader becomes even more conscious of the "before and after" picture which is so very relevant to the subject.

The power of the slave narrative results from the fact that the authors were often able to write their stories shortly after escaping to freedom. With the journey still fresh in their minds they were able to transmit a great sense of urgency to their works. The element of recall was not too important because seldom do these writers dwell at length on their childhood experiences, instead they tend to concentrate upon one or two incidents of adulthood. Since many of these ex-slaves were supported or used by abolitionists once they reached free territory, their works frequently end with a plea for a particular anti-slavery organization. This is especially true in instances where the narrative itself grew out of the lecture notes of the ex-slaves who were constantly booked as speakers at anti-slavery rallies. The power of the narrative is further enhanced by the underlying mood of loneliness which permeates these works. The excessive loneliness of slave life was initially occasioned by the separation of tribesmen so that there could be no communication between them. Later the loneliness was a result of the slaves' own awareness that their condition was at variance with the current doctrines of freedom in America and expressed the general spirit of hopelessness which was a constant companion in the slave quarters. As he prepared for his journey, the escaping slave could confide in few around him. And as he left his family and friends, he departed not only with the knowledge that he would probably never see them again but also with the fears which face the man who pursues an untraveled road alone.

The slave narrative should not be confused with the multitude of slave biographies and ghostwritten narratives which began appearing regularly during the 1840's and 1850's and continued to the end of the century. There are similarities between these works and the slave narrative; however, the biographies, which frequently were issued in collected editions, follow the thematic structure of the "success story" perhaps more so than the narrative. The central purpose of the emphasis upon success was to provide a means of identification for black Americans and foment a sense of accomplishment for them in spite of the hardships. One such work, *The Black Man, His Antecedents, His Genius and His Achievements,* was edited by ex-slave William Wells Brown, the second edition of which appeared in 1863. Even the abolitionist Lydia Maria Child issued a series of biographical studies in *The Freedmen's Book* (Boston, 1865). Many of these collected biographies attempted to gain historical perspective by surveying the lives of European blacks as well as those in America and, at the same time, by including information about their African forebears.

The ghostwritten slave narratives are legion and are—perhaps— better known today than authentic ones. Almost without exception they were written by sympathetic whites who used the works as a forum for the expression of their own anti-slavery sentiments. However, the narrative of Nat Turner, *The Confessions, Trial and*

Execution of Nat Turner, the Negro Insurrectionist . . . , was written by T.R. Gray, a pitiless southerner to whom Turner dictated his story during the last days of his life; but this type of narrative is a deviation from the usual pattern. The ghostwritten narratives tend to be far more didactic and sentimental than those actually written by ex-slaves. The title pages often give a clue to the extent of "editorial assistance" received. The authentic slave narratives are apt to note on the title page of the first edition some such phrase as "written by himself." These assertions were used not only to assure the reader of reliability but also to make certain that the reader was aware that the author would receive any monetary value from the sale of the book. When one considers that many of these stories were written in order to obtain money to secure the freedom of family members who remained enslaved, one can understand why the authorial distinction became important. On the other hand, phrases such as "related to," "edited by," "dictated to," and "narrated to" are just a few of the terms used to indicate additional help. Under many circumstances the editorial assistant is unnamed as in the case of the narrative of Andrew Jackson who was born free but who was kidnapped by his mother's ex-master. After escaping to Wisconsin, Jackson went to New York where he became engaged in the work of the anti-slavery movement, and in 1847 his work, *Narrative and Writings of Andrew Jackson of Kentucky Containing an Account of His Birth and Twenty-Six Years of His Life While a Slave, Narrated by Himself, Written by a Friend,* was published at Syracuse, New York. Of the known editorial assistants perhaps none has become more a part of American sentimental literature than Lydia Maria Child who edited Harriet Jacobs' *Incidents in the Life of a Slave Girl* (Boston, 1861). The work was especially appealing to those who viewed slavery as a testimony to the moral decay of the South for the incidents of the story hinged upon the role of the white wife once her husband had acknowledged his relationship with a female slave. Northern abolitionists viewed these women as having been wronged by the mental cruelty of husband and master, and as being victimized by a system over which they had little or no control.

The slave narratives, both authentic and ghostwritten, were significant in establishing certain beliefs about slavery, beliefs which were challenged by John Pendleton Kennedy's *Swallow Barn* (1832) and by the "plantation tradition" in American literature. Irwin Russell, Joel Chandler Harris, and Thomas Nelson Page were just a few of the southern white writers who were responsible for the establishment of the myth of the contented slaves and the wealthy slaveowners as well as the general aura of romance which surrounded the "Big House" and the slave quarters. The slave narrative denies this idyllic setting. Instead of lush green fields with singing slaves working hard but happily, the narratives portray the poverty of the land as well as the poverty of many slaveholders who are forced by circumstances to work side by side with their slaves in order to eke a living from the land. Seldom do the narratives portray the common myth of the big plantation house staffed by authoritarian house slaves and beautiful women in billowing gowns. The setting of a *Gone with the Wind* is practically non-existent in these works. Southern white women are not described as being beautiful nor benevolent. In fact, they tend to be far more brutal and mean than the men who are coarse frontiersmen. The southern "gentleman" is just as rare as the southern "lady." Much of the complaint of the narrative centers upon the irony of a brutal people "owning" human beings who are far superior in breeding and manners. There is little in the narratives to support the theory that the slaves were contented. Numerous accounts were given of slave rebellions which were more frequent than has been commonly imagined. The nature of these rebellions varied in kind and in intensity, but all of them re-enforced the idea that self-preservation became an important issue among the slaves. The narratives further highlighted the methods of deceit employed by the slaves. Many of these incidents have become an integral part of American folklore in the form of the primitive witty animal story associated with American slaves. These animal stories, popularized by Joel

Chandler Harris who recorded them as he heard them, illustrate how weak animals can defy and outwit stronger ones. In many cases the narrators make it clear that deceit *per se* is only admirable in so far as it permitted some salvation from the horrors of slavery. In the midst of an immoral society the use of deception, they reasoned, became the least of all possible evils.

Significantly, the narratives—especially the authentic ones—stress a loyalty to American democratic ideals as the slaves understood these principles and a loyalty to religious doctrines as these were interpreted. Consequently any master who remotely demonstrated either a knowledge of American ideals or a Christian spirit was rewarded with the loyalty of his slaves who, at the same time, were working diligently to break the chains of slavery. It is perhaps this characteristic more than any other which has led later generations to think that the slaves were "contented," but the narratives emphasize the universal distaste which all slaves held for their condition of servitude; they simply differed in their methods of alleviating a bad situation. The same longing for freedom, the frustration, the faith in religion as well as the underlying note of pathos which are evident in the spirituals are also present in the slave narratives. The only difference is the narratives were written by those who were fortunate enough to succeed in the first step toward earthly freedom.

II

No cursory survey of the slave narrative can do justice to the hundreds which appeared during the nineteenth century. It is difficult for the twentieth-century reader to envision the proliferation of these works; however, the narratives tended to deal with a limited number of themes and were structurally—and often stylistically—similar. The focal point of many of the narratives centered on the method of escape devised by the author. Often the escape forms the climax of the story which then concludes with the usual propaganda of the anti-slavery movement. The element of adventure and the presence of suspense made them thrilling accounts.

That the authors added some fiction to their stories is to be suspected, but the fiction served to enhance the recitation of their experiences.

In the early days of the anti-slavery· movement the names of Lewis and Milton Clarke were well-known. Both men were ardent abolitionists, and both were responsible not only for winning a number of converts to the cause of abolition but also for aiding in the escapes of innumerable slaves. Their frequent use of the Underground Railroad is well-told in *Narratives of the Sufferings of Lewis and Milton Clarke, Sons of a Soldier of the Revolution During a Captivity of More than Twenty Years Among Slaveholders of Kentucky, One of the So-Called Christian States of North America* (Boston, 1846). It is now difficult to ascertain the validity of their story because an editor was apparently instrumental in organizing the material. As the title page indicates the book was dictated to someone "by themselves." Yet, the discussion of the Underground Railroad does reveal the extensiveness of its use.

The validity of John Brown's story might also be questioned. Edited by Chameronzow in London, the book appeared as *Slave Life in Georgia: A Narrative of the Life, Sufferings and Escapes of John Brown, A Fugitive Slave Now in England* around 1855 and is written in an unnatural style. The story, however, reveals the mobility of the central character, a mobility which was not uncommon during the days of slavery. Brown—according to the story —was a slave not only in Virginia but also in Georgia and in Louisiana. After taking the Underground Railroad to Canada, he sailed for England. Henry Bibb also relied heavily upon the Underground Railroad. In his *Narrative of the Life and Adventures of Henry Bibb an American Slave* (1849) he recounted the number of times that he not only escaped but also returned in an effort to rescue others, especially his family. Although he was recaptured with a degree of regularity, he constantly sought new routes of freedom and eventually became an ardent anti-slavery worker in New England, New York, and the Midwest.

The escape of Henry Box Brown provided another unusual chapter in the history of slave escapes. Published first in Boston in 1849, the *Narrative of Henry Box Brown . . .* recounts how he fled slavery "enclosed in a box three feet long and two feet wide." Shipped in this manner from Richmond to Philadelphia, Brown became a star attraction at the meetings of various abolition societies. Whether or not Brown actually wrote his story is a moot point. The Boston edition which was "written from a statement of facts made by himself" is longer than the English edition "written by himself" and which appeared in 1851. It is interesting to note that the English edition is less sentimental and more tightly constructed than that of 1849.

Of all of the records of escape perhaps the journey made by William and Ellen Craft was the most daring. Published in London in 1860, *Running A Thousand Miles for Freedom; or The Escape of William and Ellen Craft from Slavery* became an immediate success. The plan which they devised was indicative of their ingenuity. Both had been born in Georgia and enslaved there. In 1848 they decided that their only solution for a normal life was to escape to the North. Ellen, who was a light-skinned slave, constantly ran the risk of being called into the master's house to perform services which violated her own marriage; furthermore, she ran the risk of being sold if she refused. Slavery, however, had no respect for the institution of marriage among slaves; and there was nothing that William could do to protect his wife. Out of their miserable condition their plan of escape was conceived. Ellen, dressed as a man, played the role of a wealthy planter whose illness demanded that he go to the North in order to receive medical attention. William traveled along as the servant of the "planter." Leaving their master's plantation in a carriage, they journeyed to Philadelphia after stopping each night in various hotels along the way. It is difficult for the modern reader to imagine the tension under which the two slaves moved, but in *Running A Thousand Miles for Freedom* they try to communicate their fear of possible discovery. Necessarily they had to travel more slowly to avoid the arousal of suspicion, and night travel—the salvation of many escaping slaves—was forbidden. Once in Philadelphia, they dropped the disguise and went on to Boston and later to England where their education was completed and where the narrative was written. The circumstances of their escape are so unusual and the style so developed that one might question the validity of their story; however, the letters which they wrote to abolitionists in America demonstrate their ability to write and their perfection of the stylistic devices of their book.

When William Grimes fled slavery he was older than the usual fugitive. During his fortieth year, he escaped from Savannah, Georgia, stowed away on a Boston-bound ship in 1814. The *Life of William Grimes, the Runaway Slave* (1825), like so many other narratives, was written to aid its author financially, but in this rather brief story Grimes gives a detailed picture of the inhumanity and the cruelty of slavery. And like a limited number of narratives, this work emphasizes the mental torture and the extreme fears which are necessarily a part of slavery.

Another theme used in the narratives dealt with the sordidness of slavery. First published in 1836, Charles Ball's *Slavery in the United States. A Narrative of the Life and Adventures of Charles Ball, A Black Man* was widely read and went through a series of editions. It was one of the few narratives which included a description of the African homeland; however, Ball's major emphasis is upon exposing the problems of slavery, and his own life is secondary. While all of the slave narratives might have been subtitled "Dark Deeds of American slavery," Anderson's work is one of the few whose stated purpose is as an exposé. *Life and Narrative of William Anderson or Dark Deeds of American Slavery* (Chicago, 1857) purports to be a history of slavery from an inside view. These two works treat in detail a theme which is present in varying degrees in most of the slave narratives. At the same time they make clear the contradictory nature of the ideal of America with the reality of slavery as a social system.

Both James W.C. Pennington and S.H. Platt combine the sor-

didness of slavery with their own success stories to present still
another type of indictment against slavery. On the surface Pennington's work, *The Fugitive Blacksmith, or Events in the History
of James W.C. Pennington, Pastor of a Presbyterian Church,
Formerly a Slave in the State of Maryland, United States* the second edition of which appeared in London (1849), is an obvious
success story recounting the subject's rise in life, but the bitterness
of the slave sections completely overshadow those which deal with
his successful ministry. The extent of his rise in fortune becomes
even more apparent when one remembers that he received an
honorary degree from the University of Heidelberg. As one of the
early abolitionists, Pennington's anti-slavery activities did much to
give a sense of direction to the movement in New York. His writing
style shows the strong influence of his indoctrination in a latter-
day Puritanism. The close logic and careful reasoning so often
associated with the Puritan preacher of the seventeenth century
are present in his work. Many of his published sermons are reminiscent of those of Cotton Mather and Samuel Willard. When, however, he applied this technique to his anti-slavery lectures and to
his autobiography, he produced works which were meticulously
argued but which lacked any sense of the emotional so common
in anti-slavery materials. Very similar in tone is *The Martyrs and
The Fugitive, or a Narrative of the Captivity, Sufferings and Death
of an African Family and the Escape of Their Son* by the Reverend
S.H. Platt. As a success story it does relate the rise of the minister,
but the subjugation of the slave family, the types of tortures and
indignities to which the family was exposed, and the family's
inability to survive these odds form the real story of Platt. In technique, however, Platt's work differs from that of Pennington; Platt
substituted emotional appeals for the cold logic of Pennington.

Quite a few of the slave narratives are in reality spiritual autobiographies. Here the author is primarily concerned with relating
the story of his conversion and with demonstrating the grace
which he received as a result of his conversion to Christianity. In
these works, as in all of the narratives which deal even remotely

with religious life, the authors make it quite plain that they understood the difference between Christianity as professed by the masters and slavery's social system and that which they perceived as
representing the truth of religion. In the spiritual autobiography
material which does not bear upon the author's religious life is
either omitted or subordinated to a discussion of the providential
nature of a Christian life. An early autobiography of this type appeared in England in 1774. If he had not been so intent upon
detailing the facts of his conversion and his life among the friends
of the Countess of Huntingdon, Gronniosaw could have included
some pertinent facts of his African life and his sojourn in New
York as a slave. Instead *A Narrative of the Most Remarkable
Particulars in the Life of James Albert Ukawsaw Gronniosaw, an
African Prince* is filled with platitudes. Dedicated to the Countess,
the book acknowledges its indebtedness to John Bunyan who was
Gronniosaw's literary model. Thus the story is primarily concerned
with the journey of a Christian believer rather than with the journey of an African prince through American servitude to English
freedom.

Essentially *The Life, Experiences, and Gospel Labors of the
Right Reverend Richard Allen* (Philadelphia, 1833) is also a
spiritual autobiography, but it is far more extended than the usual
book of this nature. Allen not only makes clear his own life but
recounts the story of an age with especial emphasis upon the
formation of the Negro Methodist Church in this country. In terms
of his own contributions Allen's work is extremely important and,
in spite of the fact that it is a late work in terms of his career, the
reminiscences of the grand old patriarch are extremely significant.
*The Narrative of John Quincy Adams, When In Slavery and Now
As A Freeman* (Harrisburg, 1872) is also an example of the
spiritual autobiography which combines elements of the success
story in order to get its message across.

In 1825 the second edition of *The Narrative of Some Remarkable Incidents in the Life of Solomon Bayley, formerly a Slave in
the State of Delaware, North America,* "written by himself," ap-

peared in London. Bayley was a slave not only in Delaware but also in Virginia. Eventually he was able to buy his freedom and to emigrate to Liberia. His story is far more religious than the usual slave narrative, but perhaps more important Bayley analyzes his own psychological reactions to his enforced servitude. Was it really a mandate of God that human beings suffer in such a manner? And if so, why did God select such a type of punishment? Bayley does not have definitive answers to these two questions which underlie his work, but at least in his search for answers there is more obvious reliance upon the things of the spirit. It is quite apparent that Bayley used the Bible not only as the foundation for his writing technique which shows traces of the stylistic devices employed in the King James version but also as the basis for his logical analysis of the slavery system. The effects of slavery upon the mind of man were further explored in *Narrative of William Hayden Containing a Faithful Account of His Travels for a Number of Years Whilst a Slave in the South* (Cincinnati, 1846). Hayden demonstrates the use of religion as a panacea for his earthly troubles and credits his religion with being the force which enabled him to keep his sanity in a totally insane situation.

In 1845 the first edition of the *Narrative of the Life of Frederick Douglass* appeared in Boston. Douglass, who became one of the most articulate of the anti-slavery leaders, had been born in Maryland and had spent his formative years there. With few exceptions his masters had been hard and his overseers cruel. But he had managed to learn to read and to write prior to his escape. From his escape in 1838 to the writing of the narrative Douglass had spent time in New York then in New Bedford, Massachusetts, as a common day laborer. Finally he became an anti-slavery agent who was at the disposal of William Lloyd Garrison. By 1845 he had sufficiently become adept at language usage, having published a number of open letters in the anti-slavery journals of the day and having lectured extensively, that one reading his story would not guess that he had been out of slavery only a few short years.

Initially the *Narrative of the Life of Frederick Douglass* was similar to every other slave narrative. The popularity of the form assured Douglass of an audience. Furthermore, Douglass had become an accomplished, well-known speaker, and this also aided in the sales of his book. On the surface, the book is merely a story of the escape of one man from slavery and his journey toward freedom; however, Douglass had the ability to make his story more than just a personal one, he had the ability to transcend his life in such a way that the slave condition became symbolic of the degradation of man, and his escape became equated to man's eternal search for that which is better, man's never-ceasing desire to be free. In spite of the greater sense of universality which Douglass was able to include in his narrative, a form which by definition is highly personal and subjective, the story is told with an alarming air of simplicity. As a successful lecturer, Douglass had learned the significance of the simply-stated idea and the value of relating emotion-filled incidents. He uses this to great advantage in his work. He had also learned the importance of the uses of humor to increase the pathos of his story. Hence, his narrative is one of the few to use elements of humor consciously and deliberately in order to control the thinking of the reader. The result was that Douglass' story was perhaps far more successful than the most famous of the slave narratives of the period. No doubt this was in part due to the commanding presence of Douglass, but in a larger measure this was also due to the document itself.

Two years later Douglass issued another autobiography entitled *My Bondage and My Freedom.* Longer than the earlier work, it is also a more sophisticated one. The spontaniety of the *Narrative of the Life of Frederick Douglass* is replaced by the studied attempt to evoke a given response in the reader. At the same time, the later work is far more specific about his life as a slave and about slavery in Maryland. As the work of a man who was surer of himself, *My Bondage and My Freedom* is an adequate testimony to Douglass' own growth in the anti-slavery movement and as a writer. The qualities which are apparent in the first autobiography are developed with all of the certainty which can proceed from a man who is convinced of the righteousness and justice of his cause. Douglass' use of incident is still as meaningful as in the former work. The use of the rhetorical question and the extensive use of description which were to characterize the power of Douglass' orations and informal speeches were transferred to his writing and became outstanding characteristics of his written prose. The long rolling sentences and the use of poetic prose were distinguishing features of his style as he constantly reminded America of the ambiguous position of a Christian nation involved in the maintenance of slavery.

Two more distinct editions of his autobiography appeared. Each one was entitled the *Life and Times of Frederick Douglass*. The first appeared in 1881 and the second in 1892. Much of the fire and a great deal of urgency of his first autobiographical studies were replaced by the reminiscences of an old man who is looking back into a far distant past. There are occasional flashes of the qualities which made the *Narrative of the Life of Frederick Douglass* and *My Bondage and My Freedom* outstanding, but for the most part they are the work of a man who has already told his story and has told it well. Included in these last two autobiographies are a number of speeches which Douglass had given on specific occasions. While the inclusion of his oratory is important from the historical point of view, it does nothing to add to the narrative quality of the works. Instead it tends to interrupt the action sufficiently often so that one becomes aware—perhaps for the first time in Douglass' writing—of excessive wordiness. There can be nothing quite so dull as the reproduction of a powerful speech thirty or forty years after its delivery.

By far one of the most remarkable men of letters produced by nineteenth-century America was William Wells Brown. His career had an inauspicious beginning in the throes of slavery. Perhaps in response to numerous demands Brown presented his story in a series of slightly varied autobiographies, but the major facts remained more or less the same. After having been born in Kentucky, he was soon sent to Missouri where he grew up. His jobs as a slave were many, and he eventually found himself in St. Louis in the same newspaper office with Elijah P. Lovejoy. When he was taken to Cincinnati, he found escape relatively easy as he "followed the North Star" until he reached the area near Lake Erie. Once a free man he spent time working and studying; eventually he became a lecturer for the anti-slavery movement. Hence, when he became associated in 1843 with the Western New York Anti-Slavery Society, he was still a young man but one who was able to tell the story of American slavery. *Narrative of the Life of William W. Brown, A Fugitive Slave* first appeared in 1847 and was published by the Massachusetts Anti-Slavery Society. The book was an immediate success for, instead of the didactic approach so common to slave narratives, Brown simply let the starkness and reality of his story preach his sermon for him. Three other American editions (two in 1848 and one in 1849) quickly followed as Brown expanded his narrative, and in 1849 the London edition appeared. Throughout all of the editions Brown never lost his original outrage at the indignities of slavery, and the narrative is one of the most bitter accounts in the annals of the slave narrative. His portrait of the slave trader is terrifying as the reader becomes more and more convinced that those men who dealt in the marketplace of human flesh were essentially depraved excuses for humanity.

Brown's career as a professional writer started by accident. In 1849 he went to England with the intention of returning to America during the following year; however, in 1850 the Fugitive Slave Law was passed and Brown had a choice of remaining abroad or returning to America where he was likely to be returned to slavery. Thus until 1854 he remained in Europe and earned a living by his writing and lecturing. His works were instantly popular not only because they were written by a fugitive slave but also because Brown had mastered the art of narration. Nothing written by him, however, rivalled his *Clotel; or, The President's Daughter: A Narrative of Slave Life in the United States* (1853) for sheer sensationalism and irony. For those who had wept three years earlier as Harriet Beecher Stowe related the story of *Uncle Tom's Cabin* Brown provided still further insights into the atrocities of slavery. And his novel, the first so recorded by an American Negro, was all the more effective because it was apparent that Brown utilized his own experiences as related in his autobiography as the basis for his novel. The use of Thomas Jefferson's name and the probability that he had fathered a child by a slave woman annoyed those who looked upon Jefferson as a great bastion of freedom; yet, Brown used Jefferson and interspersed his narrative with quotations from Jefferson's more notable documents of freedom to further his belief in the ambiguity of the American experience. The melodrama of *Clotel* . . . is overshadowed by the realism of it, and the novel represents one of the first exercises in American realism.

Before his death in 1884 Brown wrote additional novels, plays, and became one of the early historians of Negro life in America. There were, of course, historians who were far more aware of the demands of research. William C. Nell, for example, studied governmental papers and as many primary sources as were available to him before writing his *The Colored Patriots of the American Revolution, with Sketches of Several Distinguished Colored Persons: to Which is Added a Brief Survey of the Conditions and Prospects of Colored Americans* (1855). Although his writing is tedious and labored, he presented an excellent factual account of the Negro in America up to that time. Other men were also working in the realm of fact rather than propaganda—Martin Delany, Jesse Glasgow, Lewis H. Putnam, John B. Meachum, William T. Catto, William Douglass, to name a few—but no writer up to his time rivalled Brown in his ability to tell a story whether that story was based upon fact or fiction.

Samuel Ringgold Ward's narrative, *Autobiography of a Fugitive Negro: His Anti-Slavery Labours in the United States, Canada, and England* (London, 1855), is a slave narrative only in the loosest sense of the term. Ward's days in slavery were limited to a few in his infancy since his parents escaped from Maryland when he was three years old. That he had been born in slavery is, of course, true; but that he had never suffered the actual indignities of slavery is equally true. Like Lemuel Haynes (1753-1833), Ward became a Congregational minister and pastor of an all-white church. Unlike Haynes who had a distinguished career as a theologian but who was so involved in the problems expressed by his most famous and most publicized sermon, "Universal Salvation . . ." (1806) and in his Puritan mysticism that he did not assume a role as a racial leader, Ward became actively engaged in the anti-slavery movement. At the same time he was considerably concerned about the lives of free Negroes in the country. Ward's autobiography is one of the first full-length studies of Negroes. Devoting very little time and space to his own life, Ward used most of the book to discuss the positions of the Negro, enslaved and free, in American society. While he also was a product of the Puritan plain style, Ward was a far more appealing writer than Lemuel Haynes. Ward interspersed his closely argued case with personal reminiscences and with illustrations which made his work —on the whole—far more interesting than the theological treatises of Haynes.

Ward's work in the anti-slavery movement was strongly motivated by his belief that every Negro had a responsibility to protest against the evils of a slave society and against the injustice of northern discriminatory practices. Had Ward remained in the United States he might have offered serious competition to Frederick Douglass because he had a similar fondness for the same type of rhetorical devices and was reported to have been an electrifying orator; however, after spending years lecturing in England, Ward moved to Jamaica where his American anti-slavery activities appeared to have ended.

Toward the end of the nineteenth century Peter Randolph's autobiography was published in Boston. It was in part a re-issue of a work which he had written before the Civil War. In the early 1850's he had published *Sketches of Southern Life, or, Illustrations of the Peculiar Institution.* Prior to the publication of this work

Randolph had been freed by his owner. Making his way to Boston, he became another authoritative voice on the ways of slavery. His work then, topically arranged, presents the sociology of slavery as he investigated all facets of slave life. He was particularly interested in the caste system which existed among the slaves themselves. Later Randolph added more autobiographical material, and the complete work, *From Slave Cabin to the Pulpit, The Autobiography of Rev. Peter Randolph: The Souther Question Illustrated and Sketches of Slave Life,* appeared in 1893. By this time, of course, the interest in slavery had shifted its emphasis from the abolition of it to the historicity and validity of stories about it. Randolph's well-written work made it clear that the stories circulated about the days of slavery were in a large measure true ones as he dealt with the factors of everyday life in the slave quarters.

Perhaps the last of the great slave narratives was published in 1900 by Booker T. Washington. *Up From Slavery: An Autobiography* is not the usual slave narrative in the sense that it was published surreptitiously while the author, who was still nominally a slave, lived in free territory and worked for the anti-slavery movement. Rather it is in the tradition of the American success story, first popularized by Benjamin Franklin's *Autobiography* and later used by a group of slave writers who were intent upon recording their journeys not only from slavery to freedom but also from obscurity to fame. These stories tend to emphasize the hardships which must be overcome and the type of individual strength necessary for the long climb upward. The story by Washington is simply told and in its opening pages is similar to other slave narratives. As the book opens he tells of his early life in the slave quarters of a Virginia plantation, of his mother and his unknown white father. Then he tells of the day of emancipation. Brief though this section is, he gives a graphic portrayal of the slaves, who already knew freedom was coming, patiently waiting to be told about it. Those first confused days after emancipation are well-presented as he begins his own personal search for an education. Through it all the family structure is held intact as all members aid one another. By the time he goes to Hampton Institute and describes the experience there, his story becomes extremely didactic; and the remainder of the book—dealing with the Tuskegee experiment and his attempt to raise money for it—does not have the interest of some of the lesser known autobiographies. However, as an insight into the singular commitment of Washington *Up From Slavery* is highly successful.

Throughout his writing career as well as his oratorical career, Washington made use of the simple analogy and the extended metaphor. Perhaps the very simplicity of these devices led readers and listeners later to misunderstand what he had said, but for a given moment in Negro history he had the power to hold vast audiences through his repetitive devices. As a speaker and as a writer the monotony of his repetitions did not rival the rhetorical embellishments of a Frederick Douglass, but Washington spoke and wrote with a single motivation—to convince his audience of the validity of his ideas. And this he did so simply yet with such power that no one who heard him could doubt his sincerity.

Ultimately a consideration of nineteenth-century American literature must take into account the highly popular slave narrative which gained wide circulation. They coincided with the sentimental period of our literary national life, a period when the public enjoyed reading of hardships which had to be overcome. At the same time—because of the nature of the subject matter—the reality of slavery made the narrative the first collected body of protest literature in America. The protest element gained authenticity as many publishers advertised these works as "inside views" of slavery. While there are those who would dismiss the narrative as a completely spurious invention on the part of fanatical abolitionists, there is enough evidence to support the reliability of a number of these documents which, from a literary standpoint, include all of the characteristics of nineteenth-century American literature and provide the missing-link—on a popular level—between the western adventure stories of the early years of the nineteenth century and the didactic sentimental novel of the latter part

of the century. Obviously, these works were imitated and used to
great advantage by abolitionists. Yet publishers were careful to
check the validity of the stories which they accepted for publication. Too many hoaxes were sure to weaken the case for the anti-
slavery movement; hence, many of the narratives carry sworn
affidavits attesting to the truth of writer. In spite of these precau-
tions there are several notable exceptions where authors deliberately
took advantage of an unsuspecting public. Sometimes the author
became a victim of an ex-slave who wished a profit from the
popularity of the slave narrative as in the case of John Greenleaf
Whittier who was responsible for the publication in 1838 of *The
Narrative of James Williams,* a work which was later suppressed
by the American Anti-Slavery Society when it was proved to be a
completely false story. On the whole, however, the power of the
slave narrative lies in the skill of the writers to tell with stark
simplicity of their search for freedom.

The narratives as early studies in American realism suffer because of the intense subjectivity of the authors; however, the noted
historian, John Hope Franklin, asserts in *From Slavery to Freedom*
(New York, 1947) "the largest and perhaps most significant group
of Negro writers were ex-slaves—fugitive or manumitted—who
told the story of their experiences in 'narratives.' . . . Despite their
subjectivity, they are an important source for the study of slavery
in America (pp. 229-230)." Yet, those who are impressed with
the realistic movement as developed by William Dean Howells
and as practiced by Crane, Norris, and the host of early twentieth-
century novelists cannot fail to be struck by the similarities of
these later works and the slave narratives which flourished between
the 1830's and 1860's. The authors of these forthright narratives
unconsciously gave direction to what was to become a dominant
movement in American Literature.

III

While the slave narrative continued to appear in the years following the Civil War, its major appeal was spent as the immediacy

of the social situation which had inspired so many of the early writers had passed. This is not, however, to suggest that the form held no attraction for readers. The very popular *Behind the Scenes; or, Thirty Years a Slave, and Four Years in the White House* by Elizabeth Keckley, who presented one of the best contemporary portraits of Mary Todd Lincoln, appeared after 1865, and one of the most lucid success stories which contains elements of the slave narrative appeared in 1900 when Booker T. Washington issued his *Up From Slavery* which is still considered a classic of American Literature. But after the war, the major concern shifted from abolition to integration into American life. Many of the antebellum prose writers continued to work after the Civil War, and many began their writing careers at this time; but almost without exception their prose was practical and utilitarian. If the period after the war did not produce a series of individually outstanding writers, it did produce one of the most notable bodies of literature dealing with the freedom of man's spirit and the rights of man. The period in its intensity is matched only by the eighteenth-century writings which preceded the American Revolution. The utilitarian purpose of much of the prose of the Revolution explains the absence of a number of literary giants *per se* but in a collected form these works constitute a unique reading experience in the documents of freedom. And so it was in the latter part of the nineteenth century when Negroes sought acceptance into the life of America.

There were, of course, a number of factors operative against Negroes during this period. Perhaps Rayford Logan has best described the period as *The Nadir*. At any rate, the persecutions did not stop with the end of slavery, but as Negroes in America were forced to rely on their own resources, they cemented the foundations which had been laid by their slave as well as free ancestors, and no matter how antagonistic the white culture may have been by 1900 that same culture could not deny the existence nor the contribution of some of America's oldest citizens to the progress of this nation. Just as the slave narrative was an American innovation born out of the need to give expression to the views of former slaves so the prose which evolved after the Civil War was developed because of the need to communicate ideas to the freedmen as well as to those who had been free for some time. If the prose can be characterized, its central theme is the writers' concern for the execution of the precepts of democracy. Negroes were aware of the discrepancy between the ideal and the real, between the America of the Declaration of Independence and the America of the untold restrictive Black Codes which limited, in many instances, the movements of black men in the United States. Thus, the prose of freedom addressed itself to this ambiguity.

Much stress has been placed on the general status of the slaves who were freed with little or no preparation for the responsibilities of freedom. History books recount the tales of how the unscrupulous both in the North and in the South manipulated the emancipated slaves. At the same time little mention is made of the phenomenal progress which took place between the end of the Civil War and the opening years of the twentieth century. It was a progress which has been unmatched in modern history. Schools and colleges multiplied incredibly quickly as much emphasis was placed on education. Church memberships increased to the point that national churches were able to support schools, journals, and publishing houses. Through the educational and religious phases of life Negroes were able to make a place for themselves in the American sun.

In these days when the need for identification was so very great, the role of the Negro church and its ministers cannot be minimized. Up to this time the minister had served as the leader in the community and had given—in addition to spiritual leadership—a sense of direction to his parishioners. After the Civil War he assumed political as well as cultural leadership. With the proliferation of writers committed to the prose of freedom the ministers produced some worthwhile written documents. And frequently their works received widespread circulation because, unlike other writers, they had a built-in public. While much of the prose produced in the latter part of the nineteenth century was as pedestrian as that which flooded the colonies prior to the Revolutionary War, there were some excellent works written. In this period of cultural development the Methodist and Baptist Churches assumed the leadership. According to W. E. B. Du Bois in his early study *The Negro Church,* which appeared as an Atlanta University Publication in 1903, membership in the A.M.E. Church rose by over 500,000 in the twenty-five-period 1876-1901. In 1876 there were 172,806 members and in 1901, 688,354 (p. 126). At the same time DuBois recorded the phenomenal growth of the Baptist Church which by 1894 had 1,604,310 communicants (p. 111). Nor was growth confined merely to the end of the last century. Today the largest Baptist group, the National Baptist Convention, U.S.A., Inc., has 6,300,000 members.

One of the earliest writers influenced by Methodism was Jupiter Hammon whose poetry echoes with the Calvinistic approach popular in the eighteenth century. Even Phillis Wheatley's work, Puritan though it was, shows the influence of the Countess of Huntingdon who entertained the poet while Phillis was in England. Vassa, whose eighteenth-century slave narrative is one of the better ones, spent years working in the Methodist cause after his conversion. But by far the most significant name in Methodism is that of Richard Allen who died in 1831. With Absalom Jones he was responsible for the formation of the African Methodist Church, and when this group was finally recognized in 1816 he became its first bishop. Allen had made his place in American literature in the latter part of the eighteenth century when his first book co-authored with Absalom Jones, *A Narrative of the Proceedings of the Black People during the Late Awful Calamity in Philadelphia; and a Refutation of Some Censures Thrown Upon Them in Some Late Publications . . . ,* appeared in 1794. This was an early defense of the role of Negroes in American civilization and was a direct answer to Matthew Carey's charge that Negroes who were not susceptible to yellow fever should have done more during the Philadelphia epidemic of 1792-93. The clarity of style and the use of ironic devices make this work an effective answer to the critics of Negro Americans. Throughout his career Allen fought against the idea of colonization, and he produced a series of essays and letters stating his position. Interestingly enough, David Walker used Allen's "Letter on Colonization" as part of the argument in his *Appeal* . . . against African colonization.

Among the outstanding Methodist clergymen after the Civil War was Daniel Alexander Payne. Like Albery A. Whitman, who is sometimes thought of as the most outstanding Negro poet before Dunbar and who also was a Methodist minister, Payne also wrote poetry. His work appeared in *The Liberator* in the 1840's and demonstrated a degree of power which might have led to fame as a poet if he had taken time to perfect his technique. But he was more interested in his life as an educator. As a freeborn Negro in Charleston, South Carolina, Payne was subjected to the restrictions which surrounded free blacks in the North as well as in the South; however, he managed to get a semblance of education in his native city. For six years, 1829-1835 he conducted a school for his people until the 1835 law was passed in South Carolina which prohibited education for Negroes. By 1853 he had moved North and had become a bishop of the A.M.E. church. From this time on he assumed an active role in religious and educational circles. His story is well-presented in his autobiography, *Recollections of Seventy Years* (1888), which should take its place in American literature as one of the outstanding autobiographical studies of the nineteenth century. The book was a product of his very conscientious effort to keep an adequate journal throughout his life. Although the book was written from the vantage point of the aging Payne, the reminiscent quality of the book is subordinated to the vitality of the man which emerges from the work. Because of Payne's involvement in the major social, religious, and educational problems of his day, the book also portrays the vitality of the age. At the same time the book records one of the most complete analyses of the growth and development of a people. In the same year which saw the publication of his autobiography he issued *Sermons Delivered by Bishop Daniel A. Payne*. The work is significant as an indication of the close logic employed by Negro ministers during the period. As a printed example of pulpit oratory it should do much toward dispelling the idea of the Negro minister as an illiterate image-builder.

As a church historian Payne made two notable contributions: *The Semi-Centenary and the Retrospection of the African Methodist Episcopal Church* (1886) and *History of the African Methodist Episcopal Church* (1891). Both works indicate that Payne was aware of the demands of scholarship, and both are extremely readable accounts. The simplicity of style sometimes lulls the reader into thinking that the writer is uninformed, but the reader soon realizes that these eye-witness acounts are heavily documented. Unlike some of the other church historians of the period, Payne did not rely on emotional appeals to get his story across. But Payne was simply one of a host of Negro Methodist preachers during the century who spent time recording the type of material which they thought necessary for a people struggling in those days to assert the dignity of the individual and to grasp some means of identification. These writer-preachers include Josiah Henson (reportedly the model for Harriet Beecher Stowe's Uncle Tom) and Jermain Wesley Loguen, a bishop of the church, who recorded their stories and in so doing recorded the history of an age.

The development of the Baptist Church had its beginnings in the South in 1776 with the establishment of an independent Baptist unit in Petersburg, Virginia. By 1790 churches had been established in Williamsburg, Virginia, in Silver Bluff, South Carolina, and in Savannah, Georgia. Five years later a Negro Baptist Church was founded in Lexington, Kentucky. Although the church in the South suffered from the number of restrictions which were placed against public gatherings in the nineteenth century, George Lisle and Andrew Bryan were early Baptist clergymen who did much toward the development of the church. As slaves Lisle and Bryan were dependent upon their masters, but both men were significant as Baptist leaders among their own people. The century also saw the rise of the Baptist church in the North. By 1809 there were churches in New York, Philadelphia, and Boston. Due to the autonomous nature of the Baptist church few ministers achieved national prominence in these early years; yet, it must be remembered that on a local level they had great influence and wielded enormous power.

Of the many Baptist ministers who were instrumental on the local level in organizing churches and of the host who took the time to record their impressions during the nineteenth century, Jeremiah Asker and George Washington Williams have earned a place in American writing. In 1862 Asker's narrative was published. Entitled *An Autobiobraphy, with Details of a Visit to England* the author recounts the trials of his ministry in Providence, Rhode Island, and in Philadelphia, Pennsylvania. Although the work did not become as famous as the published autobiography of Richard Allen which appeared many years after his death when Allen had become a historical personage, the autobiography of Asker is really the story of a little discussed era not only in Negro Baptist life but also of northern free Negroes. Significantly Asker, in spite of his excellent treatment in England, was insistent upon casting his fortunes with America as he explains in his book his belief that the American dream could become an American reality.

This idea was further explored by George Washington Williams, a Baptist minister who became a historian. *The History of the Negro Race in America from 1619 to 1880* appeared in 1883. And six years later he issued *A History of the Negro Troops in the War of the Rebellion* (1889). Other histories had, of course, preceded his, but Williams brought to his work not only a fidelity to the facts and documents of history but also a style which, while not that of the "plain style" of a William Bradford, eloquently placed his subject in a total concept of universal man. In his Preface to his first work he asserted that a history of Negroes in America was needed because there were so many plentiful records which had remained untouched and because the race appeared to be "the most vexatious problem in North America." He continued:

. . . in every attempt upon the life of the nation whether by foes from without or within, the Colored people had always displayed a matchless patriotism and an incomparable heroism in the cause of Americans. . . (p. v)

His final reason for writing his *History of the Negro Race in America,* according to the Preface, was based upon the fact that "such a history would give the world more correct ideas of the Colored people, and incite the latter to greater effort in the struggle of citizenship and manhood." The first volume of the two-volume works ends on a prophetic note:

Race prejudice is bound to give way before the potent influences of character, education, and wealth. And these are necessary to the growth of the race. Without wealth there can be no leisure, without leisure there can be no thought, and without thought there can be no progress. The future work of the Negro is twofold: subjective and objective. Years will be devoted to his own education and improvement in America. He will sound the depths of education, accumulate wealth, and then turn his attention to the civilization of Africa (p. 391).

While modern readers may decry the insertion of the frequent oratorical flights of fancy which appear in Williams' book, no one can ignore the scholarship upon which the book was based nor its clarity of expression. In the style of the nineteenth-century historian, Williams was also convinced that a work of history was more than a compendium of facts; it was an integral part of a literary tradition. And there were others who apparently agreed with him. Initially published by G. P. Putnam's Sons, the *History . . .* became immediately successful. The liveliness of presentation, the smoothness of writing technique, and the objectivity of the story did much toward gaining readers and favorably impressing the critics.

In his study of the role of the Negro soldier during the Civil War Williams concentrated on the large group who actually participated in the conflict. Once again relying heavily upon existing documents, Williams was able to write a highly readable account. Modern critics are sometimes misled by his "Preface" which is highly emotional and subjective, but the work itself is as detached as the later work of the modern scientific historian. His "Preface," of course, does set the tone for his belief in the greatness of the Negro soldier.

The part enacted by the Negro soldier in the war of the Rebellion is the romance of North American history. It was midnight and noonday without a space between; from clanging chains to crushing arms; from passive submission to the cruel curse of slavery to the brilliant aggressiveness of a free soldier; from a chattel to a person; from the shame of degradation to the glory of military exaltation; and from deep obscurity to material immortality. No one in this era of fraternity and Christian civilization will grudge the Negro soldier these simple annals of his trials and triumphs in a holy struggle for human liberty. Whatever praise is bestowed upon his noble acts will be sincerely appreciated, whether from former foes or comrades in arms. For by withholding just praise they are not enriched, nor by giving are they thereby impoverished (pp. xiii-xiv).

During the time that Williams' histories were being published and gaining popularity a group of Baptist clergymen were working as hard to record accurate material about themselves and their church. Out of their efforts grew the National Baptist Convention, U.S.A., Inc. which was destined to become the most powerful Negro organization in America and probably in the world. Throughout the nineteenth century the "convention movement" was extremely fashionable. A group of like-minded people would gather for the express purpose of discussing some issue of mutual concern. This was especially true in the days before the abolition of slavery for free Negroes of the North found this to be an effective means of communicating with each other as well as with white America. Toward the end of the century some of these conventions moved toward becoming permanent bodies, and what to become the National Baptist Convention was one of these. Organized in 1880, the Convention has met in annual session ever since. While the men who took part were outstanding clergymen, few of them achieved national prominence as writers or historians. Yet it is significant that they were quite aware of the importance of writing and history. In the 1886 call to the convention, which is annually reprinted in the *Proceedings* of the Convention, six reasons were given for having the meeting. Two of these reasons indicate that the founders of the organization were cognizant of the role to be played by Negro writers. Not only were they "to encourage our literary men and women, and promote the interest of Baptist litera-ture," but also they were "to give an opportunity for the best thinkers and writers to be heard." With the establishment of its own publishing house the Convention has been able to foster denominational scholarship.

Of the many contributors to the prose of freedom in the latter part of the nineteenth century W. E. B. DuBois stands as a giant. Although the greater bulk of his work was completed in the twentieth century, DuBois produced two works, one historical and the other sociological, in the closing years of the nineteenth century which would have assured his place in history even if he had not accomplished anything else. First published as the initial volume in the Harvard Historical Studies in 1896 his *The Suppression of the African Slave Trade to the United States of America, 1638-1870* is still considered a monumental work. Three years later he pub-lished for the Publications of the University of Pennsylvania: Series of Political Economy and Public Law his *The Philadelphia Negro* which is a detailed survey of the role of Negroes in an urban environment. Both books made invaluable surveys of little-studied areas of Negro life, and both were the results of impeccable scholar-ship. While the latter study depends rather heavily upon statistical data, DuBois' clarity of expression and his use of ironic devices—characteristics which were to mark his later writing style—are evidenced in these two books. Although these books did not be-come a part of the popular reading tradition, they did indicate the capabilities of the scholar who had chosen a little-known area for study.

From an historical point of view the Washington-DuBois controversy has been thoroughly—if not adequately—discussed. Many twentieth-century readers have so committed themselves to the ideology of one man or the other that it is difficult to look at them in the same context. The fact that both men were interested in solving the problems faced by Negroes in America and the fact that each man offered solutions which were made in the light of his own experiences have been lost in the more emotional interpretations. Logically one would not expect the life of an ex-slave from Virginia to be similar to that of a free resident of Great Barrington, Massachusetts nor can the appeal of each man necessarily be made to the same group. The Washington-DuBois conflict perhaps points out most clearly the tragedy of thinking that there must be one approach or one spokesman for a group with varied experiences and backgrounds. Nor were Washington and DuBois diametrically opposed to one another early in their careers. Washington made his appeal to the host of southern ex-slaves who had shared his experience and who desired, for one reason or the other, to cast their fortunes in the South. DuBois, on the other hand, made his appeal to the "Talented Tenth." But that controversy is not central here. Both Washington and DuBois as writers demonstrate some interesting patterns, and from their work one can determine a great deal about the prose of freedom which followed the slave narrative after the Civil War.

CHAPTER IV

And the Poets Came Forth: Tendencies in Nineteenth-Century Negro Poetry

SOMEWHAT LATER than Jupiter Hammon and Phillis Wheatley another slave poet gained recognition in both the North and the South. George Moses Horton, like Hammon, was owned by a family who bequeathed him from one member to another. Although the Horton family lived in North Carolina, George Moses was given a great deal of freedom to roam about the countryside and to attend the religious meetings of the community. Eventually the Hortons allowed him "to hire out" and work for other people with the provision that he send most of his money to them. Unlike Hammon, Horton was apparently far more "earthy." He spent some time in Chapel Hill where he not only became a well-known character on the campus of the University of North Carolina but also learned to read and to write while working for the president of the university. According to the popular legend concerning his life in Chapel Hill, Horton wrote love poems for the students enrolled at the college, and they paid him pennies for his efforts. What his career would have been had he not prostituted his talents by writing these penny-ballads can only be imagined. Various northern abolitionists used Horton's work as an indication that his poetic talents were being crushed by slavery and as a means of collecting funds for his liberation. It seems, however, that enough money was never collected, and Horton did not receive his freedom until the close of the Civil War when he immediately moved to Philadelphia.

His first published volume appeared in 1829 when, according to the Preface, he was thirty-two years old. Entitled *Hope of Liberty,* it contained twenty-one poems. The volume was issued in Philadelphia in 1837 as *Poems by a Slave.* A third issue of this volume appeared in Boston in 1838 in conjunction with a collection of Phillis Wheatley's work and was entitled *The Memoir and Poems of Phillis Wheatley, a Native African and a Slave: Also Poems by a Slave.* The last published volume by Horton appeared in 1865 in Raleigh, North Carolina, and was entitled *Naked Genius.* Containing 132 poems, *Naked Genius* included some poems which had been published earlier in *Hope of Liberty* and in the popular newspapers of the day. Between 1829 and 1865 Horton published a great deal, but his publishing record does not reflect his total output for he seldom published the works written on the campus of the University of North Carolina. Like Wheatley, Horton apparently had a good ear for poetic rhythms, and it is not surprising to find in his work echoes of currently popular poets of his day.

There is a lightness in Horton's work which is not characteristic of the work of either Hammon or Wheatley; yet he, too, could be seriously concerned about matters of religion and freedom. In "On the Truth of the Savior" Horton tries to poetically analyze the power of the miracles of Jesus Christ. Employing an almost perfect ballad stanza, Horton asserts that the miracles are just as real as Christ Himself. At the same time his poetic diction indicates something of the nature of the difference between his treatment of a religious subject and that of Wheatley or Hammon.

> E'en John the Baptist did not know
>   Who Christ the Lord could be,
> And bade his own disciples go,
>   The strange event to see.
>
> They said, art thou the one of whom

'Twas written long before?
Is there another still to come,
  Who will all things restore?

This is enough, without a name—
  Go, tell him what is done;
Behold the feeble, weak and lame,
  With strength rise up and run.

This is enough—the blind now see,
  The dumb Hosannas sing;
Devils far from his presence flee,
  As shades from morning's wing.

See the distress'd, all bathed in tears,
  Prostrate before him fall;
Immanuel speaks, and Lazarus hears—
  The dead obeys his call.

This is enough—the fig-tree dies,
  And withers at his frown;
Nature her God must recognize,
  And drop her flowery crown.

At his command the water blushed,
  And all was turned to wine,
And in redundance flowed afresh,
  And owned its God divine.

Behold the storms at his rebuke,
  All calm upon the sea—
How can we for another look,
  When none can work as he?

This is enough—it must be God,
  From whom the plagues are driven;
At whose command the mountains nod
  And all the Host of Heaven.

  The plaintive note of the spiritual is heard in Horton's "On Liberty and Slavery."

Alas! and am I born for this,
    To wear this slavish chain?
Deprived of all created bliss,
    Through hardship, toil and pain!

How long have I in bondage lain,
    And languished to be free!
Alas! and must I still complain—
    Deprived of liberty.

Oh, Heaven! and is there no relief
    This side the silent grave—
To soothe the pain—to quell the grief
    And anguish of a slave?

Come Liberty, thou cheerful sound,
    Roll through my ravished ears!
Come, let my grief in joys be drowned,
    And drive away my fears.

Say unto foul oppression, Cease:
    Ye tyrants rage no more,
And let the joyful trump of peace,
    Now bid the vassal soar.

Soar on the pinions of that dove
    Which long has cooed for thee,
And breathed her notes from Afric's grove,
    The sound of Liberty.

Oh, Liberty! thou golden prize,
    So often sought by blood—
We crave thy sacred sun to rise,
    The gift of nature's God!

Bid Slavery hide her haggard face,
    And barbarism fly:
I scorn to see the sad disgrace
    In which enslaved I lie.

Dear Liberty! upon thy breast,
    I languish to respire;

And like the Swan unto her nest,
I'd to thy smiles retire.

Oh, blest asylum—heavenly balm!
Unto thy boughs I flee—
And in thy shades the storm shall calm,
With songs of Liberty!

Horton's experiences formed the basis for much of what he wrote. Seldom was he content to select a subject and to view it without introducing the personal element. In *Naked Genius* he published his self-portrait.

GEORGE MOSES HORTON, MYSELF

I feel myself in need
Of the inspiring strains of ancient lore,
My heart to lift, my empty mind to feed,
And all the world explore.

I know that I am old
And never can recover what is past,
But for the future may some light unfold
And soar from ages blast.

I feel resolved to try,
My wish to prove, my calling to pursue,
Or mount up from the earth into the sky,
To show what Heaven can do.

My genius from a boy,
Has fluttered like a bird within my heart;
But could not thus confined her powers employ,
Impatient to depart.

She like a restless bird,
Would spread her wings, her power to be unfurl'd,
And let her songs be loudly heard,
And dart from world to world.

By the time of Horton's death in 1883 two major trends were

discernible in American Negro poetry. One trend was evident in
the poetry of Hammon, Wheatley, and Horton in which the neoclassical tradition was merged with other popular literary traditions
and with primitive Christianity to produce a poetry which was
essentially religious or a poetry which structurally followed the
known patterns of English poetry. The other trend, evident in the
spirituals, was primarily based upon an oral tradition and employed a structure which depended—in a large measure—upon
repetition and biblical imagery for its effectiveness. The former
tradition, which included the slave poets, evolved from a literate
group whereas the latter one developed—in all probability—after
the more stringent laws against education had been passed. While
this second tradition was not completely a result of illiteracy, it
was most popular among those who were not as proficient in the
formal art of communication; hence, the narrative element, an
element which is extremely important in a folk literature, was
emphasized. Although the slave poets tend to be remembered
today because of their uniqueness in their society, there were other
poets who produced a large body of work. In fact, before Dunbar
was introduced to the American reading public by William Dean
Howells in the 1890's a number of these poets had achieved a
degree of fame and now serve to bridge the poetic gap between the
eighteenth-century work of Hammon and Wheatley and that of
Dunbar.

Of these poets Mrs. Frances Ellen Watkins Harper probably
achieved more fame and popularity. Born in Baltimore, Maryland
in 1825 of free parents, she was educated in one of the schools
for free children which had been established in that city. Frances
Watkins spent a few years teaching in Ohio and in Pennsylvania,
and in 1860 she married Fenton Harper. By the time of her marriage she had become determined to devote her life to the causes
of emancipation and to writing. In her poetry two themes occupied
most of her attention. Either she dealt with anti-slavery subjects
or with religion.

Her *Poems on Miscellaneous Subjects,* first issued in 1854, went through several editions. In 1857 she added to the collection, and by 1871 it was published as the "twentieth edition." It seems apparent from the letters of the day that she distributed this book during her many lectures in order to gain additional funds for her work in the anti-slavery movement. Such widespread distribution may well explain her popularity as ·a poet during the period. A large number of the poems which appear in *Poems on Miscellaneous Subjects* are narrative; however, there are a few lyrics included. Just as Wheatley demonstrated great fidelity to Pope, her literary model, so Harper demonstrated an equally faithful fidelity to Longfellow, her selected literary mentor. She also published two collections simply entitled *Poems.* One appeared in 1871 and included short verse which had not been included in her first volume. The other appeared in 1900 and contained what she considered to be her best work.

Moses: A Story of the Nile represents her most ambitious and her most symbolic work. Published before 1869, it never mentions the Negro's position in America nor the problems which immediately occurred as a result of the Emancipation Proclamation; yet it is quite obvious that the poem is an attempt to use the story of Moses very much as the poets of the spirituals had done in order to emphasize the need for a racial leader. The poem begins as a dramatic one; however, the narrative element soon becomes dominant. When the poem opens, Moses reveals to the king's daughter who has supervised his growing up that soon he must leave her. He desires to guide his people and to help them out of Egypt. When she objects to his leaving, Moses appeals to her love for him and indicates that if she really loves him as a mother might love her child, then she will not stand in his way, she will not prevent his doing what must be done. Reluctantly she grants him permission to return to his own people. From this point the poem simply recounts the story of Moses. The effectiveness of the poem is considerably heightened by the symbolic interpretation of Moses' contribution to and for the freedom of his people.

Perhaps of all of her work *Sketches of Southern Life,* which first appeared in 1872 and subsequently in 1888 and 1896, is the most original. While much of her poetry tends to be didactic and to use characters only as a means for getting a "message" to the reader, in *Sketches of Southern Life* Harper is far more subtle. The work consists of a series of poems which are unified through two characters: Aunt Chloe and Uncle Jacob. Both of these characters are similar to some of Dunbar's in the sense that they capture the essence of primitive life in America. Yet, Aunt Chloe, who tends to comment on the major issues of the day, and Uncle Jacob, who is the more mystical of the two, do not use dialect. In this respect Harper anticipates James Weldon Johnson who also rejected dialect in favor of what he was later to define as the "Negro idiom."

The more consciously anti-slavery poems appear in her first volume. Two poems appear entitled "The Slave Mother." In one a mother laments as her child is taken away and is given to a slave trader. In the other a fugitive mother kills her baby when she senses that she is to be recaptured and sent back into slavery. Both are effective anti-slavery ballads because they concentrate upon the very emotional relationship between mother and child; however, both are somewhat marred by the author's own deliberate intrusion as she comments on the action. "The Fugitive's Wife" recounts the terror and agonizing despair of a female slave whose husband is planning to make a run toward freedom. The experiences of a slave who had heard of a plot to escape but who had elected to be beaten to death rather than reveal the secrets of his fellow slaves is simply told in "The Tennessee Hero." In all of these poems Harper is able to penetrate the feelings of a people haunted and broken by the chains of slavery. Unlike the typical abolitionist she does this without becoming mawkishly sentimental. In each poem she builds her case by letting each tragic example of the effects of slavery serve as an indication of the broken bodies and broken spirits which resulted because of slavery's inhumanity to man. In "The Slave Auction," for example, she presents the

impact of human sales upon families and concludes the poem by
pointing out the terror of such sales.

> The sale began—young girls were there,
>   Defenceless in their wretchedness,
> Whose stifled sobs of deep despair
>   Revealed their anguish and distress.
>
> And mothers stood with streaming eyes,
>   And saw their dearest children sold;
> Unheeded rose their bitter cries,
>   While tyrants bartered them for gold.
>
> And woman, with her love and truth—
>   For these in sable forms may dwell—
> Gaz'd on the husband of her youth,
>   With anguish none can paint or tell.
>
> And men, whose sole crime was their hue,
>   The impress of their Maker's hand,
> And frail and shrinking children, too,
>   Were gathered in that mournful band.
>
> Ye who have laid your love to rest,
>   And wept above their lifeless clay,
> Know not the anguish of that breast,
>   Whose lov'd are rudely torn away.
>
> Ye may not know how desolate
>   Are bosoms rudely forced to part,
> And how a dull and heavy weight
>   Will press the life-drops from the heart.

Included also in the collection of predominantly anti-slavery verse
is "Eliza Harris" which first appeared in *Frederick Douglass'
Paper* on December 25, 1853. It is a narrative poem which retells
the story of Eliza Harris of *Uncle Tom's Cabin* as she is crossing
the Ohio River on large floating sheets of ice with the bloodhounds
steadily pursuing her on her dash for freedom.

Like a fawn from the arrow, startled and wild,
A woman swept by us, bearing a child;
In her eye was the night of a settled despair,
And her brow was o'ershaded with anguish and care.

She was nearing the river—in reaching the brink,
She heeded no danger, she paused not to think;
For she is a mother—her child is a slave—
And she'll give him his freedom, or find him a grave!

It was a vision to haunt us, that innocent face—
So pale in its aspect, so fair in its grace;
As the tramp of the horse and the bay of the hound,
With the fetters that gall, were trailing the ground!

She was nerv'd by despair, and strengthened by woe,
As she leap'd o'er chasms that yawn'd from below;
Death howl'd in the tempest, and rav'd in the blast,
But she heard not the sound till the danger was past.

Oh! how shall I speak of my proud country's shame?
Of the stains on her glory, how give them their name?
How say that her banner in mockery waves—
Her "star spangled banner"—o'er million of slaves?

How say that the lawless may torture and chase
A woman whose crime is the hue of her face?
How the depths of the forest may echo around,
With the shrieks of despair, and the bay of the hound?

With her step on the ice, and her arm on her child,
The danger was fearful, the pathway was wild;
But, aided by Heaven, she gained a free shore,
Where the friends of humanity open'd their door.

So fragile and lovely, so fearfully pale,
Like a lily that bends to the breath of the gale,
Save the heave of her breast, and the sway of her hair,
You'd have thought her a statue of fear and despair.

In agony close to her bosom she press'd
The life of her heart, the child of her breast:—

Oh! love from its tenderness gathering might,
Had strengthen'd her soul for the dangers of flight.

But she's free!—yes, free from the land where the slave
From the hand of oppression must rest in the grave;
Where bondage and torture, where scourges and chains
Have plac'd on our banner indelible stains.

The bloodhounds have miss'd the scent of her way;
The hunter is rifled and foil'd of his prey;
Fierce jargon and cursing, with clanking of chains,
Make sounds of strange discord on Liberty's plains.

With the rapture of love and fulness of bliss,
She placed on his brow a mother's fond kiss:—
O poverty, danger and death she can brave,
For the child of her love is no longer a slave!

Mrs. Harper's faith in the eventual solution of human problems
is perhaps best exemplified by "The Present Age" which, though
one of her later poems, is most reminiscent of Longfellow.

Say not the age is hard and cold—
    I think it brave and grand;
Where men of diverse sects and creeds
    Are clasping hand in hand.

The Parsee from his sacred fires
    Besides the Christian kneels;
And clearer light to Islam's eyes
    The word of Christ reveals.

The Brahmin from his distant home
    Brings thoughts of ancient lore;
The Bhuddist breaking bonds of caste
    Divides mankind no more.

The meek-eyed sons of far Cathay
    Are welcome round the board;
Not greed, nor malice drives away
    These children of our Lord.

And Judah from whose trusted hands
   Came oracles divine;
Now sits with those around whose hearts
   The light of God doth shine.

Japan unbars her long sealed gates
   From islands far away
Her sons are lifting up their eyes
   To greet the coming day.

The Indian child from forests wild
   Has learned to read and pray;
The tomahawk and scalping knife
   From him have passed away.

From centuries of servile toil
   The Negro finds release,
And builds the fanes of prayer and praise
   Unto the God of Peace.

England and Russia face to face
   With Central Asia meet;
And on the far Pacific coast,
   Chinese and natives greet.

Crusaders once with sword and shield
   The Holy Land to save;
From Moslem hands did strive to clutch
   The dear Redeemer's grave.

A battle greater, grander far
   Is for the present age;
A crusade for the rights of man
   To brighten history's page.

Where labor faints and bows her head,
   And want consorts with crime;
Or men grown faithless sadly say
   That evil is the time.

There is the field,
   For every earnest heart;

To side with justice, truth and right
    And act a noble part.

To save from ignorance and vice
    The poorest, humblest child;
To make our age the fairest one
    On which the sun has smiled;

To plant the roots of coming years
    In mercy, love and truth;
And bid our weary, saddened earth
    Again renew her youth.

Oh! earnest hearts! toil on in hope,
    'Till darkness shrinks from light;
To fill the earth with peace and joy,
    Let youth and age unite;

To stay the floods of sin and shame
    That sweep from shore to shore;
And furl the banners stained with blood,
    'Till war shall be no more.

Blame not the age, or think it full
    Of evil and unrest;
But say of every other age,
    "This one shall be the best."

The age to brighten every path
    By sin and sorrow trod;
For loving hearts to usher in
    The commonwealth of God.

In "A Grain of Sand" is demonstrated Harper's characteristic of finding a lesson or a moral in everything around her.

Do you see this grain of sand
Lying loosely in my hand?
Do you know to me it brought
Just a simple loving thought?
When one gazes night by night

On the glorious stars of light,
Oh how little seems the span
Measured round the life of man.

Oh! how fleeting are his years
With their smiles and their tears;
Can it be that God does care
For such atoms as we are?
Then outspoke this grain of sand
"I was fashioned by His hand
In the star lit realms of space
I was made to have a place.

"Should the ocean flood the world,
Were its mountains 'gainst me hurled
All the force they could employ
Wouldn't a single grain destroy;
And if I, a thing so light,
Have a place within His sight;
You are linked unto His throne
Cannot live nor die alone.

In the everlasting arms
Mid life's dangers and alarms
Let calm trust your spirit fill;
Know He's God, and then be still."
Trustingly I raised my head
Hearing what the atom said;
Knowing man is greater far
Than the brightest sun or star.

"Truth" also shows her ability to find a moral lesson from ordinary objects; at the same time the poem also indicates her attempt to vary her stanza pattern by shifting from the trochaic rhythmic structure of "A Grain of Sand" to the more common iambic tetrameter. As is frequently typical in didactic poetry of this name, the poet permits an image—in this case the image of the rock and the seed—to occupy the bulk of the work; then in the last stanza the meaning of the image is revealed.

A rock for ages, stern and high
Stood frowning 'gainst the earth and sky,
And never bowed his haughty crest
When angry storms around him prest.
Morn, springing from the arms of night,
Had often bathed his brow with light,
And kissed the shadows from his face
With tender love and gentle grace.

Day, pausing at the gates of rest,
Smiled on him from the distant West,
And from her throne the dark-browed Night
Threw round his path her softest light.
And yet he stood unmoved and proud,
Nor love, nor wrath, his spirit bowed;
He bared his brow to every blast
And scorned the tempest as it passed.

One day a tiny, humble seed—
The keenest eye would hardly heed—
Fell trembling at that stern rock's base,
And found a lowly hiding-place.
A ray of light, and drop of dew,
Came with a message, kind and true;
They told her of the world so bright,
Its love, its joy, and rosy light,
And lured her from her hiding place,
To gaze upon the earth's glorious face.

So, peeping timid from the ground,
She clasped the ancient rock around,
And climbing up with childish grace,
She held him with a close embrace;
Her clinging was a thing of dread;
Where'er she touched a fissure spread,
And he who'd brested many a storm
Stood frowning there, a mangled form.

A Truth, dropped in the silent earth,
May seem a thing of little worth,

Till, spreading round some mighty wrong,
It saps its pillars proud and strong,
And o'er the fallen ruin weaves
The brightest blooms and fairest leaves.

When Goethe died, he reportedly uttered the words: "light, more light." From these words Harper wrote "Let the Light Enter."

"Light! more light! the shadows deepen
And my life is ebbing low,
Throw the windows widely open:
Light! more light! before I go.

"Softly let the balmy sunshine
Play around my dying bed,
E'er the dimly lighted valley
I with lonely feet must tread.

"Light! more light! for Death is weaving
Shadows 'round my waning sight,
And I fain would gaze upon him
Through a stream of earthly light."

Not for greater gifts of genius;
Nor for thoughts more grandly bright,
All the dying poet whispers
Is a prayer for light, more light.

Heeds he not the gathered laurels,
Fading slowly from his sight;
All the poet's aspirations
Center in that prayer for light.

Gracious Savior, when life's day-dreams
Melt and vanish from the sight,
May our dim and longing vision
Then be blessed with light, more light.

Occasionally Frances Harper used the ballad meter with varying degrees of success. In the ballad of "Vashti" she was able to adhere more strictly to the form; however, in "The Dying Bond-man" she tells the story of a dying slave with the simplicity which is characteristic of her anti-slavery poems. This is one of the few poems in which she does not insert her own comments. Both of these ballads are indicative of her strong interest in contemporary problems. Long a supporter of women's· rights, Harper tells in "Vashti" the story of a young woman who dared to disobey her husband who was also her king. In both ballads the central characters are intent upon gaining freedom.

VASHTI

She leaned her head upon her hand
    And heard, the King's decree—
"My lords are feasting in my halls;
    Bid Vashti come to me.

I've shown the treasures of my house,
    My costly jewels rare,
But with the glory of her eyes
    No rubies can compare.

"Adorn'd and crown'd I'd have her come,
    With all her queenly grace,
And, 'mid my lords and mighty men,
    Unveil her lovely face.

"Each gem that sparkles in my crown,
    Or glitters on my throne,
Grows poor and pale when she appears,
    My beautiful, my own."

All waiting stood the chamberlains
    To hear the Queen's reply.
They saw her cheek grow deathly pale,
    But light flash'd to her eye:

"Go, tell the King," she proudly said,
    "That I am Persia's Queen,
And by his crowds of merry men
    I never will be seen.

"I'll take the crown from off my head
  And tread it 'neath my feet,
Before their rude and careless gaze
  My shrinking eyes shall meet.

"A queen unveil'd before the crowd!—
  Upon each lip my name!—
Why, Persia's women all would blush
  And weep for Vashti's shame!

"Go back!" she cried, and waved her hand,
  And grief was in her eye:
"Go, tell the King," she sadly said,
  "That I would rather die."

They brought her message to the King;
  Dark flash'd his angry eye;
'Twas as the lightning ere the storm
  Hath swept in fury by.

Then bitterly outspoke the King,
  Through purple lips of wrath—
"What shall be done to her who dares
  To cross your monarch's path?"

Then spake his wily counsellors—
  "O King of this fair land!
From distant Ind to Ethiop,
  All bow to your command.

"But if, before thy servants' eyes,
  This thing they plainly see,
That Vashti doth not heed thy will
  Nor yield herself to thee,

"The women, restive 'neath our rule,
  Would learn to scorn our name,
And from her deed to us would come
  Reproach and burning shame.

"Then, gracious King, sign with thy hand
  This stern but just decree,

That Vashti lay aside her crown,
  Thy Queen no more to be."

She heard again the King's command,
  And left her high estate;
Strong in her earnest womanhood,
  She calmly met her fate,

And left the palace of the King,
  Proud of her spotless name—
A woman who could bend to grief
  But would not bow to shame.

THE DYING BONDMAN

Life was trembling, faintly trembling
On the bondman's latest breath,
And he felt the chilling pressure
Of the cold, hard hand of Death.

He had been an Afric chieftain,
Worn his manhood as a crown;
But upon the field of battle
Had been fiercely stricken down.

He had longed to gain his freedom,
Waited, watched and hoped in vain,
Till his life was slowly ebbing—
Almost broken was his chain.

By his bedside stood the master,
Gazing on the dying one,
Knowing by the dull grey shadows
That life's sands were almost run.

"Master," said the dying bondman,
"Home and friends I soon shall see;
But before I reach my country,
Master write that I am free;

"For the spirits of my fathers
Would shrink back from me in pride,

If I told them at our greeting
I a slave had lived and died;—

"Give to me the precious token,
That my kindred dead may see—
Master! write it, write it quickly!
Master! write that I am free!"

At his earnest plea the master
Wrote for him the glad release,
O'er his wan and wasted features
Flitted one sweet smile of peace.

Eagerly he grasped the writing;
"I am free!" at last he said.
Backward fell upon the pillow,
He was free among the dead.

When she died in 1911, Frances Ellen Watkins Harper had lived and worked through the last days of slavery, through the Civil War, through Reconstruction with all of its attendant problems, and on into the twentieth century. She was essentially optimistic in the Longfellow tradition, but her optimism was not totally unjustified. She had seen progress being made, and as a popular lecturer and poet she had played an important role in that progress. If her poetry appears too moralistic for the modern temperament, it must be remembered that didactic poetry was at one time the most popular poetic type. If she appears too concerned about the contemporary problems of her day, it must be remembered that she belonged to a poetic tradition which maintained that poetry was not a form separate from the ordinary materials and concerns of everyday life. She was a woman who believed in causes. When the Civil War was over and abolitionism was no longer relevant, she turned her attention to women's rights and to the Women's Christian Temperance Union. She did not wholly ignore the problems of the freedmen, but she felt—as did others then—that these problems were well on the way to being solved. Her greatest contribution, however, remains in the area of anti-slavery literature, and when she wrote "Bury Me In a Free Land," she had no doubt that America would one day be a completely free country.

> Make me a grave where'er you will,
> In a lowly plain, or a lofty hill;
> Make it among earth's humblest graves,
> But not in a land where men are slaves.
>
> I could not rest if around my grave
> I heard the steps of a trembling slave;
> His shadow above my silent tomb
> Would make it a place of fearful gloom.
>
> I could not rest if I heard the trwad
> Of a coffle gang to the shambles led,
> And the mother's shriek of wild despair
> Rise like a curse on the trembling air.
>
> I could not sleep if I saw the lash
> Drinking her blood at each fearful gash,
> And I saw her babes torn from her breast,
> Like trembling doves from their parent nest.
>
> I'd shudder and start if I heard the bay
> Of bloodhounds seizing their human prey,
> And I heard the captive plead in vain
> As they bound afresh his galling chain.
>
> If I saw young girls from their mother's arms
> Bartered and sold for their youthful charms,
> My eye would flash with a mournful flame,
> My death-paled cheek grow red with shame.
>
> I would sleep, dear friends, where bloated might
> Can rob no man of his dearest right;
> My rest shall be calm in any grave
> Where none can call his brother a slave.
>
> I ask no monument, proud and high,
> To arrest the gaze of the passers-by;

> All that my yearning spirit craves,
> Is bury me not in a land of slaves.

A second outstanding poet who immediately preceded Dunbar was James Madison Bell whose anti-slavery activities included aiding John Brown plan the raid on Harper's Ferry. Because of his so-called radical position Bell lived in Canada during the six years before the Civil War, but even while there most of his energies were directed toward the cause of abolition. In 1864 he published his first long poem, *The Day and the War,* which appeared as a pamphlet and which praised Lincoln while commemorating the Emancipation Proclamation. Two other long poems, *The Progress of Liberty* (1866) and *The Triumph of Liberty* (1870), dealt with various aspects of freedom and of the anti-slavery movement. Due to Bell's reliance upon different specific occasions for his poetic subjects, much of what he wrote is outdated; however, he still has value as a poetic experimentalist.

Ordinarily Bell used the eight-line stanza which consisted of two quatrains with alternating rhyme. Toward the end of *The Progress of Liberty* he shifted first to a ten-line stanza which was composed of five couplets, then to a twelve-line stanza which consisted of four couplets and a quatrain of alternating rhyme patterns. The result of this is not only a variety of patterns but a greater freedom for the poet. As the poem opens there is an invocation to Liberty which is personified as having a "charm so great" that "one radiant smile, one look at thine/ can change the drooping bondsman's fate,/ and light his brow with hope divine." His invocation continues as he recounts the effects of Liberty.

> His manhood, wrapped in rayless gloom,
>   At thy approach throws off its pall,
> And rising up, as from the tomb,
>   Stands forth defiant of the thrall.
> No tryant's power can crush the soul
>   Illumed by thine inspiring ray;

The fiendishness of base control
Flies thy approach as night from day.

Then in a stanza strangely reminiscent of the spiritual, Bell heralds liberty:

Ride onward, in thy chariot ride,
Thou peerless queen; ride on, ride on—
With Truth and Justice by thy side—
From pole to pole, from sun to sun!
Nor linger in our bleeding South,
Nor domicile with race or clan;
But in thy glorious goings forth,
By thy benignant object Man—

Of every clime, of every hue,
Of every tongue, of every race,
'Neath heaven's broad, ethereal blue;
Oh! let thy radiant smiles embrace,
Till neither slave nor one oppressed
Remain throughout creation's span,
By thee unpitied and unblest
Of all the progeny of man.

Later he moves into the ten-line stanza:

We fain would have the world aspire
To that proud height of free desire,
That flamed the heart of Switzer's Tell
(Whose archery skill none could excell),
When once upon his Alpine brow,
He stood reclining on his bow,
And saw, careering in his might—
In all his majesty of flight—
A lordly eagle float and swing
Upon his broad, untrammeled wing.

Finally the poem reaches the concluding twelve-line stanza:

> He bent his bow, he poised his dart,
> With full intent to pierce the heart;
> But as the proud bird nearer drew,
> His stalwart arm unsteady grew,
> His arrow lingered in the groove—
> The cord unwilling seemed to move,
> For there he saw personified
> That freedom which had been his pride;
> And as the eagle onward sped,
> O'er lofty hill and towering tree,
> He dropped his bow, he bowed his head;
> He could not shoot—'twas Liberty!

Bell's best work is contained in his long poems where, with the precision of one always faithful to dates and events, his fluency and conscious style are more obvious. In 1901 he issued *The Poetical Works of James Madison Bell* which includes not only his three long works but also a collection of short didactic poems none of which match the epic sweep or effectiveness of the early works. While the central motivations for Bell's major works have passed, one can still discern in his work the poet's interest in Negro history and in eliminating all barriers in America which are based upon race or creed. In another day at another time Bell may have produced an outstanding historical romance, but his anti-slavery sentiments were so strong that everything in his long poems was subordinated to his message.

Of the major Negro poets who preceded Dunbar, Albery A. Whitman is perhaps the least known today. Like Bell, he also appeared to use Sir Walter Scott as a model; but unlike Bell, he seemed to turn to the Byron of *Childe Harold* for additional patterns. His early life was spent in bondage. Born in 1851 apparently in Kentucky, he was enslaved until 1863, but writing of his early life in *The Rape of Florida* (1884) Whitman said: "I enjoyed the inestimable blessings of cabin life and hard work during the whole of my early days. I was in bondage,—*I never was a slave,*—the infamous laws of a savage despotism took my substance—what of that? (p. 4)" After receiving his freedom he taught in a small school and eventually became a minister. The extent of his fame is demonstrated by the fact that he was selected in 1893 to compose a poem for the World's Columbian Exposition. For that occasion in Chicago he read his "The Freedman's Triumphant Song."

Whitman published three long poems and one collection of verse. The first of his publications, *Not a Man, and Yet a Man,* may well have the distinction of being one of the longest poems in American literature. Structurally the poem, consisting of almost three hundred pages, seems to be patterned after the neoclassical works of the eighteenth century. The narrative is told by means of the heroic couplet; however, the mood is far more romantic than neo-classical. The setting is Saville, a village of the Middle West; life is rugged but at the same time the descriptions tend to emphasize the idyllic nature of the setting. The protagonist of the poem is Rodney, a slave owned by Sir Maxey the wealthiest man in the village. Sir Maxey's daughter, Dora, is captured by the Indians of a nearby town and is saved by the heroic Rodney. While he is happy to have his daughter back safely, Sir Maxey is extremely unhappy because in a moment of anxiety during the captivity of Dora he had promised to marry her to the man who could save her. Dora who believes she has fallen in love with her rescuer insists that her father keep his promise. Instead Sir Maxey gives Rodney to a slave trader with instructions that the slave is to be sold into the deep South. Rodney eventually finds himself in Florida on a plantation where he meets Leona, another slave. The two fall in love, and after a series of harrowing escapades manage to get to Canada and thus to assured freedom. As fate would decree, in Canada the two lovers find themselves being protected and supported by Dora who now admits that she had mistakenly imagined herself in love with Rodney when in reality she simply respected him and felt sorry for his people.

Whitman admitted the influence of Byron and Spenser, but it appears from the poem that his knowledge of Spenser was a second-

hand one for his use of the nine-line Spenserian stanza is more
reminiscent in tone of Byron than of Spenser. In an apologetic
dedicatory statement which appears in *The Rape of Florida,* Whitman interestingly analyzed his own work.

[Concerning] the 'stately verse,' mastered only by Spenser, Byron, and
a very few other great poets, I may seem to have 'rushed in where
angels fear to tread.' To this view of the matter, I will say by way of
defense: some Negro's sure to do everything that any one else has ever
done, and as none of the race have executed [sic] a poem in the 'stately
verse,' I simple *venture in.*

It would be advantageous to discover exactly how extensive was
Whitman's actual reading background. As a student at Wilberforce
he was probably exposed to the literary masters; yet, it becomes
extremely difficult to ascertain how much he is indebted to them
if at all. There is enough originality in all of his work to preclude
any conscious imitation. On the other hand, in *Not a Man, and
Yet a Man* there appear to be traces of Dwight's *Greenfield Hill* in
the celebration of the countryside as well as of Goldsmith's *The
Deserted Village.* When he describes the Indian settlement, Whitman seems to approximate Longfellow. Even vestiges of Scott's
The Lady of the Lake seem discernible. Whitman may have had
an excellent ear for poetic sound and may have absorbed the
popular works of his period. In spite of the fact that he may have
incorporated the sounds which he liked best into his own work,
Not a Man, Yet a Man is an exciting adventure story which is
indicative of the sustained poetic powers of Whitman. While Dora
and her father are stereotypes, both Rodney and Leona emerge
as warmly human creations. Rodney, whose story unifies the entire
work, is far more believable than the usual romantic hero in a work
of this nature.

Occasionally Whitman employed dialect in the poem, a dialect
rather similar to Dunbar's but which within the context of the
poem is more forced than natural. For example, while Rodney is

waiting for the arrival of the slave trader, the narrator describes the scene through the use of dialect which the poet puts in iambic tetrameter couplets rather than in the heroic couplet and Spenserian stanza of the bulk of the poem.

> In yonder room is Rodney tied,
> Where stands a locust on dis side.
> De white folks sell him in de morn,
> An' he'll be left yer, shore's yer born,
> Go see him, gal, bid him farewell,
> An' tell him what yer's got to tell,
> An' I'll stand here, de outside by,
> An' keep watchout wid open eye.

The dialect inconsistencies are apparent even in this short passage. Fathiful representation of language would decree that if *an'* is used *stan'* rather than *stand* should also be used.

His second poem, *The Rape of Florida,* was revised in 1885 as *Twasinta's Seminoles; or, The Rape of Florida.* The narrative deals with the Seminoles' loss of Florida and is an adventure story after the manner of Byron. The theme deals primarily with the search for another home; however, several allusions are made to the fact that the Seminoles frequently aided runaway slaves. The following sections from Canto I illustrate how faithfully Whitman employed the Spenserian stanza:

VI

> The sable slave, from Georgia's utmost bounds,
> Escapes for life into the Great Wahoo.
> Here he has left afar the savage hounds
> And human hunters that did late pursue;
> There in the hommock darkly hid from view,
> His wretched limbs are stretched awhile to rest,
> Till some kind Seminole shall guide him thro'
> To where by hound nor hunter more distrest,
> He in a flow'ry home, shall be the red man's guest.

X

Fair Florida! whose scenes could so enhance—
Could in the sweetness of the earth excel!
Wast thou the Seminole's inheritance?
Yea, it was thee he loved, and loved so well!
'Twas 'neath thy palms and pines he strove to dwell.
Not savage, but resentful to the knife,
For these he sternly struggled—sternly fell!
Thoughtful and brave, in long uneven strife,
He held the verge of manhood mid the heights of life.

XI

A wild-born pride endeared him to thy soil!
When roamed his herds without a keeper's care—
Where man knew not the pangs of slavish toil!
And where thou didst not blooming pleasures spare,
But well allotted each an ample share,
He loved to dwell: Oh! isn't the goal of life
Where man has plenty and to man is fair?
When free from avarice's pinch and strife,
Is earth not like the Eden-home of man and wife?

XXVIII

The poorest negro coming to their shore,
To them was brother—their own flesh and blood,—
They sought his wretched manhood to restore,—
They found his hidings in the swampy wood,
And brought him forth—in arms before him stood,—
The citizens of God and sovran earth,—
They shot straight forward looks with flame imbued,
Till in him manhood sprang, a noble birth,
And warrior-armed he rose to all that manhood's worth.

Before publishing his last long work, *The Octoroon: An Idyl of
the South* in 1901, Whitman issued *Twasinta's Seminoles; or The
Rape of Florida* again in 1890 in which appeared *Not a Man, Yet*

a Man as well as a group of unpublished short poems which were collected under the title "Drifted Leaves." *The Octoroon: An Idyl of the South,* subtitled "An Epic in Two Parts," deals with the forbidding story of the love of a young white man for one of his father's slaves. The environment will not permit the fulfillment of this love, and Whitman mournfully concludes:

> The hedges may obscure the sweetest bloom—
> The orphan of the waste—the lowly flower:
> While in the garden, faint for want of room,
> The splendid failure pines within her bower.
> There is a wide republic of perfume,
> In which the nameless waifs of sun and shower,
> That scatter wildly through the fields and woods,
> Make the divineness of the solitudes.

Whitman's implicit faith in his people was perhaps best stated in his introductory remarks in the 1884 edition of *The Rape of Florida:*

I have yielded to the firm belief that the Negro has a future: I abhor the doctrine that he is but a cipher in the sum of the world's greatness —a captive in the meshes of dominating influences. . . . The time has come when all the 'Uncle Toms' and 'Topsies' ought to die. Goody-goodness is a sort of man worship: ignorance is its inspiration, fear its ministering spirit, and beggary its heritage (pp. 3-4).

Perhaps nowhere in nineteenth-century Negro literature has a more positive statement been uttered. Whitman died in 1902 before the writers of the Harlem Renaissance re-echoed his firm belief; however, he lived long enough to see the freedmen accomplish things which would have been considered impossible in 1863.

In addition to Harper, Bell, and Whitman there were other nineteenth-century poets who were not as prolific as these three but who did—at times—produce some interesting and significant works. For those who today maintain that the "black-is-beautiful" cult is a modern phenomenon, the June 8, 1827, issue of *Freedom's Journal* is of value. In this magazine appeared the short work of an anonymous poet who identified himself merely as "a son of Africa." Entitled "The Black Beauty," the poem attempts to place the color of skin in its proper perspective. In couplets of irregular trochaic trimeter the anonymous poet plays upon two words: *black* and *beauteous.*

> Black I am, oh! daughters fair!
> But my beauty is most rare.
> Black, indeed, appears my skin,
> Beauteous, comely, all within:
> Black when by affliction press'd,
> Beauteous, when in Christ I rest;
> Black, by sin's defiling blood,
> Beauteous, wash'd in Jesus' blood;
> Black I am in my own eyes,
> Beauteous in my Lord's I rise:
> Black I am to men, 'tis true,
> Beauteous in the angel's view:
> Black, if Jesus frowns a while,
> Beauteous, when I see him smile;
> Black, while in the tomb I lie,
> Beauteous, when I mount the sky.

The anti-slavery newspapers and magazines published numerous poems by free and enslaved Negroes. While both Wheatley and Horton published some work in these journals, many of the poems which appeared were used simply as "fillers" and have little or no merit. Furthermore, little is known of these writers many of whom possibly may not have even been Negroes. For example, in five issues of *The Liberator* (December 5, 1833; January 4, 1834; June 27, 1835; March 11 and June 16, 1837) there were printed poems by Ada who was reported as being "a young lady of color." But her identity is otherwise unknown. On February 16, 1833, John Boyd of the Bahamas published his "The Vanity of Life" in *The Liberator*. Unlike many of the more ephemeral poets, Boyd did publish in 1834 in London a volume of his poems all of which seem faint echoes of the early work of Milton whose work he may have known. "A Colored Female of the Barbadoes" published two poems in the *Emancipator* for September 27, 1837. All of these poems are in the sentimental anti-slavery tradition and exhibit neither great originality nor a thorough knowledge of poetic technique.

From approximately 1840 to the end of the Civil War a great deal of verse was written by those opposed to slavery, but much of it was written by men who really were not poets in the strictest sense of the term. William Wells Brown, the first Negro professional novelist, wrote "Fling Out the Anti-Slavery Flag" which appeared in the London edition (1849) of his *Narrative*. This abolition hymn gained popularity merely because it appeared in one of the most famous of the slave narratives of the period. Frederick Douglass, the orator, is not usually associated with poetry in spite of the poetic prose which seems to characterize so much of his oratory; however, in a speech which he delivered in New York (May, 1857) dealing with the Dred Scott decision, he included two stanzas of verse which do seem to follow his general rhetorical pattern. The purpose of the inserted short poem was to further emphasize and explain to his audience the possible results of slave rebellions.

> The fires thus kindled may be revived again;
> The flames are extinguished, but the embers remain;
> One terrible blast may produce an ignition,
> Which shall wrap the whole South in wild conflagration.
>
> The pathway of tyrants lies over volcanoes;
> The very air they breathe is heavy with sorrows;
> Agonizing heart-throbs convulse them while sleeping,
> And the wind whispers Death, as over them sleeping.

The earliest political satire in Negro literature was written by a Presbyterian minister, the Reverend Mr. Elymas Payson Rogers. *The Repeal of the Missouri Compromise Considered* was published in 1856. There is very little internal evidence in the poem that its author is a Negro; however, there are sympathetic references to the outstanding Negroes who were—at that time—active in the anti-slavery movement. Rogers achieved the type of detachment which is helpful and effective in satiric writing. In the section devoted to the description of America in 1820, the year of the Missouri Compromise, Rogers in iambic tetrameter couplets portrays the North and the South in this manner:

> "I want the land," was Freedom's cry:
> And Slavery answered, "So do I!
> By all that's sacred, I declare
> I'll have my just and lawful share.
> The Northern cheek should glow with shame,
> To think to rob me of my claim;
> And if my claim you dare deny,
> I'll knock the Union into Pi!"
> The Northern faces did not glow,
> Because they were composed of dough:
> But such a tall and horrid threat,
> Their equilibrium upset.

Unlike the other poets who believed that the Negro had a place in America, James M. Whitfield believed that the salvation of the race rested in complete escape from America. Toward this goal he worked diligently to promote the cause of migration to Central America. When the Colored Colonization Convention, sometimes referred to as the National Emigation Convention of Colored Men, was called in 1854, he strongly supported its platform and was quite vocal in defending the convention against the attacks of Frederick Douglass and others who were opposed to it. The year before his involvement in this colonization plan, in 1853, he published *America and Other Poems*.

The title poem, "America," is an ode which points out the irony of the country being called "land of liberty" when so many of its inhabitants are enslaved. Beginning with the Revolutionary War, Whitfield shows how Negroes have aided the country which has made them slaves:

America, it is to thee,
Thou boasted land of liberty,—
It is to thee I raise my song,
Thou land of blood, and crime, and wrong.
It is to thee my native land,
From which has issued many a band
To tear the black man from his soil,
And force him here to delve and toil;
Chained on your blood-bemoistened sod,
Cringing beneath a tyrant's rod,
Stripped of those rights which Nature's God
   Bequeathed to all the human race,
Bound to a petty tyrant's nod,
Because he wears a paler face.
Was it for this that freedom's fires
Were kindled by your patriot sires?
Was it for this they shed their blood,
On hill and plain, on field and flood?
Was it for this that wealth and life
Were staked upon that desperate strife,
Which drenched this land for seven long years
With blood of men, and women's tears?
When black and white fought side by side,
   Upon the well-contested field,—
Turned back the fierce opposing tide,
   And made the proud invader yield—
When, wounded, side by side they lay,
   And heard with joy the proud hurrah
From their victorious comrades say
   That they had waged successful war,
The thought ne'er entered in their brains

That they endured those toils and pains,
To forge fresh fetters, heavier chains
For their own children, in whose veins
Should flow that patriotic blood,
So freely shed on field and flood.
Oh, no; they fought, as they believed,
     For the inherent rights of man;
But mark, how they have been deceived
     By slavery's accursed plan.
They never thought, when thus they shed
     Their heart's best blood, in freedom's cause,
That their own sons would live in dread,
     Under unjust, oppressive laws:
That those who quietly enjoyed
     The rights for which they fought and fell,
Could be the framers of a code,
     That would disgrace the fiends of hell!
Could they have looked, with prophet's ken,
     Down to the present evil time,
     Seen free-born men, uncharged with crime,
Consigned unto a slaver's pen—
Or thrust into a prison cell,
With thieves and murderers to dwell—
While that same flag whose stripes and stars
Had been their guide through freedom's wars
As proudly waved above the pen
Of dealers in the souls of men!

Then the poet proceeds to the unfulfilled promises of the years following the Revolutionary War, the years of indecision. He is convinced that Christianity has not helped those who believe one doctrine and practice another.

And manhood, too, with soul of fire,
And arm of strength, and smothered ire,
Stands pondering with brow of gloom,
Upon his dark unhappy doom,

Whether to plunge in battle's strike,
And buy his freedom with his life,
And with stout heart and weapon strong,
Pay back the tyrant wrong for wrong
Or wait the promised time of God,
    When his Almighty ire shall wake,
And smite the oppressor in his wrath,
And hurl red ruin in his path,
And with the terrors of his rod,
    Cause adamantine hearts to quake.
Here Christian writhes in bondage still,
    Beneath his brother Christian's rod,
And pastors trample down at will,
    The image of the living God.

Whitfield's ode finally concludes:

Almighty God! thy aid impart,
And fire anew each faltering heart,
And strengthen every patriot's hand,
Who aims to save our native land.
We do not come before thy throne,
    With carnal weapons drenched in gore,
Although our blood has freely flown,
    In adding to the tyrant's store.
Father! before thy throne we come,
    Not in panoply of war,
With pealing trump, and rolling drum,
    And cannon booming loud and far;
Striving in blood to wash out blood,
    Through wrong to seek redress for wrong;
For while thou'rt holy, just and good,
    The battle is not to the strong;
But in the sacred name of peace,
    Of justice, virtue, love and truth,
We pray, and never mean to cease,
    Till weak old age and fiery youth
In freedom's cause their voices raise,

> And burst the bonds of every slave;
> Till, north and south, and east and west,
> The wrongs we bear shall be redressed.

The total despair of Whitfield is evidenced in another poem which appeared in *America and Other Poems.* "The Misanthropist," an early pessimistic poem of social protest, blames the religiously oriented society of America for the plight of Negroes. He ends the poem by describing the uselessness and alienation of life in America.

> But mine must still the portion be,
> However dark and drear the doom,
> To live estranged from sympathy,
> Buried in doubt, despair, and gloom;
> To bare my breast to every blow,
> To know no friend, and fear no foe,
> Each generous impulse trod to dust,
> Each noble aspiration crushed,
> Each feeling struck with withering blight,
> With no regard for wrong or right,
> No fear of hell, no hope of heaven,
> Die all unwept and unforgiven,
> Content to know and dare the worst,
> Which mankind;s hate, and heaven's curse,
> Can heap upon my living head,
> Or cast around my memory dead;
> And let them on my tombstone trace,
> "Here lies the Pariah of his race."

Although *America and Other Poems* was an extremely successful volume, Whitfield spent the remainder of his life as a crusader for the cause of colonization. He was firmly convinced that in America the democratic principles would never be realized. Nor was he alone. There did develop among some of the poets of the period, notably Charles L. Reason and George B. Vashon, a questioning of the foundations of America. While Reason and

Vashon, both college professors, did not scorn America to the extent that they advocated complete withdrawal, they did use their work as a means of positively insisting upon freedom for all. In "Freedom," a rather elaborate ode, Reason attempts to trace the desire for freedom from the ancient Greeks to the struggle of Toussaint L'Ouverture. And he concludes that even though superior forces have sometimes been arrayed against those who fight for freedom, any force which is opposed to freedom will be defeated. In "Vincent Oge" Vashon portrayed the freedom fighter of Haiti as a martyr in the cause of justice. Both Reason and Vashon were convinced that freedom would prevail even at the cost of great bloodshed. Both of these poems were published in the 1854 edition of *Autographs for Freedom,* the short-lived anti-slavery annual which was edited and published by Julia Griffiths, an Englishwoman who came to this country to aid the abolitionists.

Because of the popularity of verse as a means of social protest and the apparent ease with which many of these books were published, the years after the Civil War saw a group of undistinguished volumes presented to the American reading public. Most of these books were crude imitations, but they do demonstrate the presence of poetic activity. In 1867 two versified attempts to survey biblical literature appeared and today are little more than historical curiosities; however, in both instances the writers presented a rather strange combination of prose and poetry. Lorenzo D. Blackson's contribution, *The Rise and Progress of the Kingdoms of Light and Darkness; or the Reigns of Kings Alpha and Abadon,* was referred to by an ambitious bookseller as "the Negro's *Pilgrim's Progress.*" The similarity between Bunyan and Blackson is purely coincidental as Blackson's King Alpha, who is first God then Christ, battles King Abadon, who is Satan. The battle extends from the days of Adam and Eve to the nineteenth century in America. At the end of the long story, Blackson inserts an equally long poem which summarizes the narrative in rather simple quatrains. One Mr. B. Clark is the other poet who attempted to survey biblical literature and world history in a work entitled *The Past, Present, and Future in Prose and Poetry.* These examples can be multiplied during the closing years of the nineteenth century; hence when Dunbar's work began to appear in the 1890's, when he was hailed as a national literary figure, he brought a new vitality to a literary form which had become saturated with imitative historical poems and poorly-executed hymns. Yet the literary activity of the century provided later writers with a poetic tradition upon which they could build.

CHAPTER V

The Masking of the Poet

WHEN DUNBAR finished high school in Dayton, Ohio, the city of his birth, it seemed that he was doomed to spend his life as an elevator operator, but friends and acquaintances soon recognized his great literary ability and encouraged him to submit poems to the popular magazines and journals of his day. Eventually, in 1893, *Oak and Ivy* was published privately. The volume did not become an immediate success, but at least his work was before a reading public, small though that public was. His next volume, *Majors and Minors,* was issued early in 1896 by an obscure publisher in Toledo, Ohio, and was no more successful, but it was sent to William Dean Howells, long considered the dean of American letters, who in turn—because he was so impressed—wrote the review which was destined to place Dunbar's name before the American reading public. Later that same year *Lyrics of Lowly Life* appeared, published by Dodd, Mead, and Company with the now famous introduction by Howells. Although he was only twenty-four years old at the time, Dunbar had achieved the type of acclaim frequently reserved for much older writers.

From 1896 until his death in 1906 Paul Lawrence Dunbar was the subject of numerous essays and extensive readings—both public and private—as he became, for many people, the symbol of Negro authorship in the United States. Some referred to him as the very first Negro writer in America; others who had heard of Phillis Wheatley allowed that he was the second writer; but all agreed that he was the first truly to interpret Negro life in the country. In many ways Dunbar's success saddened him because he knew that there had been other writers before him and almost without exception it was his dialect poetry which drew white America to him. This poetry which was thought of as a "representative interpretation of Negro life" was such a small portion of his total output.

In time Negroes repudiated Dunbar although many can still recall the twilight evenings when "Little Brown Baby" or "When Malindy Sings" was read to them. These were the private moments of racial consciousness which could not be shared with other Americans. At the same time that there has been a private acceptance of Dunbar, on a public literary and intellectual level, however, he is often rejected as a mere dialect versifier, as one who did not even attempt to write of his people in a realistic way. But this attitude was not always the case. At one time there were numerous Dunbar Societies which flourished as young men and women gathered to read his poetry. The many schools and projects in the country which bear his name attest to a respect which did exist. Aside from attacking his lack of realism, there are others who accuse him of deliberately falsifying his picture of his race in order to pacify white readers. As time went on, these accusations multiplied so that today Dunbar symbolizes for many the plantation tradition in literature, a tradition held in disrepute especially when practiced by a Negro. George Washington Cable, Irwin Russell, Joel Chandler Harris, and Thomas Nelson Page are excused for their work in the plantation tradition because they were white and were not expected to know anything else. But not so in the instance of Dunbar. For a Negro to do this is now considered unforgivable because, it is felt, he had a rare opportunity to get before the American reading public a realistic analysis of the racial problems of America and an honest portrayal of Negro characters.

Dunbar himself was aware of the dilemma which faced him. While he had no way of knowing that he would eventually be categorized with others who used the minstrel tradition in a derisive manner, he was frequently unhappy about the widespread acceptance of his dialect verse to the exclusion of his other verse. One of the best contemporary accounts of Dunbar's personal attitude is provided in James Weldon Johnson's autobiography *Along This Way*. Writing in 1933 of Dunbar's early visit to his home, Johnson recorded:

> We talked again and again about poetry. I told him my doubts regarding the further possibilities of stereotyped dialect. He was hardly less dubious than I. He said, 'You know, of course, that I didn't start as a dialect poet. I simply came to the conclusion that I could write it as well, if not better, than anybody else I knew of, and that by doing so I should gain a hearing. I gained the hearing, and now they don't want me to write anything but dialect.' There was a tone of self-reproach in what he said; and five years later, in his fatal illness, he sounded that same tone more deeply when he said to me, 'I've kept on doing the same things, and doing them no better. I have never gotten to the things I really wanted to do.' (pp. 160-61).

But in spite of the pessimism which frequently gripped Dunbar, he was able to accomplish a great deal during his short life.

Those who would now dismiss Dunbar's work fail to remember that he wrote at a time when the romantic tradition was still in vogue in America, at a time when stories of the ante-bellum South were still appearing in popular magazines. Dunbar, who himself was not a southerner, did not write from his own personal experiences, but rather from the stories which his mother, who had been a slave in Kentucky, told him; hence, the assertion that he wrote from personal observation and participation is not valid. He had not really known what the aftermath of slavery in the South was actually like. One of his literary models was James Whitcomb Riley with whom he developed a friendship, and much of what Dunbar wrote in terms of the plantation tradition was simply the Riley vernacular transposed into stories of the South. Furthermore, Dunbar was aware of the publishing situation in the 1890's and the early years of the twentieth century, and much of his work was geared toward popular tastes rather than toward social criticism.

Yet, he did produce a large body of work which consists of a series of realistic portrayals of some of the problems of American life. Dunbar was not oblivious to the racial problem in this country. That he did not devote his entire literary career to it, of course, is regretted by many today; but no one who has read "We Wear the Mask," "The Haunted Oak," "Frederick Douglass" or the sonnets addressed to Harriet Beecher Stowe, Booker T. Washington, and Robert Gould Shaw can forget their subtlety nor doubt the deep concern of Dunbar for his own people.

Perhaps nowhere did his recognition of his own life and work become more apparent than in the short poem "The Poet."

> He sang of life, serenely sweet,
>> With, now and then, a deeper note.
>> From some high peak, nigh yet remote,
> He voiced the world's absorbing beat.
>
> He sang of love when earth was young,
>> And love, itself, was in his lays.
>> But ah, the world, it turned to praise
> A jingle in a broken tongue.

Dunbar did sing of "life, serenely sweet" in most of his poems, short stories, and novels, but it was the "jingle in a broken tongue" by which he became famous and for which he is now remembered.

I

For a well-known poet Dunbar produced an unusually large body of fiction, and it can be divided primarily into two types. There are those stories in which he appeared to concern himself mainly with white characters and their world, stories which do not deal with specific aspects of Negro life. In some of these stories the characters could have been anybody and the situations frequently applicable to white and black alike. Those who look at this fiction and deplore the lack of Negro characters are inadvertently supporting the thesis that the Negro artist must and should produce either works which are within the mold of social protest or which are circumscribed not only by the time and place but also by the race of the author. Dunbar was not, in this fiction, intent upon renouncing his race neither was he attempting to ignore those problems which he saw daily but rather he was operating within the framework of his own belief that the literary artist who happens to be a Negro is not bound by the limitations of purely racial subjects. With this view of literary art Dunbar produced *The Uncalled* (1898), *The Love of Landry* (1900), *The Fanatics* (1901), *Ohio Pastorals,* five short stories which appeared in *Lippincott's Monthly Magazine* from August (1901) to December (1901), and numerous short stories within his short story collections.

The Uncalled first appeared in *Lippincott's Monthly Magazine* (May, 1898) before it appeared in book form. As a first novel, it suffers from the usual self-consciousness which one tends to ascribe to such works. In many ways it appears to be autobiographical in the sense that the protagonist, Frederick Brent, is faced with the problem of whether or not to enter the ministry, a question which Dunbar also faced. The novel is set in Dexter, a small town in Ohio, and the central action surrounds Frederick's need to find himself. In spite of his own wishes he does attend a seminary and become a minister, but eventually he rejects the life of hypocrisy for a more meaningful life. The purpose of *The Uncalled,* if this popular slick magazine story can be said to have a purpose, is the revelation of the pettiness and deceitfulness which exist in a small town. The central theme focuses upon Frederick's growing awareness of himself and of the world around him.

Years before the formal attack-on-the-village school of fiction, popularized by Edgar Lee Masters and Sinclair Lewis, Dunbar had investigated the same problems and situations. However, when it was discovered that the author of *The Uncalled* was *THE* Paul Laurence Dunbar of dialect poetry, some critics were visibly upset as they asserted that the novel failed because the author should have written about his own people. Ironically the characters are not given racial labels, but it was assumed that the novelist intended that the characters be white. Perhaps this type of critical attitude is best exemplified by Vernon Loggins writing in his *The Negro Author in America* (New York, 1931). Claiming that Dunbar should have "painstakingly avoided" writing stories without Negro characters, Loggins continued: "All of the bubbling spontaneity which he showed in his tales on blacks is replaced . . . by cheap conventional story-telling, with echoes of Dickens and the popular magazine, and with an English which is often downright faulty." The "faulty English" which Loggins found is simply an English devoid of dialect or peculiar mannerisms; it is a language which cannot be racially identified. While he asserted that it "came as a great disappointment to Dunbar's admirers," Loggins was forced to admit that the novel had "some commercial success (p. 316)." And it was commercial success for which Dunbar aimed inasmuch as he had selected the role of professional writer for his occupation.

The Love of Landry appeared in 1900. The characters are white easterners who go West. The attitude of some white Americans is briefly introduced with no attempt on the part of the novelist to either deny or support the portrayal presented. While on the west-bound train Mildred Osborne, the protagonist, comments rather sadly upon the life of a porter, and her father scoffs at her for being sympathetic by asserting:

'Poor coloured man! Why Mildred, that man gets more out of life than I do. He has a greater capacity for enjoyment, with the paradox that less satisfies it. You think it humiliates him to take a tip? Not in the least. That's his business. He courteously fleeces us, and then laughs about it, no doubt . . . (p. 38)'

The major action is set in Colorado, and once the characters, especially Mildred Osborne, get there, they begin to lose the superficialities which had bound them to the East and to civilization. They become "real" people once again as they become aware of the beauty of nature, a beauty which eluded them in the East. The story is not at all spectacular. Dunbar uses an old ruse for having his characters "find" themselves, but in terms of the back-to-nature tradition which he uses in the novel, it is as successful as any of this type. Most certainly, the novel demonstrates all of the weaknesses of the romantic novel at the turn of the century.

His third novel, *The Fanatics* (1901) does touch more upon racial questions, but once again primarily from a "white" point of view. The novel deals with the conflict between two families in a small town in Ohio. Bradford Waters and his family are Union sympathizers, and Stephen Van Doren and his family support the Confederacy. The conflict between these two families is symbolic of the general conflict in the border town which is almost evenly divided between northern and southern supporters. The hostility between the two families is intensified because Bob Van Doren is in love with Mary Waters. When Bob joins the Confederate Army, Bradford Waters insists that Mary, his daughter, reject Bob's love and end her engagement to him. Mary refuses because she claims that she loves Bob and "not his politics." But Bradford Waters does not take kindly to his rebellious daughter and rejects her. After the Civil War, however, the two families become re-united and "live happily ever after."

As a story dealing with the effects of the Civil War upon a community, the novel demonstrates once again that Dunbar understood the psychology of the small town and that he understood the self-righteous northerner even better. For example, there was a growing concern in Dorbury, Ohio, the place of the action, about the many Negroes who poured into the town. As is noted in the novel:

Ohio, placed as she was, just on the border of the slave territory, was getting more than her share of this unwelcome population, and her white citizens soon began to chafe at it (p. 158).

Eventually one character, Raymond Stothard, complains about the refugees and actually voices a prevailing attitude:

'All the niggers in the South are crowding in on us, and pretty soon, we won't have a place to lay our heads. They'll undercharge the laborer and drive him out of house and home. They will live on leavings, and the men who are eating white bread and butter will have to get down to the level of the black hounds.'

Stothard continues his lament by claiming:

'The whole war is on their account. If it hadn't been for them, we'd have been friends with the South today, but they've estranged us from our brothers, rent the country asunder, and now they're coming up here to crowd us out of our town (pp. 165-66).'

As is typical of the romantic and sentimental novel, the characters of Dunbar's novel are overdrawn. The Negroes who stream into the town as refugees from the war are used primarily in the local color tradition; only Nigger Ed, the town crier who goes to war, emerges as a warmly human character. Dunbar, the author, remains detached from all of his characters as he views the fanatics on both sides; yet he demonstrates quite clearly the hypocrisy of the North as well as the paradoxical position in which most Negroes are forced in northern communities. And he concludes that the North is really no different in attitudes from the South.

Little can be said for the five stories which comprise *Ohio Pastorals.* "The Motification of the Flesh," "The Independence of Silas Bollender," "The White Counterpane," "The Minority Committee," and "The Visiting of Mother Danbury" are stories which employ some of the more popular techniques of the day and as they appeared in five successive issues of *Lippincott's Monthly Magazine* they are simply entertaining fillers in the magazine. No single characteristic distinguishes them from the host of magazine stories which were popular at the time.

The second type of fiction which Dunbar wrote was in the plantation tradition after the manner and formula of Joel Chandler Harris, Thomas Nelson Page, Irwin Russell, and George Washington Cable. In four collections of short stories, *Folks From Dixie* (1898), *The Strength of Gideon and Other Stories* (1900), *In Old Plantation Days* (1903), and *The Heart of Happy Hollow* (1904), Dunbar presents a sentimental picture of the Old South. His portrait of ante-bellum days is similar to those which followed the conventional local color methods. This tradition presented imagined characters in typical situations when the South was thought of as being divided into two classes: the slaves and the masters. Seldom are the unpleasant aspects of life displayed. Of all of the men who dealt successfully with this world of masters and slaves, Dunbar was the only non-southerner in the group. As the observant outsider, Dunbar never permitted his characters to become clowns merely for the sake of humor. Even though he really did not know the characters about whom he wrote, from his mother's stories he was able to present them sympathetically and gently; his plantations stories (as much of his dialect poetry) show more obviously the influence of James Whitcomb Riley than they do of the plantation school of southern writers. When Dunbar wrote of the days following the Civil War when Negroes were migrating in large numbers to northern cities, he was insistent upon the contrast between the more pleasing side of life in the South with the harshness of life in northern cities. This was partially due to Dunbar's own belief in an agrarian way of life as opposed to that in an industrial community.

His first collection of short stories, *Folks From Dixie,* is most apparently influenced by the then-popular plantation tradition. Many of the stories are set in Kentucky where his mother had been enslaved. While the stories are typical of their genre, Dunbar demonstrates a far more sensitive understanding of his characters than Russell, Page, Cable, or Harris ever did. Thus while most of the twelve stories of the collection are traditional in the sense that they portray—in a large measure—the happy and contented relationship between master and slave, the differences (both social and intellectual) between house and field slaves, the narratives are presented with far greater knowledge of some of the basic problems which existed before and after the Civil War. Dunbar, who did not have first-hand knowledge of either slavery or those days following in the South, was content to employ the usual stereotypes: the young master or the considerate master who sold his slaves only in a financial crisis, the beautiful mistress who spent much time in the slaves' quarters taking care of the ill and educating the young, the poor white overseer who was hated by master and slave alike, the house slaves—especially the "Mammy" and the butler—who controlled everybody and everything in the "Big House," and the general aura of gentility which pervaded the idea of southern life and manners.

Although his stories in this collection included in varying degrees all of these stereotypes, he did analyze such themes as the effects of religion and church life in such stories as "Anner Lizer's Stumblin' Block," "The Ordeal at Mt. Hope" which was also a strong plea for industrial education, "Mt. Pisgah's Christmas Possum," and "The Trial Sermons on Bull-Skin." The idealized portrait of loyalty and dedication is best exemplified in "The Colonel's Awakening" where ex-slaves aid their old master who has lost his mind, his fortune, and his sons during the Civil War. The same theme is evident in "The Intervention of Peter" where Peter, an old respected slave, prevents a duel between two southern "gentlemen," and in "Nelse Hatton's Revenge" where another ex-slave aids a former master who had seemed so terrible prior to the Civil War. He further explored the exploitation of Negroes by Negroes in such stories as "Aunt Mandy's Investment," and in "Jimsella" he presented the problem of life in the North, a problem which he was to treat at greater length in *The Sport of the Gods.* Just as "The Ordeal at Mt. Hope" is a form of social protest so also is "At Shaft 11" where Dunbar pleads with Negroes to stay out of labor unions. The success of these stories, once one passes the superficialities of the local color tradition, is in Dunbar's ability to distinguish the true meaning of the actions of his characters from those actions which are assumed for the sake of expediency. No white writer of the plantation tradition was ever able to do this.

The Strength of Gideon and Other Stories consists of twenty stories. Life on the plantation is treated in "Viney's Free Papers," "The Case of 'Ca'line': A Kitchen Monologue," "Uncle Simon's Sunday Out," "The Fruitful Sleeping of the Rev. Elisha Edwards," and "Jim's Probation." Once again Dunbar portrays the loyalty of the ex-slaves for their old masters in such stories as "Mammy Peggy's Pride," and in the title story of the collection "The Strength of Gideon." A number of the narratives of this collection deal with the inability of Negroes to adjust to northern urban environments and with the role of Negroes in politics during the days of Reconstruction. "An Old Time Christmas," "The Trustfulness of Polly," "The Finding of Zach," "The Faith Cure Man," "Silas Jackson," "The Finish of Patsy Barnes," and "One Man's Fortune" portray the disillusionment with life in the North. "One Man's Fortune" is especially interesting today for it deals with a young man who had listened to all of the injunctions to "get an education" only to discover that education has little or no value for him. He becomes aware that society still looks at him as a Negro rather than as a man. Dunbar makes it clear that the initial efforts toward aiding the freedman after the Civil War was soon replaced by a general spirit of indifference. Political aspirations are treated realistically in "Mr. Cornelius Johnson, Office Seeker," "A Mess of Pottage," and "A Council of State." In "The Ingrate" Dunbar sympathetically presents the story of a slave who has escaped to Canada but who later returns to the United States in order to join the Union Army and to help others gain their freedom. The story, which is probably patterned after the life of his father, is significantly one of his strongest attacks on the institution of slavery.

With *In Old Plantation Days* Dunbar returns to the basic type of *Folks From Dixie*. While in his second collection of short stories Dunbar introduced far more realistic portrayals of character and situations as well as more stories of social protest, his third volume re-echoes the traditionalism of the first. Stuart Mordaunt's plantation is the background for most of the stories which adhere to the conventional concept of good masters, happy and contented slaves, and cruel overseers. A very few of the stories, most notably "A Judgment of Paris," "Silent Samuel," and "The Way of a Woman," deal with those days of adjustment in norther cities after the Civil War.

Dunbar concerned himself more with racial problems in *The Heart of Happy Hollow* than he had done in his earlier collections. Happy Hollow is described in the introduction to the volume:

> Happy Hollow; are you wondering where it is? Wherever Negroes colonize in the cities or villages, North or South, wherever the hod carrier, the porter, and the waiter are the society men of the town; wherever the picnic and the excursion are the chief summer diversion, and the revival the winter time of repentance, wherever the cheese cloth veil obtains at weddings, and the little white hearse goes by with black mourners in the one carriage behind, there—there—is Happy Hollow. Wherever laughter and tears rub elbows day by day, and the spirit of labour and laziness shake hands, there—there—is Happy Hollow.

It is ironic that Dunbar should have called his village "Happy Hollow" because if one can say true happiness existed here, it was of the most hollow variety. People groped for a method which would alleviate, no matter how briefly, the problems of their lives in an environment which was essentially hostile. For this reason the small things of life took on added significance as the characters were bound together in their search for anything which would help them. The people of Happy Hollow were a serious lot, laughter was seldom, tears came often as they were often forced to mask their true feelings in order to survive. They were exploited by the unscrupulous and ignored by the supposedly sympathetic. With no one to whom they might turn, they lived—or rather, they existed— from day to day. The pathos of the collection is perhaps best exemplified by "The Lynching of Jube Benson." Dunbar firmly believed, as he demonstrated in so many of his stories, that the role of the writer was to tell a good story; consequently, he did not view fiction as primarily a social instrument. Yet, in spite of the functional restrictions which he placed upon his own work and upon himself, probably nowhere in American literature has the protest against lynching been more plaintively revealed. The anger and rancor occasioned by the action is submerged in the author's own sense of disbelief which is passed on to the reader who shares in the shock of the action.

The Lynching of Jube Benson

Gordon Fairfax's library held but three men, but the air was dense with clouds of smoke. The talk had drifted from one topic to another much as the smoke wreaths had puffed, floated, and thinned away. Then Handon Gay, who was an ambitious young reporter, spoke of a lynching story in a recent magazine, and the matter of punishment without trial put new life into the conversation.

"I should like to see a real lynching," said Gay rather callously.

"Well, I should hardly express it that way," said Fairfax, "but if a real, live lynching were to come my way, I should not avoid it."

"I should," spoke the other from the depths of his chair, where he had been puffing in moody silence. Judged by his hair, which was freely sprinkled with gray, the speaker might have been a man of forty-five or fifty, but his face, though lined and serious, was youthful, the face of a man hardly past thirty.

"What! you, Dr. Melville? Why, I thought that you physicians wouldn't weaken at anything."

"I have seen one such affair," said the doctor gravely; "in fact, I took a prominent part in it."

"Tell us about it," said the reporter, feeling for his pencil and notebook, which he was, nevertheless, careful to hide from the speaker.

The men drew their chairs eagerly up to the doctor's, but for a minute he did not seem to see them, but sat gazing abstractedly into the fire; then he took a long draw upon his cigar and began:

"I can see it all very vividly now. It was in the summertime and about seven years ago. I was practicing at the time down in the little town of Bradford. It was a small and primitive place, just the location for an impecunious medical man, recently out of college.

"In lieu of a regular office, I attended to business in the first of two rooms which I rented from Hiram Daly, one of the more prosperous of the townsmen. Here I boarded and here also came my patients—white and black—white from every section, and blacks from 'nigger town,' as the west portion of the place was called.

"The people about me were most of them coarse and rough, but they were simple and generous, and as time passed on I had about abandoned my intention of seeking distinction in wider fields and determined to settle into the place of a modest country doctor. This was rather a strange conclusion for a young man to arrive at, and I will not deny that the presence in the house of my host's beautiful young daughter, Annie, had something to do with my decision. She was a girl of seventeen or eighteen, and very far superior to her surroundings. She had a native grace and a pleasing way about her that made everybody that came under her spell her abject slave. White and black who knew her loved her, and none, I thought, more deeply and respectfully than Jube Benson, the black man of all work about the place.

"He was a fellow whom everybody trusted—an apparently steady-going, grinning sort, as we used to call him. Well, he was completely under Miss Annie's thumb, and as soon as he saw that I began to care for Annie, and anybody could see that, he transferred some of his allegiance to me and became my faithful servitor also. Never did a man have a more devoted adherent in his wooing than did I, and many a one of Annie's tasks which he volunteered to do gave her an extra hour with me. You can imagine that I liked the boy, and you need not wonder any more that, as both wooing and my practice waxed apace, I was content to give up my great ambitions and stay just where I was.

"It wasn't a very pleasant thing, then, to have an epidemic of typhoid break out in the town that kept me going so that I hardly had time for the courting that a fellow wants to carry on with his sweetheart while he is still young enough to call her his girl. I fumed, but duty was duty, and I kept to my work night and day. It was now that Jube proved how invaluable he was as coadjutor. He not only took messages to Annie, but brought sometimes little ones from her to me, and he would tell me little secret things that he had overheard her say that made me throb with joy and swear at him for repeating his mistress's conversation.

But, best of all, Jube was a perfect Cerberus, and no one on earth could have been more effective in keeping away or deluding the other young fellows who visited the Dalys. He would tell me of it afterwards, chuckling softly to himself, 'An', Doctah, I say to Mistah Hemp Stevens, " 'Scuse us, Mistah Stevens, but Miss Annie, she des gone out," an' den he go outer de gate lookin' moughty lonesome. When Sam Elkins come, I say, "Sh, Mistah Elkins, Miss Annie, she done tuk down," an' he say, "What, Jube, you don' reckon hit de———" Den he stop an' look skeert, an' I say, "I feared hit is, Mistah Elkins," an' sheks my haid ez solemn. He goes outer de gate lookin' lak his bes' frien' done daid, an' all de time Miss Annie behine de cu'tain ovah de po'ch des a-laffin' fit to kill.'

"Jube was a most admirable liar, but what could I do? He knew that I was a young fool of a hypocrite, and when I would rebuke him for these deceptions, he would give way and roll on the floor in an excess of delighted laughter until from very contagion I had to join him—and, well, there was no need of my preaching when there had been no beginning to his repentance and when there must ensue a continuance of his wrong-doing.

"This thing went on for over three months, and then, pouf! I was down like a shot. My patients were nearly all up, but the reaction from overwork made me an easy victim of the lurking germs. Then Jube loomed up as a nurse. He put everyone else aside, and with the doctor, a friend of mine from a neighboring town, took entire charge of me. Even Annie herself was put aside, and I was cared for as tenderly as a baby. Tom, that was my physician and friend, told me all about it afterward with tears in his eyes. Only he was a big, blunt man, and his expressions did not convey all that he meant. He told me how Jube had nursed me as if I were a sick kitten and he my mother. Of how fiercely he guarded his right to be the sole one to 'do' for me, as he called it, and how, when the crisis came, he hovered, weeping but hopeful, at my bedside until it was safely passed, when they drove him, weak and exhausted, from the room. As for me, I knew little about it at the time, and cared less. I was too busy in my fight with death. To my chimerical vision there was only a black but gentle demon that came and went, alternating with a white fairy, who would insist on coming in on her head, growing larger and larger and then dissolving. But the pathos and devotion in the story lost nothing in my blunt friend's telling.

"It was during the period of a long convalescence, however, that I came to know my humble ally as he really was, devoted to the point of abjectness. There were times when, for very shame at his goodness to me, I would beg him to go away, to do something else. He would go, but before I had time to realize that I was not being ministered to, he would be back at my side, grinning and puttering just the same. He manufactured duties for the joy of performing them. He pretended to see desires in me that I never had, because he liked to pander to them, and when I became entirely exasperated and ripped out a good round oath, he chuckled with the remark, 'Dah, now, you sholy is gittin' well. Nevah did hyeah a man anywhaih nigh Jo'dan's sho' cuss lak dat.'

"Why, I grew to love him, love him, oh, yes, I loved him as well—oh, what am I saying? All human love and gratitude are damned poor things; excuse me, gentlemen, this isn't a pleasant story. The truth is usually a nasty thing to stand.

"It was not six months after that that my friendship to Jube, which he had been at such great pains to win, was put to too severe a test.

"It was in the summertime again, and, as business was slack, I had ridden over to see my friend, Dr. Tom. I had spent a good part of the day there, and it was past four o'clock when I rode leisurely into Bradford. I was in a particularly joyous mood and no premonition of the impending catastrophe oppressed me. No sense of sorrow, present or to come, forced itself upon me, even when I saw men hurrying through the almost deserted streets. When I got within sight of my home and saw a crowd surrounding it, I was only interested sufficiently to spur my horse into a jog trot, which brought me up to the throng, when something in the sullen, settled horror in the men's faces gave me a sudden, sick thrill. They whispered a word to me, and without a thought save for Annie, the girl who had been so surely growing into my heart, I leaped from the saddle and tore my way through the people to the house.

"It was Annie, poor girl, bruised and bleeding, her face and dress torn from struggling. They were gathered round her with white faces, and oh! with what terrible patience they were trying to gain from her fluttering lips the name of her murderer. They made way for me and I knelt at her side. She was beyond my skill, and my will merged with theirs. One thought was in our minds.

" 'Who?' I asked.

"Her eyes half opened. 'That black——' She fell back into my arms dead.

"We turned and looked at each other. The mother had broken down and was weeping, but the face of the father was like iron.

" 'It is enough,' he said; 'Jube has disappeared.' He went to the door and said to the expectant crowd, 'She is dead.'

"I heard the angry roar without swelling up like the noise of a flood, and then I heard the sudden movement of many feet as the men separated into searching parties, and laying the dead girl back upon her couch, I took my rifle and went out to join them.

"As if by intuition the knowledge had passed among the men that Jube Benson had disappeared, and he, by common consent, was to be the object of our search. Fully a dozen of the citizens had seen him hastening toward the woods and noted his skulking air, but as he had grinned in his old good-natured way, they had, at the time, thought nothing of it. Now, however, the diabolical reason of his slyness was apparent. He had been shrewd enough to disarm suspicion, and by now was far away. Even Mrs. Daly, who was visiting with a neighbor, had seen him stepping out by a back way, and had said with a laugh, 'I reckon that black rascal's a-running off somewhere.' Oh, if she had only known!

" 'To the woods! To the woods!' that was the cry; and away we went, each with the determination not to shoot, but to bring the culprit alive into town, and then to deal with him as his crime deserved.

"I cannot describe the feelings I experienced as I went out that night to beat the woods for this human tiger. My heart smoldered within me like a coal, and I went forward under the impulse of a will that was half my own, half some more malignant power's. My throat throbbed drily, but water or whisky would not have quenched my thirst. The thought has come to me since, that now I could interpret the panther's desire for blood and sympathize with it, but then I thought nothing. I simply went forward and watched, watched with burning eyes for a familiar form that I had looked for as often before with such different emotions.

"Luck or ill-luck, which you will, was with our party, and just as dawn was graying the sky, we came upon our quarry crouched in the corner of a fence. It was only half light, and we might have passed, but my eyes caught sight of him, and I raised the cry. We leveled our guns and he rose and came toward us.

"'I t'ought you wa'n't gwine see me,' he said sullenly; 'I didn't mean no harm.'

"'Harm!'

"Some of the men took the word up with oaths, others were ominously silent.

"We gathered around him like hungry beasts, and I began to see terror dawning in his eyes. He turned to me, 'I's moughty glad you's hyeah, Doc,' he said; 'you ain't gwine let 'em whup me.'

"'Whip you, you hound,' I said, 'I'm going to see you hanged,' and in the excess of my passion I struck him full on the mouth. He made a motion as if to resent the blow against such great odds, but controlled himself.

"'W'y, Doctah,' he exclaimed in the saddest voice I have ever heard, 'w'y, Doctah! I ain't stole nuffin' o' yo'n, an' I was comin' back. I only run off to see my gal, Lucy, ovah to de Centah.'

"'You lie!' I said, and my hands were busy helping others bind him upon a horse. Why did I do it? I don't know. A false education, I reckon, one false from the beginning. I saw his black face glooming there in the half light, and I could only think of him as a monster. It's tradition. At first I was told that the black man would catch me, and when I got over that, they taught me that the devil was black, and when I recovered from the sickness of that belief, here were Jube and his fellows with faces of menacing blackness. There was only one conclusion: This black man stood for all the powers of evil, the result of whose machinations had been gathering in my mind from childhood up. But this has nothing to do with what happened.

"After firing a few shots to announce our capture, we rode back into town with Jube. The ingathering parties from all directions met us as we made our way up to the house. All was very quiet and orderly. There was no doubt that it was, as the papers would have said, a gathering of the best citizens. It was a gathering of stern, determined men, bent on a terrible vengeance.

"We took Jube into the house, into the room where the corpse lay. At the sight of it he gave a scream like an animal's, and his face went the color of storm-blown water. This was enough to condemn him.

We divined rather than heard his cry of 'Miss Ann, Miss Ann; oh, my God! Doc, you don't t'ink I done it?'

"Hungry hands were ready. We hurried him out into the yard. A rope was ready. A tree was at hand. Well, that part was the least of it, save that Hiram Daly stepped aside to let me be the first to pull upon the rope. It was lax at first. Then it tightened, and I felt the quivering soft weight resist my muscles. Other hands joined and Jube swung off his feet.

"No one was masked. We knew each other. Not even the culprit's face was covered, and the last I remember of him as he went into the air was a look of sad reproach that will remain with me until I meet him face to face again.

"We were tying the end of the rope to a tree, where the dead man might hang as a warning to his fellows, when a terrible cry chilled us to the marrow.

" 'Cut 'im down, cut 'im down; he ain't guilty. We got de one. Cut him down, fu' Gawd's sake. Here's de man; we foun' him hidin in de barn!'

"Jube's brother, Ben, and another Negro came rushing toward us, half dragging, half carrying a miserable-looking wretch between them. Someone cut the rope and Jube dropped lifeless to the ground.

" 'Oh, my Gawd, he's daid, he's daid!' wailed the brother, but with blazing eyes he brought his captive into the center of the group, and we saw in the full light the scratched face of Tom Skinner, the worst white ruffian in town; but the face we saw was not as we were acustomed to see it, merely smeared with dirt. It was blackened to imitate a Negro's.

"God forgive me; I could not wait to try to resuscitate Jube. I knew he was already past help; so I rushed into the house to the dead girl's side. In the excitement they had not yet washed or laid her out. Carefully, carefully, I searched underneath her broken fingernails. There was skin there. I took it out, the little curled pieces, and went with it into my office.

"There, determinedly, I examined it under a powerful glass, and read my own doom. It was the skin of a white man, and in it were embedded strands of short brown hair or beard.

"How I went out to tell the waiting crowd I do not know, for something kept crying in my ears, 'Blood guilty! Blood guilty!'

"The men went away stricken into silence and awe. The new prisoner attempted neither denial nor plea. When they were gone, I would have helped Ben carry his brother in, but he waved me away fiercely. 'You he'ped murder my brothah, you dat was his frien'; go 'way, go 'way! I'll tek him home myse'f.' I could only respect his wish, and he and his comrade took up the dead man and between them bore him up the street on which the sun was now shining full.

"I saw the few men who had not skulked indoors uncover as they passed, and I—I—stood there between the two murdered ones, while all the while something in my ears kept crying, 'Blood guilty! Blood guilty!'"

The doctor's head dropped into his hands and he sat for some time in silence, which was broken by neither of the men; then he rose, saying, "Gentlemen, that was my last lynching."

Whatever the shortcomings of this story may be, no man committed to the plantation tradition could have told it.

Dunbar's last novel is neither a "white" novel nor is it truly in the plantation tradition. *The Sport of the Gods* first appeared in the May (1901) issue of *Lippincott's Monthly Magazine* and was subsequently published in book form in the United States and as *The Jest of Fate* in England during the following year. While the situations described are not always believable, it is the most naturalistic of all of Dunbar's fiction. The Berry Hamilton family is forced by circumstances to move away from home because Berry has been accused of stealing money from his employer's brother and for which he is sentenced to ten years in prison. Before his trial, which is a farce, he is rejected not only by Maurice Oakley, his employer who knows that he has always been a good and honest worker, but also by the Negro community which fears reprisals if anyone should show mercy or sympathy for the Hamiltons. Dunbar does not find white rejection unusual, but he attacks those Negroes who are afraid to support Hamilton or to acknowledge his integrity.

It seems a strange irony upon the force of right living, that this man, who had never been arrested before, who had never even been suspected of wrongdoing, should find so few who even at the first telling doubted the story of his guilt.

The A.M.E. church, of which he had been an honest and active member, hastened to disavow sympathy with him, and to purge itself of contamination by turning him out. His friends were afraid to visit him and were silent when his enemies gloated. . . . In the black people of the town the strong influence of slavery was still operative, and with one accord they turned away from one of their own kind upon whom had been set the ban of the white people's displeasure. . . . Not then, not now, nor has it ever been true, although it has been claimed, that negroes either harbour or sympathize with the criminal of their kind. They did not dare do it before the sixties. They do not dare do it now. They have brought down as a heritage from the days of their bondage both fear and disloyalty (pp. 48-50).

Thus victimized by both Negro and white society, Hamilton goes to prison, and his wife and two children escape to New York City in a search for anonymity. In the city they are caught in a web of conditions over which they have no control, and the closely-knit family is doomed to defeat. Pathetically each character tries to hold the ideals which he had maintained in his southern home, but the urban environment is too much and takes its toll as these unsuspecting people go down one by one. As Dunbar observes in the novel:

Whom the gods wish to destroy they first make mad. The first sign of the demoralization of the provincial who comes to New York is his pride at his insensibility to certain impressions which used to influence him at home. First, he begins to scoff, and there is no truth in his views nor depth in his laugh. But by and by, from mere pretending it becomes real. He grows callous. After that he goes to the devil very cheerfully (p. 88).

The son, Joe, becomes involved in the life of the Banner Club and eventually kills a jaded chorus girl whom he had been dating. The daughter, Kitty, becomes a chorus girl and loses not only her beauty but also her ideals. Even Mrs. Hamilton is not secure as she becomes entangled with another man whom she finally marries. Through the good offices of an inquisitive newspaper reported, Berry Hamilton is freed from prison, and in a contrived situation Mrs. Hamilton's second husband is killed thereby paving the way for the reunion of the broken couple. Through a series of intricate sub-plots the mystery of the stolen money is revealed, and Oakley in an attempt to protect his brother (who had gambled his money away and then lied about it) and his family name loses his mind. As the story ends, Berry and his wife are once again in the old house near the Oakleys and as they sit there "together with clasped hands listening to the shrieks of the madman across the yard," they think "of what he had brought to them and to himself." Dunbar concludes the novel: "It was not a happy life, but it was all that was left to them, and they took it up without complaint, for they know they were powerless against some Will infinitely stronger than their own (p. 255)."

Throughout the novel Dunbar makes it quite clear that the "cheerful" journey to the devil is not really the doing of the characters themselves but rather is a result of the hypocrisy and deceitfulness of a society which can imprison a man because he is black thus forcing the man's family to face a world for which the members of the family are not prepared. Underlying the action of *The Sport of the Gods* is a powerful message to white and black America.

Before one dismisses Dunbar's short stories and novels for what he did not do, one must consider what he accomplished. For the first time an American Negro writer gained widespread acceptance with the reading public. He wrote at a time when the romantic tradition was still currently in vogue and when realism and naturalism were just beginning to make an impact. Romantic though much of his work is, there is in his fiction a growing awareness not only of the social problems of America but most specifically of the problems created by an urban society. The city as an evil force reached its culmination in *The Sport of the Gods,* but throughout his writing career he attempted to deal with the influence of the city upon men. By veiling his views of life and masking his ideas of society frequently behind raceless or white characters, he was able to produce in rapid succession four novels which enjoyed a measure of success. With great understanding Dunbar, in his short stories, became the interpreter of various facets of Negro life in America. Committed to the popular in fiction, he took the well-liked plantation tradition which was not original with him and made it peculiarly his own. While one may smile or even laugh at some of the antics of his slave characters, one can never forget that beneath the humor there is the unspoken assertion: I, too, am a man.

II

Just as Dunbar's fiction can be divided into two major types so also can his poetry. On the one hand, Dunbar wrote in standard English using traditional and innovative poetic forms, and on the other hand, he wrote in dialect. Yet, whether he used standard English or dialect, his subjects were unlimited. His first collection of verse, in fact his first published work, was *Oak and Ivy*. It contained fifty-six poems many of which were to appear in later collections. He had just finished high school and some of the poems suffer from youthful exhuberance and from a lack of maturity. Furthermore, there is the inevitable imitation, especially of James Whitcomb Riley, one of his favorite poets. Unfortunately, this is demonstrated not only by subject matter but also by a dialect which is a combination of Indiana Hoosier speech with that of the southern Negro as Dunbar imagined that speech to be. But in some of the poems, which Dunbar included in subsequent volumes, he shows his magnificent poetic qualities.

Significantly *Oak and Ivy* opens with "Ode to Ethiopia" in which the poet manifests his profound interest in and deep concern for his people.

> O Mother Race! to thee I bring
> This pledge of faith unwavering,

This tribute to thy glory.
I know the pangs which thou didst feel,
When Slavery crushed thee with its heel,
    With thy dear blood all gory.

Sad days were those—ah, sad indeed!
But through the land the fruitful seed
    Of better times was growing.
The plant of freedom upward sprung,
And spread its leaves so fresh and young—
    Its blossoms now are blowing.

On every hand in this fair land,
Proud Ethiope's swarthy children stand
    Beside their fairer neighbour;
The forests flee before their stroke,
Their hammers ring, their forges smoke,—
    They stir in honest labour.

They tread the fields where honour calls;
Their voices sound through senate halls
    In majesty and power.
To right they cling; the hymns they sing
Up to the skies in beauty ring,
    And bolder grow each hour.

Be proud, my Race, in mind and soul;
Thy name is writ on Glory's scroll
    In characters of fire.
High 'mid the clouds of Fame's bright sky
Thy banner's blazoned folds now fly,
    And truth shall lift them higher.

Thou has the right to noble pride,
Whose spotless robes were purified
    By blood's severe baptism.
Upon thy brow the cross was laid,
And labour's painful sweat-beads made
    Consecrating chrism.

> No other race, or white or black,
> When bound as thou wert, to the rack,
>   So seldom stooped to grieving;
> No other race, when free again,
> Forgot the past and proved them men
>   So noble in forgiving.
>
> Go on and up! Our souls and eyes
> Shall follow thy continuous rise;
>   Our ears shall list thy story
> From bards who from thy root shall spring,
> And proudly tune their lyres to sing
>   Of Ethiopia's glory.

Although there is in the poem a youthful tendency toward overemphasis and a stilted poetic diction, "Ode to Ethiopia" does reflect an awareness of racial pride which remained with Dunbar throughout his life.

His diversity of interest is manifested in *Oak and Ivy* and his ability to produce pure lyrical poetry in the manner of the romantic tradition is seen in a number of poems included in this volume. One such poem is "October" whose poetic diction is unusual and frequently unexpected. The poet speaks, for example, of the "roguish Sun." Excesses of language, a recurring Dunbar fault, and an innovative rhyme pattern are also evident here. He uses an eight-line stanza which in reality consists of two rather dissimilar quatrains with a rhyme scheme of *ababccdd*.

> October is the treasure of the year,
>   And all the months pay bounty to her store;
> The fields and orchards still their tribute bear,
>   And fill her brimming coffers more and more.
> But she, with youthful lavishness,
> Spends all her wealth in gaudy dress,
>   And decks herself in garments bold
>   Of scarlet, purple, red, and gold.

She heedeth not how swift the hours fly,
  But smiles and sings her happy life along;
She only sees above a shining sky;
  She only hears the breezes' voice in song.
Her garments trail the woodlands through,
And gather pearls of early dew
    That sparkle, till the roguish Sun
    Creeps up and steals them every one.

But what cares she that jewels should be lost,
  When all of Nature's bounteous wealth is hers?
Though princely fortunes may have been their cost,
  Not one regret her calm demeanor stirs.
Whole-hearted, happy, careless, free,
She lives her life out joyously,
    Nor cares when Frost stalks o'er her way
    And turns her auburn locks to gray.

There is a general spirit of optimism which pervades so many of his poems. In "Merry Autumn" Dunbar negates the sadness which is often associated with the fall of the year.

It's all a farce,—these tales they tell
  About the breezes sighing,
And moans astir o'er field and dell,
  Because the year is dying.

Such principles are most absurd,—
  I care not who first taught 'em;
There's nothing known to beast or bird
  To make a solemn autumn.

In solemn times, when grief holds sway
  With countenance distressing,
You'll note the more of black and gray
  Will then be used in dressing.

Now purple tints are all around;
  The sky is blue and mellow;

And e'en the grasses turn the ground
From modest green to yellow.

The seed burrs all with laughter crack
On featherweed and jimson;
And leaves that should be dressed in black
Are all decked out in crimson.

A butterfly goes winging by;
A singing bird comes after;
And Nature, all from earth to sky,
Is bubbling o'er with laughter.

The ripples wimple on the rills,
Like sparkling little lasses;
The sunlight runs along the hills,
And laughs among the grasses.

The earth is just so full of fun
It really can't contain it;
And streams of mirth so freely run
The heavens seem to rain it.

Don't talk to me of solemn days
In autumn's time of splendor,
Because the sun shows fewer rays,
And these grow slant and slender.

Why, it's the climax of the year,—
The highest time of living!—
Till naturally its bursting cheer
Just melts into thanksgiving.

In "A Drowsy Day" the poet recounts the effects of nature upon the sensitive soul:

The air is dark, and the sky is gray,
The misty shadows come and go,
And here within my dusky room
Each chair looks ghostly in the gloom.

Outside the rain falls cold and slow—
Half-stinging drops, half blinding spray.

Each slightest sound is magnified,
    For drowsy quiet holds her reign;
The burnt stick in the fireplace breaks,
The nodding cat with start awakes,
    And then to sleep drops off again,
Unheeding Towser at her side.

I look far out across the lawn,
    Where huddled stand the silly sheep;
My work lies idle at my hands,
My thoughts fly out like scattered strands
    Of thread, and on the verge of sleep—
Still half awake—I dream and yawn.

What spirits rise before my eyes!
    How various of kind and form!
Sweet memories of days long past,
The dreams of youth that could not last,
    Each smiling calm, each raging storm,
That swept across my early skies.

Half seen, the bare, gaunt-fingered boughs
    Before my window sweep and sway,
And chafe in tortures of unrest.
My chin sinks down upon my breast;
    I cannot work on such a day,
But only sit and dream and drowse.

While "A Drowsy Day" provides a rather traditional approach to nature which is distinguished merely by the poet's ability to repeat the usual cliches, "Sunset," which also is an early poem, shows Dunbar's use of a seven-line stanza and is one his more effective poems of nature.

The river sleeps beneath the sky,
    And clasps the shadows to its breast;

The crescent moon shines dim on high;
And in the lately radiant west
The gold is fading into gray.
Now stills the lark his festive lay,
And mourns with me the dying day.

While in the south the first faint star
Lifts to the light its silver face,
And twinkles to the moon afar
Across the heaven's graying space,
Low murmurs reach me from the town,
As Day puts on her sombre crown,
And shakes her mantel darkly down.

Dunbar, like many poets of his day, had a great tendency to moralize and to find lessons in each little experience. "The Sparrow" furnishes an example of the type of poem in which the instruction appears in the second stanza after the recounting of an experience.

A little bird with plumage brown,
Beside my window flutters down,
A moment chirps its little strain,
Then taps upon my window-pane,
And chirps again, and hops along,
To call my notice to its song;
But I work on, nor heed its lay,
Till, in neglect, it flies away.

So birds of peace and hope and love
Come fluttering earthward from above,
To settle on life's window-sills,
And ease our load of earthly ills;
But we, in traffic's rush and din
Too deeply engaged to let them in,
With deadened heart and sense plod on,
Nor know our loss till they are gone.

Another approach to didactic poetry is seen in his early definition which is simply entitled "Life."

> A crust of bread and a corner to sleep in,
> A minute to smile and an hour to weep in,
> A pint of joy to a peck of trouble,
> And never a laugh but the moans come double;
>   And that is life!
>
> A crust and a corner that love makes precious,
> With a smile to warm and the tears to refresh us;
> And joy seems sweeter when cares comes after,
> And a moan is the finest of foils for laughter;
>   And that is life!

With the excitment engendered by the World's Columbian Exposition which was held in Chicago in 1893, it is not surprising to
see that Dunbar joined the host of poets who paid poetic tribute
to the founding of America. For the occasion he composed "Columbian Ode," which was read during the Exposition and which
is included in *Oak and Ivy.* Among the poets who did appear for
that event Dunbar was probably the least known; however, his
poem still holds interest for its technique if for no other reason.
The poem is composed of three stanzas, and each stanza is a
quatrain longer than the preceding one. Thus beginning with eight
lines, he moves to twelve lines, and concludes his ode with a six-
teen-line stanza.

> Four hundred years ago a tangled waste
>   Lay sleeping on the west Atlantic's side;
> Their devious ways the Old World's millions traced
>   Content, and loved, and labored, dared and died,
> While students still believed the charts they conned,
>   And revelled in their thriftless ignorance,
> Nor dreamed of other lands that lay beyond
>   Old Ocean's dense, indefinite expanse.
>
> But deep within her heart old Nature knew

That she had once arrayed, at Earth's behest,
Another offspring, fine and fair to view,—
The chosen suckling of the mother's breast.
The child was wrapped in vestments soft and fine,
Each fold a work of Nature's matchless art;
The mother looked on it with love divine,
And strained the loved one closely to her heart.
And there it lay, and with the warmth grew strong
And hearty, by the salt sea breezes fanned,
Till Time with mellowing touches passed along,
And changed the infant to a mighty land.

But men knew naught of this, till there arose
That mighty mariner, the Genoese,
Who dared to try, in spite of fears and foes,
The unknown fortunes of unsounded seas.
O noblest of Italia's sons, thy bark
Went not alone into that shrouding night!
O dauntless darer of the rayless dark,
The world sailed with thee to eternal light!
The deer-haunts that with game were crowded then
To-day are tilled and cultivated lands;
The schoolhouse tow'rs where Bruin had his den,
And where the wigwam stood the chapel stands;
The place that nurtured men of savage mien
Now teems with men of Nature's noblest types;
Where moved the forest-foliage banner green,
Now flutters in the breeze the stars and stripes!

Interestingly, there are few dialect poems in *Oak and Ivy;* however, of those which do appear there is unmistakably the stamp of James Whitcomb Riley. "The Old Apple-Tree" is representative of Dunbar's attempt to reproduce a midwestern speech pattern, and the subject is one designed to appeal to an agrarian-oriented people.

There's a memory keeps a-runnin'
Through my weary head tonight,
An' I see a picture dancin'

In the fire-flames' ruddy light;
'Tis the picture of an orchard
    Wrapped in autumn's purple haze,
With the tender light about it
    That I loved in other days.
An' a-standin' in a corner
    Once again I seem to see
The verdant leaves an' branches
    Of an old apple-tree.

You perhaps would call it ugly,
    An' I don't know but it's so,
When you look the tree all over
    Unadorned by memory's glow;
For its boughs are gnarled an' crooked,
    An' its leaves are gettin' thin,
An' the apples of its bearin'
    Wouldn't fill so large a bin
As they used to. But I tell you,
    When it comes to pleasin' me,
It's the dearest in the orchard,—
    Is that old apple-tree.

I would hide within its shelter,
    Settlin' in some cosy nook,
Where no calls nor threats could stir me
    From the pages o' my book.
Oh, that quiet, sweet seclusion
    In its fulness passeth words!
It was deeper than the deepest
    That my sanctum now affords.
Why, the jaybirds an' the robins,
    They was hand in glove with me,
As they winked at me an' warbled
    In that old apple-tree.

It was on its sturdy branches
    That in summers long ago
I would tie my swing an' dangle

In contentment to an' fro,
Idly dreamin' childish fancies,
    Buildin' castles in the air,
Makin' o' myself a hero
    Of romances rich an' rare.
I can shet my eyes an' see it
    Jest as plain as plain kin be,
That same old swing a-danglin'
    To the old apple-tree.

There's a rustic seat beneath it
    That I never kin forget.
It's the place where me an' Hallie—
    Little sweetheart—used to set,
When we'd wander to the orchard
    So's no listen' ones could hear
As I whispered sugared nonsense
    Into her little willin' ear.
Now my gray old wife is Hallie,
    An' I'm grayer still than she,
But I'll not forget our courtin'
    'Neath the old apple-tree.

Life for us ain't all been summer,
    But I guess we've had our share
Of its flittin' joys an' pleasures,
    An' a sprinklin' of its care.
Oft the skies have smiled upon us;
    Then again we've seen 'em frown,
Though our load was ne'er so heavy
    That we longed to lay it down.
But when death does come a-callin',
    This my last request shall be,—
That they'll bury me an' Hallie
    'Neath that old apple-tree.

In his first collection of verse perhaps the only note of sadness is
expressed in "Melancholia" which uses a unique variation of the

seven-line stanza which includes the internal rhyme of the fourth
line.

> Silently without my window,
>   Tapping gently at the pane,
>   Falls the rain.
> Through the trees sighs the breeze
>   Like a soul in pain.
> Here alone I sit and weep;
> Thought hath banished sleep.
>
> Wearily I sit and listen
>   To the water's ceaseless drip.
>   To my lip
> Fate turns up the bitter cup,
>   Forcing me to sip;
> 'Tis a bitter, bitter drink,
> Thus I sit and think,—
>
> Thinking things unknown and awful,
>   Thought on wild, uncanny themes,
>   Waking dreams.
> Spectres dark, corpses stark,
>   Show the gaping seams
> Whence the cold and cruel knife
> Stole away their life.
>
> Bloodshot eyes all strained and staring,
>   Gazing ghastly into mine;
>   Blood like wine
> On the brow—clotted now—
>   Shows death's dreadful sign.
> Lonely vigil still I keep;
> Would that I might sleep!
>
> Still, oh, still, my brain is whirling!
>   Still runs on my stream of thought;
>   I am caught
> In the net fate hath set.

Mind and soul are brought
To destruction's very brink;
Yet I can but think!

Eyes that look into the future,—
   Peeping forth from out my mind,
   They will find
Some new weight, soon or late,
   On my soul to bind,
Crushing all its courage out,—
   Heavier than doubt.

Dawn, the Eastern monarch's daughter,
   Rising from her dewy bed,
   Lays her head
'Gainst the clouds' sombre shrouds
   Now half fringed with red.
O'er the land she 'gins to peep;

Come, O gentle Sleep!
Hark! the morning cock is crowing;
   Dreams, like ghosts, must hie away;
   'Tis the day.
Rosy morn now is born;
   Dark thoughts may not stay.
Day my brain from foes will keep;
Now, my soul, I sleep.

His dominant concerns and interests are first expressed in *Oak and Ivy.* The poems cover a wide range of subjects. There are some general verses on nature and on life, with the typical nineteenth-century didactic poems and a few works in dialect. The collection is not the most outstanding collection of poetry ever published in America, but as the product of a young high-school graduate the work did show a great promise for a literary future. That promise was probably realized in his second collection of verse, *Majors and Minors,* which appeared early in 1896. The collection is significant because some of his best verse, which he was to include in later volumes, appeared for the first time. Generally the volume can be characterized by Dunbar's own deepening sense of disillusionment, the presentation of life as a spiritual experience, and his growing mastery of the more technical aspects of poetry. The imitations of his former volume are replaced by far more original pieces. The book is divided into two parts: the first section consists of the poems in standard English and the second, entitled "Humor and Dialect," contains poems which range from a pathetic acceptance of life to those which are broadly humorous with little or no regard for the ultimate meaning of life. Eleven poems of this collection had appeared in *Oak and Ivy,* the remaining seventy-four were printed in book form for the first time.

The collection begins with a long narrative poem "Ione" which does contain some notable lines, but which is most distinguished by its popularly romantic mode of Longfellow and others of that school. While "Ione" did have appeal at the time of its publication, "Ere Sleep Comes Down to Soothe the Weary Eyes" has long been considered among his best work in standard English. With a mastery of iambic pentameter Dunbar considers the paradox of illusion and reality. He describes the "waking world [as] a world of lies." Using the lyrical form, the poet files a claim against society.

> Ere sleep comes down to soothe the weary eyes,
>   Which all the day with ceaseless care have sought
> The magic gold which from the seeker flies;
>   Ere dreams put on the gown and cap of thought,
> And making the waking world a world of lies,—
>   Of lies most palpable, uncouth, forlorn,
> That say life's full of aches and tears and sighs,—
>   Oh, how with more than dreams the soul is torn,
> Ere sleep comes down to soothe the weary eyes.
>
> Ere sleep comes down to soothe the weary eyes,
>   How all the griefs and heartaches we have known
> Come up like pois'nous vapors that arise
>   From some base witch's caldron, when the crone,
> To work some potent spell, her magic plies.

The past which held its share of bitter pain,
    Whose ghost we prayed that Time might exorcise,
    Comes up, is lived and suffered o'er again,
Ere sleep comes down to soothe the weary eyes.

Ere sleep comes down to soothe the weary eyes,
    What phantoms fill the dimly lighted room;
What ghostly shades in awe-creating guise
    Are bodied forth within the teeming gloom.
What echoes faint of sad and soul-sick cries,
    And pangs of vague inexplicable pain
That pay the spirit's ceaseless enterprise,
    Comes thronging through the chambers of the brair.
Ere sleep comes down to soothe the weary eyes.

Ere sleep comes down to soothe the weary eyes,
    Where ranges forth the spirit far and free?
Through what strange realms and unfamiliar skies
    Tends her far course to lands of mystery?
To lands unspeakable—beyond surmise,
    Where shapes unknowable to being spring,
Till, faint of wing, the Fancy fails and dies
    Much wearied with the spirit's journeying,
Ere sleep comes down to soothe the weary eyes.

Ere sleep comes down to soothe the weary eyes,
    How questioneth the soul that other soul,—
The inner sense which neither cheats nor lies,
    But self exposes unto self, a scroll
Full writ with all life's acts unwise or wise,
    In characters indelible and known;
So, trembling with the shock of sad surprise,
    The soul doth view its awful self alone,
Ere sleep comes down to soothe the weary eyes.

When sleep comes down to seal the weary eyes,
    The last dear sleep whose soft embrace is balm,
And whom sad sorrow teaches us to prize
    For kissing all our passions into calm,
Ah, then, no more we heed the sad world's cries,

> Or seek to probe th' eternal mystery,
> Or fret our souls at long-withheld replies,
>   At glooms through which our visions cannot see,
> When sleep comes down to soothe the weary eyes.

The poems in standard English were referred to as "the majors."
While these poems are extremely well executed, it was the poems
of humor and dialect, "the minors," by which he was to gain immediate fame. Of the dialect poems "When Malindy Sings," cast
in the form of a dramatic monologue, is perhaps most representative.

> G'way an' quit dat noise, Miss Lucy—
>   Put dat music book away;
> What's de use to keep on tryin'?
>   Ef you pratise twell you're gray,
> You cain't sta't no notes a'flyin'
>   Lak de ones dat rants and rings
> F'on de kitchen to de big woods
>   When Malindy sings.
>
> You ain't got de nachel o'gans
>   Fu' to make de soun' come right,
> You ain't got de tu'ns an' twistin's
>   Fu' to make it sweet an' light.
> Tell you one thing now, Miss Lucy,
>   An' I'm tellin' you fu' true,
> When hit comes to raal right singin',
>   'T ain't no easy thing to do.
>
> Easy 'nough fu' folks to hollah,
>   Lookin' at de lines an' dots,
> When dey ain't no one kin sence it,
>   An' de chune comes in, in spots;
> But fu' real melojous music,
>   Dat jes' strikes you' hea't and clings,
> Jes' you stan' an' listen wif me
>   When Malindy sings.

Ain't you nevah hyeahed Malindy?
  Blessed soul, tek up de cross!
Look hyeah, ain't you jokin', honey?
  Well, you don't know whut you los'.
Y' ought to hyeah dat gal a-wa'blin'.
  Robins, la'ks, an' all dem things,
Heish dey moufs an' hides dey faces
  When Malindy sings.

Fiddlin' man jes' stop his fiddlin',
  Lay his fiddle on de sh'f;
Mockin'-bird quit tryin' to whistle,
  'Cause he jes' so shamed hisse'f.
Folks a-playin' on de banjo
  Draps dey fingahs on de strings—
Bless yo' soul—fu'gits to move 'em,
  When Malindy sings.

She jes' spreads huh mouf and hollahs,
  "Come to Jesus," twell you hyeah
Sinnahs' tremblin' steps and voices,
  Timid-lak a-drawin' neah;
Den she tu'ns to "Rock of Ages,"
  Simply to de cross she clings,
An' you fin' yo' teahs a-drappin'
  When Malindy sings.

Who dat says dat humble praises
  Wif de Master nevah counts?
Heish yo' mouf, I hyeah dat music,
  Ez hit rises up an' mounts—
Floatin' by de hills an' valleys,
  Way above dis buryin' sod,
Ez hit makes its way to glory
  To de very gates of God!

Oh, hit's sweetah dan de music
  Of an edicated band;
An' hit's dearah dan de battle's
  Song o' triumph in de lan'.

It seems holier dan evenin'
    When de solemn chu'ch bell rings,
Ez I sit an' ca'mly listen
    When Malindy sings.

Towsah, stop dat ba'kin, hyeah me!
    Manydy, mek dat chile keep still;
Don't you hyeah de echoes callin'
    F'om de valley to de hill?
Let me listen, I can hyeah it,
    Th'oo de bresh of angels' wings,
Sof' an' sweet, "Swing Low, Sweet Chariot,"
    Ez Malindy sings.

When *Majors and Minors* was sent to him, William Dean Howells wanted to meet the young poet at once. Although such a meeting was not to take place for several years, the famed critic wrote a review of the work and then wrote the introduction to Dunbar's third volume of verse, *Lyrics of Lowly Life,* which was published later in 1896 and by which the poet became a celebrity. Only eleven poems of this collection were new ones. The remaining ninety-four (twenty from *Oak and Ivy* and seventy-four from *Majors and Minors*) had appeared earlier. The Howells' introduction is significant for calling public attention for Dunbar. It may well be that Howells was in a large measure responsible for making Dunbar a major writer during his day; however, it was an unfortunate introduction because Howells stressed the dialect poems or the poems which Dunbar himself thought of as "the jingles in a broken tongue." Howells begins by asserting:

I think I should scarcely trouble the reader with a special appeal in behalf of this book, if it had not specially appealed to me for reasons apart from the author's race, origin, and condition. The world is too old now, and I find myself too much of its mood, to care for the work of a poet because he is black, because his father and mother were slaves, because he was, before and after he began to write poems, an elevator-boy. These facts would certainly attract me to him as a man, if I knew him to have literary ambition, but when it came to his literary art, I must judge it irrespective of these facts, and enjoy or endure it for what it was in itself.

After a discussion of Dunbar's early life, Howells continues:

. . . here was the first instance of an American negro who had evinced innate distinction in literature. . . . [he] was the only man of pure African blood and of American civilization to feel the negro life aesthetically and express it lyrically. . . .

Yet . . . it appears to me now that there is a precious difference of temperament between the races which it would be a great pity ever to lose, and that this is best preserved and most charmingly suggested by Mr. Dunbar in those pieces of his where he studies the moods and traits of his race in its own accent of our English. We call such pieces dialect . . .

The tone, however, of *Lyrics of Lowly Life* was set by its opening poem "Ere Sleep Comes Down to Soothe the Weary Eyes" and not by the dialect poems written after the manner of Riley or those presented in a pseudo-Negro dialect.

Since so much has been made of Dunbar's dialect poems which form a very small portion of his total output and since there have been a number of imitators of Dunbar, one needs to examine the dialect tradition itself in Negro poetry. As a form of poetry it is first dependent upon an oral tradition in the sense that it is poetry designed to be heard. It is essentially formed by attempting to capture all of the peculiarities of a given speech pattern in written form. This eventually led to a phonetic representation of the speech patterns in question. Although Dunbar is credited by Howells with reproducing exact patterns of Negro speech, this is not entirely a valid observation. Vernon Loggins in his *The Negro Author in America* (1931) labored under a similar misconception. He praises the realism of Dunbar because

. . . it was inspired by sincere feeling and not by the search for novelty; his music appeals to us as more natural because we do not in any way have to associate it with white singers. His Negro dialect verse is today generally accepted as the best which has been written in America. It deserves that consideration, and will probably maintain it. For the picturesque and poetic Negro language Dunbar knew so well in rapidly passing away; he preserved a record of it at the right time (p. 349)."

A study of Dunbar's dialect will reveal that it comes closer to Riley's approach to colloquial speech than it does to the speech which it is supposed to represent. Since he did not really know the speech patterns of the characters whom he represented, Dunbar created a form which is not indicative of any particular community. His major contribution was in creating a speech pattern which could be read with minimum effort and one which would aid in the creation of character.

None of Dunbar's follower's received the acclaim of the American reading public which had been accorded to Dunbar himself, for they were not considered as effective. Most assuredly, they did not have the benefit of introductions by William Dean Howells. Yet, many of them came closer to representing the speech patterns of the plantation Negroes. Perhaps of all of the practitioners of the dialect tradition and users of it as an artistic medium James Edwin Campbell, who was older than Dunbar, did more than any other writer (including Dunbar) in correctly capturing the sounds of the speech of the plantation Negroes, especially those who spoke in the Gullah dialect. Interestingly, Campbell was also born in Ohio, but a comparison of his dialect poems with any of those by Dunbar will reveal his greater fidelity to the authentic speech patterns. At the same time Campbell's poems are not as easily read. Dunbar burlesqued standard English just enough to give regional flavor to what he was saying, but the difficulty of most of Campbell's work is due to its greater reliability upon an actual method of speech. The West Indian origin of his recorded dialect is evident in "De Cunjah Man" in the substitution of pronouns in the objective case for those which should have appeared in the nominative case.

> O chillen, run, de Cunjah man,
> Him mouf ez beeg ez fryin' pan,
> Him yurs am small, him eyes am raid,
> Him hab no toof een him ol' haid,
> Him hab him roots, him wu'k him trick,
> Him roll him eye, him mek you sick—
>> De Cunjah man, de Cunjah man,
>> O chillen, run, de Cunjah man!
>
> Him hab ur ball ob raid, raid ha'r,
> Him hide it un' de kitchen sta'r,
> Mam Jude huh pars urlong dat way,
> An' now huh hab ur snaik, de say.
> Him wrop ur roon' huh buddy tight,
> Huh eyes pop out, ur orful sight—
>> De Cunjah man, de Cunjah man,
>> O chillen, run, de Cunjah man!
>
> Miss Jane, huh dribe him f'um huh do',
> An' now huh hens woan' lay no mo';
> De Jussey cow huh done fall sick,
> Hit all done by de Cunjah trick.
> Him put ur root un' 'Lijah's baid,
> An' now de man he sho' am daid—
>> De Cunjah man, de Cunjah man,
>> O chillen, run, de Cunjah man!
>
> Me see him stan' de yudder night
> Right een de road een white moon-light;
> His toss him arms, him whirl him 'roun',
> Him stomp him foot urpon de groun';
> De snaiks come crawlin', one by one,
> Me hyuh um hiss, me break an' run—
>> De Cunjah man, de Cunjah man,
>> O chillen, run, de Cunjah man!

The mood evoked by Campbell's "When Ol' Sis' Judy Pray" is similar to that created by Dunbar's "When Malindy Sings," but the differences in dialect are still apparent. Dunbar relied more heavily upon mispelled words to transmit his idea of a unique speech pattern. Furthermore, the emotional restrictions of dialect are more apparent in Campbell's poem. In "When Malindy Sings," for example, Dunbar was able to include a range of probable responses from the humorous to the serious; however, Campbell's tone remained constant. His poems are either humorous portrayals or serious ones. There is never the combination which one finds so artfully executed in Dunbar.

> When ol' Sis' Judy pray,
> De teahs come stealin' down my cheek,
> De voice ur God widin me speak';
> I see myse'f so po' an' weak'
> Down on my knees de cross I seek,
> When ol' Sis' Judy pray.
>
> When ol' Sis' Judy pray,
> De thun'ers ur Mount Sin-a-i
> Comes rushin' down f'um up on high—
> De Debbil tu'n his back an' fly
> While sinnahs loud fur pa'don cry,
> When ol' Sis' Judy pray.
>
> When ol' Sis' Judy pray,
> Ha'd sinnah's trimble in dey seat
> Ter hyuh huh voice in sorro' 'peat:
> (While all de chu'ch des sob an' weep)
> "O Shepa'd, dese, dy po' los' sheep!"
> When ol' Sis' Judy pray.
>
> When ol' Sis' Judy pray,
> De whole house hit des rock an' moan
> Ter see huh teahs an' hyuh huh groan;
> Dar's somepin' in Sis' Judy's tone
> Dat melt all ha'ts dough med ur stone
> When ol' Sis' Judy pray.

> When ol' Sis' Judy pray,
> Salvation's light comes pourin' down—
> Hit fill de chu'ch an' all de town—
> Why, angels' robes go rustlin' 'roun',
> An' hebben on de Yurf am foun',
> When ol' Sis' Judy pray.
>
> When ol' Sis' Judy pray,
> My soul go sweepin' up on wings,
> An' loud de chu'ch wid "Glory!" rings,
> An' wide de gates ur Jahsper swings
> Twel you hyuh ha'ps wid golding strings,
> When ol' Sis' Judy pray. . . .

From the work of Dunbar to the present time dialect has been used with varying degrees of success. In Dunbar's work dialect became a means of local color by which he attempted to capture a people by means of peculiar speech patterns. While some of his poems are humorous, the majority of them are designed to portray some aspect of the ante-bellum South in as realistic manner as possible. Following the tradition of Burns and Riley, Dunbar's central concern was to get at the heart and soul of an uneducated people whose broken language often symbolized their broken bodies but seldom their broken spirits. Consequently, Dunbar relied heavily upon folk tales which emphasized the simple philosophy or upon characters whose "jingle in a broken tongue" could transmit something of the joy as well as the sorrow of their circumscribed lives. Thus Dunbar surveys the entire range of human emotions, and his poems extend from the broadly humorous to the very pathetic. Later practitioners of the dialect tradition had difficulty. Part of this was due, of course, to the antipathy which developed around the use of dialect. Many poets and readers rejected it as a tool for serious subjects because they found its use too degrading and too closely related to the minstrel tradition which they also spurned. Other poets used it only as a means of evoking tears, and still others used it as a means of the comic. In time it came to be used purely as a means of humor. However, throughout the history of its entire use, no matter what the particular approach of the poet, it substantially covered the same types of subjects. It tended to deal with the limited social lives of the characters or with some aspect of religion or with instances of shrewdness as a master or some other character gets outwitted. Infrequently it dealt with some aspect of nature.

Among the followers of Dunbar there have been some notable examples of dialect poetry, but all of them have demonstrated the necessary limitations imposed by dialect itself as a means of artistic expression. As dialect and its practitioners are judged, it must be remembered that Dunbar had once sadly remarked that his dialect poetry, which he himself did not acknowledge as his most significant work, was the only way to get "them" to listen to him. What he was noting were the inevitable problems which Negro writers have faced in this country especially among publishers, critics, and readers who expect something *unique* from the pens of Negro writers and who wish to emphasize all of their own preconceived stereotypes. Furthermore, comic though the dialect tradition might be and even perhaps ineffectual, it must also be remembered that Dunbar was writing at a time when the philosophy of the local colorists was still in vogue with its insistence upon the recording of externals in order to portray the times and the community.

By the 1920's the dialect tradition had all but disappeared among Negro poets. James Weldon Johnson, who had been one of Dunbar's closest friends, unwittingly led the fight against the "jingles in a broken tongue" by indicating the differences between dialect and idiom. While he agreed that the experiences of a people and the primitive element had artistic validity, Johnson assumed that dialect could not really get to the heart of folk experiences because it relied too heavily upon external characteristics and because it had too long been associated with type characters and humor. Certainly this is true of his own dialect poetry which never seems quite as faithful as that of Dunbar in spite of the fact that

Johnson asserted in his autobiography, *Along This Way* (1933), that he regarded himself as Dunbar's disciple (p. 160). When he published his first volume of poetry, Johnson referred to his dialect poetry as "Jingles and Croons." Yet, Johnson returned to the idiomatic expression of the spirituals and the early slave sermons and out of this he developed a poetic diction which is not only realistic but which does more to capture the "soul" of a people. In 1927 he published *God's Trombones: Seven Negro Sermons in Verse* and introduced his book by maintaining:

At first thought, Negro dialect would appear to be the precise medium for those old-time sermons; however, as the reader will see, the poems are not written in dialect. My reason for not using dialect is double. First, although the dialect is the exact instrument for voicing certain traditional phases of Negro life, it is, and perhaps by that very exactness, a quite limited instrument. Indeed, it is an instrument with but two complete stops, pathos and humor. This limitation is not due to any defect of the dialect as dialect, but to the mould of convention in which Negro dialect in the United States has been set, to the fixing of effects of its long association with the Negro only as a happy-go-lucky or a forlorn figure. The Aframerican poet in time might be able to break this mould of convention and write poetry in dialect without feeling that his first line will put the reader in a frame of mind which demands that the poem be either funny or sad, but I doubt that he will make the effort to do it; he does not consider it worth while. In fact, practically no poetry is being written in dialect by the colored poets of today. These poets have thrown aside dialect and discarded most of the material and subject matter that went into dialect poetry. The passing of dialect as a medium for Negro poetry will be an actual loss, for in it many beautiful things can be done, and done best; however, in my opinion, *traditional* Negro dialect as a form for Aframerican poets is absolutely dead. The Negro poet in the United States, for poetry which he wishes to give a distinctively racial tone and color, needs now an instrument of greater range than dialect; that is, if he is to do more than sound the small notes of sentimentality. . . .

The second part of my reason for not writing these poems in dialect is weightier. The old-time Negro preachers, though these actually used dialect in their ordinary intercourse, stepped out from its narrow confines when they preached. They were all saturated with the sublime phraseology of the Hebrew prophets and steeped in the idioms of King James English, so when they preached and warmed to their work they spoke another language, a language far removed from traditional Negro dialect. It was a real fusion of Negro idioms with Bible English; and in this there may have been, after all, some kinship with the innate grandiloquence of their old African tongues. To place in the mouths of the talented old-time Negro preachers a language that is a literary imitation of Mississippi cotton-field dialect is sheer burlesque. . . . (pp. 7-9)

Earlier, in 1922, when Johnson had edited *The Book of American Negro Poetry,* he had emphasized the use of an idiomatic speech in a more general way.

What the colored poet in the United States needs to do is something like what Synge did for the Irish; he needs to find a form that will express the racial spirit by symbols from within rather than by symbols from without, such as the mere mutilation of English spelling and pronunciation. He needs a form that is freer and larger than dialect, but which will still hold the racial flavor; a form expressing the imagery, the idioms, the peculiar turns of thought, and the distinctive humor and pathos, too, of the Negro, but which will also be capable of voicing the deepest and highest emotions and aspirations, and allow of the widest range of subjects and the widest scope of treatment.

Negro dialect is at present a medium that is not capable of giving expression to the varied conditions of Negro life in America, and much less is it capable of giving the fullest interpretation of Negro character and psychology. . . . (pp. 41-42)

Johnson was aided in his own poetic efforts toward the use of realistic language by the popularity of free verse. Released from the restrictive demands of set rhyme and rhythmic patterns, he was able to explore the greater possibilities of idiomatic expression.

Not relying upon "the mere mutilation of English spelling and pronunciation" nor upon "eye dialect" which is the use of a speech pattern which seems apparent at first glance but which becomes obscured at the initial attempts to read it, Johnson sought, as he asserted in *God's Trombones,* to capture that idiom which characteristically set the old Negro sermon apart from every other rhetorical effort.

III

While white America first became aware of Dunbar through Howell's popularizing his dialect verse and through his use of the plantation tradition in his short stories, it must never be forgotten that Dunbar had not closed his eyes nor turned his back upon the racial situation in America. For example, in "The Haunted Oak" the poet reveals a sensitivity to the problems of the United States that at first shocked the genteel readers of the *Century* where it first appeared in December, 1900. The poem, according to some who knew Dunbar, was occasioned by the lynching of a man for a crime which he had not committed. In the poem the mob has selected the nearest tree for its crime, an oak tree, and shortly thereafter that particular branch of the tree dies while the remainder of the tree continues to grow. Using an imperfect ballad stanza, Dunbar re-tells the old story of a lynching but from the viewpoint of the tree from which the victim has been hung.

> Pray why are you so bare, so bare,
>   Oh, bough of the old oak-tree;
> And why, when I go through the shade you throw,
>   Runs a shudder over me.
>
> My leaves were green as the best, I trow,
>   And sap ran free in my veins,
> But I saw in the moonlight dim and weird
>   A guiltless victim's pains.
>
> I bent me down to hear his sigh;
>   I shook with his gurgling moan,

And I trembled sore when they rode away,
    And left him here alone.

They'd charged him with the old, old crime,
    And set him fast in jail:
Oh, why does the dog howl all night long,
    And why does the night wind wail?

He prayed his prayer and swore his oath,
    And he raised his hand to the sky;
But the beat of hoofs smote on his ear,
    And the steady tread drew nigh.

Who is it rides by night, by night,
    Over the moonlit road?
And what is the spur that keeps the pace,
    What is the galling goad?

And now they beat at the prison door,
    "Ho, keeper, do not stay!
We are friends of him whom you hold within,
    And we fain would take him away

"From those who ride fast on our heels
    With mind to do him wrong;
They have no care for his innocence,
    And the rope they bear is long."

They have fooled the jailer with lying words,
    They have fooled the man with lies;
The bolts unbar, the locks are drawn,
    And the great door open flies.

Now they have taken him from the jail,
    And hard and fast they ride,
And the leader laughs low down in his throat,
    As they halt my trunk beside.

Oh, the judge, he wore a mask of black,
    And the doctor one of white,
And the minister, with his oldest son,
    Was curiously bedight.

> Oh, foolish man, why weep you now?
>   'T is but a little space,
> And the time will come when these shall dread
>   The mem'ry of your face.
>
> I feel the rope against my bark,
>   And the weight of him in my grain,
> I feel in the throe of his final woe
>   The touch of my own last pain.
>
> And never more shall leaves come forth
>   On a bough that bears the ban;
> I am burned with dread, I am dried and dead,
>   From the curse of a guiltless man.
>
> And ever the judge rides by, rides by,
>   And goes to hunt the deer,
> And ever another rides his soul
>   In the guise of a mortal fear.
>
> And ever the man he rides me hard,
>   And never a night stays he;
> For I feel his curse as a haunted bough,
>   On the trunk of a haunted tree.

Another indication of Dunbar's awareness of the social problems in America and another manifestation of his own racial consciousness occur in a series of poems addressed to specific individuals who, in one way or another, had been a part of the Negro's struggle in the United States. One of the first such poems appeared in *Lyrics of Lowly Life* and is entitled "Frederick Douglass."

> A hush is over all the teeming lists,
>   And there is pause, a breath-space in the strife;
> A spirit brave has passed beyond the mists
>   And vapors that obscure the sun of life.
> And Ethiopia, with bosom torn,
> Laments the passing of her noblest born.

She weeps for him a mother's burning tears—
  She loved him with a mother's deepest love.
He was her champion thro' direful years,
  And held her weal all other ends above.
When Bondage held her bleeding in the dust,
He raised her up and whispered, "Hope and Trust."

For her his voice, a fearless clarion, rung
  That broke in warning on the ears of men;
For her the strong bow of his power he strung,
  And sent his arrows to the very den
Where grim Oppression held his bloody place
And gloated o'er the mis'ries of a race.

And he was no soft-tongued apologist;
  He spoke straightforward, fearlessly uncowed;
The sunlight of his truth dispelled the mist,
  And set in bold relief each dark hued cloud;
To sin and crime he gave their proper hue,
And hurled at evil what was evil's due.

Through good and ill report he cleaved his way
  Right onward, with his face set toward the heights,
Nor feared to face the foeman's dread array,—
  The lash of scorn, the sting of petty spites.
He dared the lightning in the lightning's track,
And answered thunder with his thunder back.

When men maligned him, and their torrent wrath
  In furious imprecations o'er him broke,
He kept his counsel as he kept his path;
  'T was for his race, not for himself he spoke.
He knew the import of his Master's call,
And felt himself too mighty to be small.

No miser in the good he held was he,—
  His kindness followed his horizon's rim.
His heart, his talents, and his hands were free
  To all who truly needed aught of him.

Where poverty and ignorance were rife,
He gave his bounty as he gave his life.

The place and cause that first aroused his might
    Still proved its power until his latest day.
In Freedom's lists and for the aid of Right
    Still in the foremost rank he waged the fray;
Wrong lived; his occupation was not gone.
He died in action with his armor on!

We weep for him, but we have touched his hand,
    And felt the magic of his presence nigh,
The current that he sent throughout the land,
    The kindling spirit of his battle-cry.
O'er all that holds us we shall triumph yet,
And place our banner where his hopes were set!

Oh, Douglass, thou hast passed beyond the shore,
    But still thy voice is ringing o'er the gale!
Thou'st taught thy race how high her hopes may soar,
    And bade her seek the heights, nor faint, nor fail.
She will not fail, she heeds thy stirring cry,
She knows thy guardian spirit will be nigh,
And, rising from beneath the chast'ning rod,
She stretches out her bleeding hands to God!

In many respects the ideas of Alexander Crummell were opposed to those of Douglass. Crummell supported the theory of the
colonization of Africa by American Negroes because he felt that
this would not only permit a greater degree of freedom for Negroes
but also aid in the Christianization of Africa. Born in 1819, he
early showed signs of his great intellectual powers. Although he
had a difficult time in securing an education, he was eventually
ordained a priest of the Protestant Episcopal Church in 1844,
and in 1853 he graduated from Queen's College, Cambridge. It
was after his experience in England that he went to Africa, but
once he returned to the United States he devoted himself ex-

clusively to the cause of his people. After his death in 1898 Dunbar wrote, "Alexander Crummell—Dead."

> Back to the breast of thy mother,
> Child of the earth!
> E'en her caress can not smother
> What thou has done.
> Follow the trail of the westering sun
> Over the earth.
> Thy light and his were as one—
> Sun, in thy worth.
> Unto a nation whose sky was as night,
> Camest thou, holily, bearing thy light:
> And the dawn came,
> In it thy fame,
> Flashed up in a flame.
> Back to the breast of thy mother—
> To rest.
> Long hast thou striven;
> Dared where the hills by the lightning of heaven were riven;
> Go now, pure shriven.
> Who shall come after thee, out of the clay—
> Learned one and leader to show us the way?
> Who shall rise up when the world gives the test?
> Think thou no more of this—
> Rest!

In the sonnets addressed to Booker T. Washington, Robert Gould Shaw, and Harriet Beecher Stowe, Dunbar re-echoes the hopes and the aspirations of a people as he commends his subjects for their roles in a noble cause. In "Harriet Beecher Stowe" Dunbar is primarily concerned with the effects of *Uncle Tom's Cabin.*

> She told the story, and the whole world wept
>   At wrongs and cruelties it had not known
>   But for this fearless woman's voice alone.
>   She spoke to consciences that long had slept:

Her message, Freedom's clear reveille, swept
From heedless hovel to complacent throne.
Command and prophecy were in the tone
And from its sheath the sword of justice leapt.
Around two peoples swelled a fiery wave,
But both came forth transfigured from the flame.
Blest be the hand that dared be strong to save,
And blest be she who in our weakness came—
Prophet and priestees! At one stroke she gave
A race to freedom and herself to fame.

To the Negro soldiers of the Civil War Dunbar paid tribute in "The Unsung Heroes," a poem of eight quatrains with varying iambic and anapestic lines.

A song for the unsung heroes who rose in the country's need,
When the life of the land was threatened by the slaver's cruel greed,
For the men who came from the cornfield, who came from the plough
and the flail,
Who rallied round when they heard the sound of the mighty man of rail.

They laid them down in the valleys, they laid them down in the wood,
And the world looked on at the work they did, and whispered, "It is good."
They fought their way on the hillside, they fought their way in the glen,
And God looked down on their sinews brown, and said, "I have made them men."
They went to the blue lines gladly, and the blue lines took them in,
And the men who saw their musket's fire thought not of their dusky skin.
The gray lines rose and melted beneath their scathing showers,
And they said, " 'Tis true, they have force to do, these old slave boys of ours."

Ah, Wagner saw their glory, and Pillow knew their blood,
That poured on a nation's altar, a sacrificial flood.
Port Hudson heard their war-cry that smote its smoke-filled air,
And the old free fires of their savage sires again were kindled there.

They laid them down where the rivers the greening valleys gem.
And the song of the thund'rous cannon was their sole requiem,
And the great smoke wreath that mingled its hue with the dusky cloud,
Was the flag that furled o'er a saddened world, and the sheet that made
    their shroud.

Oh, mighty God of the Battles Who held them in Thy hand,
Who gave them strength through the whole day's length, to fight for
    their native land,
They are lying dead on the hillsides, they are lying dead on the plain,
And we have not fire to smite the lyre and sing them one brief strain.

Give, Thou, some seer the power to sing them in their might,
The men who feared the master's whip, but did not fear the fight;
That he may tell of their virtues as minstrels did of old,
Till the pride of face and the hate of race grow obsolete and cold.

A sing for the unsung heroes who stood the awful test,
When the humblest host that the land could boast went forth to meet
    the best.
A song for the unsung heroes who fell on the bloody sod,
Who fought their way from night to day and struggled up to God.

The mood of the spirituals' poetic tradition is evident in "By
Rugged Ways." While the poem asserts that in due course deliverance will come from God, the poem emphasizes the idea that the
struggle is in itself a strengthening force.

> By rugged ways and thro' the night
> We struggle blindly toward the light;
> And groping, stumbling, ever pray
> For sight of long delaying day.
> The cruel thorns beside the road
> Stretch eager points our steps to goad,
> And from the thickets all about
> Detaining hands reach threatening out.
>
> "Deliver us, oh, Lord," we cry,
> Our hands uplifted to the sky.
> No answer save the thunder's peal,

And onward, onward, still we reel.
"Oh, give us now thy guiding light";
Our sole reply, the lightning's blight.
"Vain, vain," cries one, "in vain we call";
But faith serene is over all.

Besides our way the streams are dried,
And famine mates us side by side.
Discouraged and reproachful eyes
Seek once again the frowning skies.
Yet shall there come, spite storm and shock,
A Moses who shall smite the rock,
Call manna from the Giver's hand,
And lead us to the promised land!

The way is dark and cold and steep,
And shapes of horror murder sleep,
And hard the unrelenting years;
But 'twixt our sighs and moans and tears,
We still can smile, we still can sing,
Despite the arduous journeying.
For faith and hope their courage lend,
And rest and light are at the end.

In poems of this nature, Dunbar is essentially optimistic as he views God as a helper in the fight for equality. Faith in God, the poet makes clear on a number of occasions, is a prerequisite for winning the battles of life regardless of the type of battle.

As he neared the end of his life, Dunbar wrote feverishly. Just as his fiction moved from the romanticism of the early tales to the realism of *The Sport of the Gods* so also does his poetry demonstrate a similar progression. His collections of verse show a greater sense of disillusionment and many of the poems more obviously accept the tragedy of human existence. After the publication of *Lyrics of Lowly Life,* he published three other distinct collections of verse and numerous heavily illustrated anthologies which contain, for the most part, selected poems which had appeared earlier. But it is in *Lyrics of the Hearthside* (1899), *Lyrics of Love and*

Laughter (1903), and *Lyrics of Sunshine and Shadow* (1905) that one can trace his development as a poet.

In *Lyrics of the Hearthside* the effects of his broadened experiences are evident. Some of the exhuberance of *Majors and Minors* and of *Lyrics of Lowly Life* has disappeared but in its place is a greater emphasis upon man's need not only for love but also for God. The volume also discloses a far greater technical control over the methods of poetry. The number of nature poems in the volume may well have been suggested by his 1897 voyage to England which impressed him greatly. During the latter part of 1899 *Poems of Cabin and Field* was issued and achieved almost immediate success leading to the custom of producing similar heavily illustrated books: *Candle-Lightin' Time* (1901), *When Malindy Sings* (1903), *L'il' Gal* (1904), *Howdy, Honey Howdy* (1905), *Joggin' Erlong* (1906), *Speakin' o' Christmas* (1914). The popularity of these gift books, whose titles emphasize Dunbar's dialect poetry, did much to cement in the minds of his readers the relationship between Dunbar and dialect. Yet at the same time that these poems were receiving mass circulation, Dunbar wrote some of his most outstanding poetry in standard English. No reader can truly forget the simplicity of "When Day Is Done" as the poet speaks of the inevitability of death and of the hope for a tomorrow. Appearing in *Lyrics of the Hearthside,* "When All Is Done" is representative of the type of poem included in the volume.

> When all is done, and my last word is said,
> And ye who loved me murmur, "He is dead,"
> Let no one weep, for fear that I should know,
> And sorrow too that ye should sorrow so.

> When all is done and in the oozing clay,
> Ye lay this cast-off hull of mine away,
> Pray not for me, for, after long despair,
> The quiet of the grave will be a prayer.

> For I have suffered loss and grievous pain,
> The hurts of hatred and the world's disdain,

And wounds so deep that love, well-tried and pure,
Had not the pow'r to ease them or to cure.

When all is done, say not my day is o'er,
And that thro' night I seek a dimmer shore:
Say rather that my morn has just begun,—
I greet the dawn and not a setting sun,
    When all is done.

Four years passed before Dunbar issued another distinct collection of verse. *Lyrics of Love and Laughter* is characterized by the poet's growing awareness of the effects of industrialism and commercialism on nature. Here also are included the ballad on lynching, "The Haunted Oak," as well as other more racially conscious works. The sonnet to Booker T. Washington appears in this volume.

The word is writ that he who runs may read.
What is the passing breath of earthly fame?
But to snatch glory from the hands of blame—
That is to be, to live, to strive indeed.
A poor Virginia cabin gave the seed,
And from its dark and lowly door there came
A peer of princes in the world's acclaim,
A master spirit for the nation's need.
Strong, silent, purposeful beyond his kind,
    The mark of rugged force on brow and lip,
Straight on he goes, nor turns to look behind
    Where hot the hounds come baying at his hip;
With one idea foremost in his mind,
    Like the keen prow of some on-forging ship.

A few months before his death *Lyrics of Sunshine and Shadow* was published and was to be his last distinct collection of verse. Illustrated gift books would continue to be popular and to be produced by various editors, but with the work of *Lyrics of Sunshine and Shadow* Dunbar's published career as a poet was almost

at an end. The volume is marked by the general tone of reminis-
cence which seems to pervade the book. There is a feeling that
Dunbar is trying to recapture a past day. Whether in his poems of
childhood (and there are perhaps more here than in previous
volumes) or of love or of nature the poignancy of a fruitless
search becomes most evident. By the time that this work was
published, Dunbar knew that he could not exist in such physical
pain for much longer. Perhaps he may have known that he was
dying. At any rate, it is in this volume that "Compensation"
appeared, the first stanza of which is frequently used in Dunbar
memorials.

> Because I had loved so deeply,
>   Because I had loved so long,
> God in his great compassion
>   Gave me the gift of song.
>
> Because I have loved so vainly,
>   And sung with such faltering breath,
> The Master in infinite Mercy
>   Offers the boon of Death.

Any judgment of Dunbar must consider what he accomplished
in a twelve-year period. Between his first volume of verse, *Oak and
Ivy,* and his last, *Lyrics of Sunshine and Shadow,* he produced
additional volumes of verse, four novels, four collections of short
stories, as well as uncollected stories and poems. He was in short,
a prolific writer who recognized the popular vein of American
literature and worked within that framework. That he might seem
unduly romantic and sentimental to the modern reader is a valid
observation; yet, it must be remembered that social protest fiction
and realistic portrayals of life were just beginning to gain an
audience at the time of his productivity.

Dunbar's influence was not confined to the Negro writers who
adopted dialect as a means for humorous and semi-pathetic poems
or to the Negro writers who saw in Dunbar the professional man

of letters. Those who attempted to stress the effects of the large city, especially of New York's Harlem, upon the newly-arrived southern immigrant were following his lead. In several short stories and in *The Sport of the Gods* Dunbar emphasized the disillusion- ment which was frequently the outcome of "going north." Even Carl Van Vechten acknowledged his indebtedness to Dunbar. In 1926 he wrote *Nigger Heaven.* Two years later in his introduction to James Weldon Johnson's *Autobiography of an Ex-Coloured Man,* Van Vechten acknowledged Dunbar as his literary mentor and *The Sport of the Gods* as his pattern by asserting that Dunbar had concerned himself with "the plight of a young outsider who comes to the larger New York Negro world to make his fortune, but who falls victim to the sordid snares of that world, a theme I elaborated in 1926 to fit a newer and much more intricate social system (p. vii)."

Dunbar had crowded into his short life a writing career of no mean achievement. He understood the role of the writer as being one which primarily emphasized the transmission of pleasure to the reader. If, by chance, the writer gave instruction, Dunbar felt that this was simply an additional feature. He did not view himself, as a Negro writer, as being radically different from any other writer in America. Benjamin Brawley, in his biography *Paul Laurence Dunbar* (1936), records what is perhaps one of Dunbar's most cogent observations on the role of the Negro poet in America. Ac- cording to Brawley when he was asked to compare Negro and white poetry, Dunbar gave the following explanation:

The predominating power of the African race is lyric. In that I should expect the writers of my race to excel. . . [however] their poetry will not be exotic or differ much from that of whites [because] for two hundred and fifty years the environment of the Negro has been American, in every respect the same as that of all other Americans (pp. 76-77).

Dunbar was never convinced that he was substantially different from any other male American although he recognized that his experiences, as well as those of his people, were often conditioned by matters of race. And the tragedy and the disillusionment of Americans who happened to be Negroes were nowhere more pathetically and clearly presented than in "We Wear the Mask."

> We wear the mask that grins and lies,
> It hides our cheeks and shades our eyes,—
> This debt we pay to human guile;
> With torn and bleeding hearts we smile,
> And mouth with myriad subtleties.
>
> Why should the world be overwise,
> In counting all our tears and sighs?
> Nay, let them only see us, while
>   We wear the mask.
>
> We smile, but, O great Christ, our cries
> To thee from tortured souls arise.
> We sing, but oh the clay is vile
> Beneath our feet, and long the mile;
> But let the world dream otherwise,
>   We wear the mask!

Perhaps "We Wear the Mask" is the best explanation for Dunbar's own career, because beneath the dialect poems and those in standard English is a reservoir of feeling which is often masked. Successful and famous though he became, he was never able to forget that he had sung "of love when earth was young," but that "the world . . . turned to praise a jingle in a broken tongue."

To friends he frequently spoke of being incapable of doing what he wanted to do, and one suspects that Dunbar was fully aware that he had fallen victim to the many preconceived notions of what he should be. The often-voiced disappointment which he repeatedly expressed toward the end of his life is further evidence of his own sense of non-fulfillment and inadequacy. While he always insisted that his dialect poetry was not his best poetry, he was equally insistent upon exploring those facets of Negro life in America which to him seemed important. And his own racial pride is evident in so much of what he did. But, above all else, he desired to capture those universal qualities of life which are applicable to all people in all places at all times. Ultimately the products of his extensive writing career must stand today as a silent monument to the young man who proved to America once again that the creative spirit of life is not restricted by race even though the creator may be compelled to "wear the mask."

CHAPTER VI

The Art of the Storyteller

THE YEARS BETWEEN the poetic efforts of Dunbar and the onset of the Harlem Renaissance were few indeed; yet, Negro writing in American life assumed still greater dimensions for during this period the short story and the novel—as distinct literary forms—were perfected. The art of storytelling was, of course, as old as the recorded history of Negroes. Before coming to America, Africans had been known as remarkable narrators, and many of these stories of West African origin found a place in the fables which became a part of the cultural heritage of American slavery. Narrative skill is evident not only in the fables but also in the spirituals and in the slave autobiographies. Consequently, the earliest manifestation of fiction among Negroes in America was the folk tale which was most prevalent in the South. These tales, just as the spirituals, were not recorded until the latter part of the nineteenth century. Many of the stories, no doubt, had a history which antedated the American experience, but positive identification of the place and time of origin of these early tales can be, even today, no more than speculation.

The next step in the development of the art of prose fiction was the slave narrative which was extremely popular during the mid years of the nineteenth century. While many of these works represented the true life stories of their authors, there were some which were mere fabrications, which simply used the prevailing pattern to tell an exciting story of escape and sometimes of capture. Legitimately those whose stories were obviously untrue were the first writers of fiction.

216

In 1853 William Wells Brown published *Clotel, or The President's Daughter* and Frances Ellen Watkins Harper published "Two Offers" in the September and October (1859) issues of the *Anglo-African;* thus the 1850's ushered into American culture the formal presentation of fiction by Negroes. *Clotel,* still considered the first Negro novel, was initially published in England, but because of its implication of Thomas· Jefferson as a licentious man who preyed on slave women, it was not as successful with white readers as much of Brown's earlier writing. "Two Offers" is a typical anti-slavery tract whose protagonist, a young white woman, rejects an offer of marriage in favor of a lifetime devoted to freeing the slaves. The. merit of "Two Offers" rests in its historical value rather than in its literary significance. It is among the first short stories written by a Negro in America. Both the novel by Brown and the short story by Harper indicate many of the problems which were the face the Negro writer of fiction during the nineteenth century and well into the twentieth. There had not as yet been developed a racial market for their work; at the same time white readers were reluctant to accept the Negro writer of fiction on the same basis as they accepted white writers. While this nebulous reading public was quite willing to support the writers of slave narratives and even on occasions a poet or two, there was something in the nature of fiction which made it more difficult to be accepted unless, of course, the writer were willing to make certain concessions and compromises.

Without an already-established reading public the writer of formal fiction faced a number of problems some of which had been faced by their white counterparts who also battled against the Puritan ethos which rendered fiction highly objectionable; however, by the end of the nineteenth century three patterns had emerged in fiction written by Negroes. There was the plantation tradition which included stories of the Old South, legends and folk tales. This tradition had been popularized by Joel Chandler Harris, Irwin Russell, Thomas Nelson Page, and George Washington Cable. Because of the nature of the work of these white writers who attempted in some instances to imitate the stories which they had heard from Negroes during slavery and because these writers tended to emphasize a romantic view of the days of slavery, the plantation tradition itself is currently held in disrepute. At the same time that the plantation tradition was gaining popularity, the use of legend was also being used.

Among Negro writers Lorenzo Blackson was the first to attempt a story using legend as the background. In 1867 he issued *The Rise and Progress of the Kingdoms of Light and Darkness; or, The Reigns of Kings Alpha and Abadon.* This is an interesting attempt to record the history of the universe from the "war" between God and Satan to the days immediately following the Civil War. Using the material of Milton's *Paradise Lost* and Bunyan's *Pilgrim's Progress* Blackson attempted to re-create a story in which King Alpha, first God and then Christ, eventually wins the world but only after ages and ages of battling with King Abadon or Satan. Progressing through the story are such characters as Faith, Confession, Anger, and Malice, to name a few. The tale is interrupted periodically in order that the author might insert short sermons or comments upon the action, but substantially it is a retelling of the story of man from Adam and Eve to the nineteenth century. The novel obviously suffers from the author's own limited knowledge and understanding, but it never suffers from the author's lack of enthusiasm. While Blackson's work satisfied the needs of those who maintained that fiction should be didactic, the novel was too imitative of the form which Bunyan had used to greater advantage centuries earlier.

Paul Laurence Dunbar successfully produced stories in the more popular plantation tradition. Many of his tales of the Old South were cast in the conventional local color pattern and enjoyed a degree of good fortune with them. In this respect coupled very closely with Dunbar is Charles W. Chesnutt who began his career twenty years after Blackson's novel appeared. In the August, 1887, issue of the *Atlantic Monthly* "The Goophered Grapevine" was published. This story later became one of the seven stories collected under the title *The Conjure Woman* (1899). The stories are unified by a single character, Uncle Julius, who recounts incidents of a time gone by, incidents which occurred before the Civil War. The usual sentimental reminiscing is obvious in *The Conjure Woman* but there is something about Uncle Julius which makes him far more outstanding than the usual character in this type of fiction. Certainly it is not the dialect which is as unrealistic as that used by Dunbar; yet Uncle Julius could never be confused with the host of ex-slaves who peopled this type of story. All of the tales in the collection demonstrate the painstaking artistic efforts of the author, and though many of the situations are contrived, *The Conjure Woman* shows the plantation tradition at its finest point. Chesnutt did far more with the intellectual development of his characters, and because he emphasized psychological realism rather than the local color or surface realism of Dunbar, there is far more appeal in *The Conjure Woman* for the modern reader.

A second pattern which was evident in fiction by Negroes by the end of the nineteenth century, a pattern also manifested in the work of Dunbar, was the writing of "race-less" fiction or sentimentalized stories of white characters. Since the popular fictional patterns of the nineteenth century leaned toward the romance, it was this type which was produced. In a number of his stories Chesnutt, on the other hand, evidences some influence of Henry James. Especially is this true of a story which appeared in the June, 1904, issue of *The Atlantic Monthly.* "Baxter's Procrustes" is one of the later works of Chesnutt and demonstrates his artistic maturity as well as his delightful sense of humor. As the story emerged, there is no way by which a reader could identify the race of the author.

A third fictional pattern—and from the standpoint of the twentieth century—perhaps the most important was the fiction of social protest. William Wells Brown who began his long and diversified career as an abolitionist lecturer has achieved a place in American literature as much for his attempts as for his productions. Aside from the numerous editions of his *Narrative,* already discussed in

Chapter III, Brown was the first Negro in this country to write a novel and a drama. And he was one of the early historians. His 1853 novel, *Clotel . . . ,* presents American slavery in all of its wretchedness. The sentimentalism of *Uncle Tom's Cabin* is replaced by a bitter and pessimistic realism that borders on the naturalistic approach to life. The story is set in the nineteenth century, and the opening action occurs in Virginia. Currer, a Negro woman who had been both house slave and mistress to Thomas Jefferson, has had two children by him—Clotel and Althesa. With her children Currer lives in Richmond. Although the three are slaves, they do enjoy a degree of freedom, and the daughters are being educated by a free Negro. But the lenient master dies, and Currer with Clotel and Althesa, as well as the other slaves, are to be sold. Brown traces the episodes in the lives of the three but focuses upon Clotel. As he does this, he portrays slavery in a number of states and includes the familiar sensational incidents involving slavery: inhuman slave traders, slave pens, slave rebellions, and the inevitable auction block. While Jefferson is not a character in the novel, Brown uses him and quotations from him on human liberty as on ironic commentary on the fates of his two daughters. And as the novel ends, Clotel who is being pursued by slave traders drowns herself near President Jefferson's home.

The novel suffers from the fact that Brown does not really develop any one of his characters sufficiently to permit the character to evolve naturally. Characters are introduced, and in the author's desire to present his opinion of slavery, the character becomes little more than a pawn to be moved at the will of the author. The dialogue is stilted and unrealistic. Although the starkness of the story is sometimes relieved by the bits of humor, the terror of the recounted incidents is the dominant impression provided by Brown. As an invective against slavery, *Clotel . . .* is far superior to *Uncle Tom's Cabin* which tends to reduce the matter to its simplest statement. And it may well be the complexity of situations and the multiplicity of incidents also kept *Clotel . . .* from evoking the same kind of response as Mrs. Stowe's novel. *Uncle Tom's Cabin* manages to transmit the shock of slavery to its readers whereas *Clotel* . . . couples its shock with the anger and personal involvement of the author. There was still another problem which prevented Brown's novel from achieving widespread success in England and later in America. The charge against Jefferson was never substantiated; hence, the action of the novel was occasioned by an unproved rumor. In 1864 the book was published in the United States as *Clotelle: A Tale of the Southern States,* and by this time Brown had decided to replace Jefferson with an anonymous Senator. This was partially done in order to answer the criticism levied against him for using Thomas Jefferson. To many Jefferson was a citadel of freedom, often quoted as a prophet of the rights of man and the power of human dignity. While in his personal dealings with Negroes Jefferson never achieved this type of heroic stature for at this point the discrepancy between his philosophy and his action was too apparent. Yet to many others in both England and America his was the true voice of freedom. As social protest novelists have realized throughout the years, an attacked idol falls slowly. The second edition, in spite of the change, was not much more successful than the first, and three years later a third edition appeared as *Clotelle; or, The Colored Heroine.*

Before writing his last work of fiction, Brown published *The Escape; or, A Leap for Freedom* (1858) which has the distinction of being the first drama written by an American Negro as well as a series of historical works. The first of these *The Black Man: His Antecedents, His Genius, and His Achievements* (1863) attempts to survey the accomplishments made by a group of men and consists of a series of essays about them. Four years later *The Negro in the American Rebellion: His Heroism and His Fidelity* dealt more with the Civil War than with the American Revolution. *The Rising Sun* appeared in 1874 and is a compilation of material taken from the two previous historical works. Although it sold more than 10,000 copies within a year, the tendency of Brown toward the relation of the more sensational aspects of life is still evident. But the book does represent an attempt to record the history of the race from ancient Africa through Europe, South and Central Americas, and finally to the United States. If Brown's inclination toward dramatizing incidents and episodes in a propagandistic way had not prevailed, he might have made a notable contribution to scholarship. He was not really equipped to write history but recognized the great need to recount the story of his people. As a historian he was perhaps too closely associated with some of the events which he narrated, but at least he brought to his history an understanding of American life which was an important factor in the effectiveness of his work.

His last work of fiction *My Southern Home: or, The South and Its People* defies classification. It is neither a novel nor a collection of short stories. Within the narrative Brown recounts recollections of the South in the days before and after the Civil War. Although four editions appeared between 1880 and 1884, the work is marred by the author's tendency toward propaganda even in the instances when he is obviously recording a folk tale. All of Brown's works suffer from a major flaw of social protest fiction and writing. The didactic element frequently supercedes other considerations; yet even though his work suffers from a number of defects, Brown was an excellent storyteller who had the gift for making events live.

While Brown was the foremost storyteller who achieved a measure of fame through the use of social protest before the work of Dunbar and Chesnutt later in the nineteenth century, he was not the only writer to attempt this literary form. Martin Delany, a physician who advocated the colonization of Central America as an antidote for American restrictions upon free men, made a venture into fiction. His work was published in the *Anglo-African* which was a Negro magazine modeled very much on the pattern of *The Atlantic Monthly*. For some reason not wholly explained Delany's attempt at fiction appeared serially in a rather haphazard way. The later chapters appeared in the January, 1859, issue;

subsequently, the beginning chapters appeared in February, and the last of the story ran in the July issue. Why Delany either wrote no more of it or why the *Anglo-African* published nothing further of the novel is perhaps understandable once the published portions are read. Entitled *Blake, or, The Huts of America*, the novel presents the sordidness and inhumanity of life in the slaves' quarters. Although Delany was no great storyteller, the one vivid scene which cannot fail to impress readers is a slave auction which takes place in a church. Nowhere else does the ambiguity of human slavery become more apparent.

The fiction of Brown and Delany was essentially designed as a protest against the methods and procedures of slavery, but this was not the only theme of the social novelist. The work of Frank Webb attempts to explore another facet of Negro life in America. And in many ways Chesnutt's concern with the "color line" has its first statement in Webb's *The Garies and Their Friends*. The mixed marriage of Mr. and Mrs. Garie leads only to persecution for their children and eventually to death for themselves. Victims of the most deadly forms of racial prejudice, the Garies are unable to survive in Philadelphia after their escape from the South. Many of the situations are contrived and many of the incidents are forced, but nonetheless Webb did show an understanding of the subtleties of northern racial prejudice.

In 1893 Frances E. W. Harper published a novel about the Civil War entitled *Iola Leroy; or, Shadows Uplifted*. The following year *Appointed* by Walter Stowers appeared under the pseudonym Sandra. The two novels have little to recommend them; however, in the latter one the theme of lynching plays a dominant role in the novel, a theme which is repeated through the fiction by Negro writers. Perhaps nowhere in American literature has the lynching mob been described with greater power nor with overwhelming power as the author concentrates upon describing each member of the mob who singly is nondescript and frequently weak, but once he becomes a member of the mob a pack of wild animals could not rival this group in ferocity.

While Dunbar's literary theory did not permit him to spend too much creative energy in the realm of social protest fiction, one of the most outstanding documents against the hostility of the urban northern environment occurs in *The Sport of the Gods* (1902); however, this period in the development of Negro fiction comes to a close with the work of Charles Chesnutt. He was not as prolific as Dunbar, but his fiction holds perhaps more interest for the modern reader. Racial prejudice in all of its ramifications forms the central theme of much of what Chesnutt wrote. Unlike Dunbar he did not write as many "raceless" or "white" stories neither was he as attuned to the popular tradition in American Literature. His social protest fiction consists primarily of the stories in *The Wife of His Youth, and Other Stories of the Color Line* (1899) and his three novels: *The House Behind the Cedars* (1899), *The Marrow of Tradition* (1901), and *The Colonel's Dream* (1905). The volume of short stories is held together by the central theme as Chesnutt shows the effects of racial prejudice on all of the characters. At the same time that he attacks the problem of Negro-white relationships, he also perceptibly handles the type of prejudice which exists among Negroes themselves. All three novels, set in the South, deal with the tragedy of near-white Negroes as well as with the extent of racial prejudice which is apparent in all facets of southern life.

If these early years in the development of fiction demonstrate anything at all, it is the diversity of patterns and themes which were to become a recognized part of so-called Negro fiction. From the mid-years of the nineteenth century to the opening years of the twentieth century the Negro writers of fiction were searching for themes which could best express their stories. At the same time they were faced with the necessity of creating an audience for their work. Unlike the writers whose prose of freedom found ready-made and receptive audiences, these authors frequently found themselves with a story but without a publisher or a public. With the exception of the novel of protest the art of storytelling followed so closely the already existing forms in American literature that the contributions of the storytellers became more qualitative.

As the twentieth century progressed with its emphasis upon the realistic movement—and later with its naturalistic approach to writing—a market was created for stories of the dispossessed, and the Negro storyteller had an opportunity to tell his tale. But ironically, this could be done only when he confined himself to the story his audience wanted to hear, to the analysis of the peculiar position of his race in American Life. The "race-less" fiction which asserted the right of the artist to select his subject was subordinated by demands of an insatiable public to read of the uniqueness of the Negro experience. At the end of the First World War a significant body of fiction had been produced devoted to the presentation of the futility of life in America; yet, the optimism which was frequently implicit in nineteenth-century productions gave way to a moroseness which is characteristic of social fiction. At the same time the attitude of American publishing houses precluded the possibility of another type of story being given widespread circulation.

Of these early twentieth-century novelists perhaps no one was as persistent as Sutton E. Griggs whose work is still misunderstood by white America. Griggs realized the importance of the storyteller's audience. He knew that fiction could serve as an adequate means of reaching those who might remain untouched by either a sermon or an historical treatise. He further recognized that a fiction which emphasized the independence of the mind and the dignity of the spirit would not find a welcomed place among those who were still more intent upon the promulgation of a myth than upon the dissemination of the truth. Hence Griggs, one of the outstanding Baptist clergymen of his day, used his publishing firm and received a wider audience among his own people than the fiction of either Dunbar or Chesnutt. In fact Griggs' work became so popular that later critics such as Robert Bone are faced with the difficulty of trying to explain his popularity. But anyone who has even seen the massive crowds of a Baptist annual meeting can understand how Griggs could achieve the acclaim which he did. Furthermore, Griggs capitalized on his own recognition that among his people an artist could be maintained at the same time he utilized fictional devices which were understandable to the unsophisticated reader and palatable to the more knowledgeable reader.

Much of Griggs' fiction is essentially didactic in the sense that out of the reported situations and incidents a reader could draw a model for a life-pattern. But the didacticism was the author's way of emphasizing his belief in the essential dignity and worth of his people. He was neither pro- nor anti-white. He accepted the premise that there are people of goodwill and of evil intent operative at all times. And the so-called "white element" is important in his fiction only in so far as it aids the development of the story being presented. Griggs is representative of the transitional novelists who were searching for a form and a subject matter in the first years of the twentieth century. By the time he concluded his work the "Negro novel" had gained a different sense of direction. And whether one agrees or not, this novel was to become essentially racial in nature. The idea which Dunbar had supported, the idea that the novel did not have to be a manifestation of the storyteller's racial concerns, was superceded by the novel which limited the scope of the author. Out of this evolved a fiction which was basically social. The negative reactions of the press in general toward Negro Americans, the conditions of publishing, and the attitudes of the reading public were in part responsible for the rejection of Dunbar's theory of fiction and the acceptance of purely racial matters in works written by Negroes. But the growing interest in the literature of economic and social protest during the opening years of the twentieth century provided a forum for Negro writers in America if those writers were willing to restrict their subject areas. Ultimately it was not until the Harlem Renaissance that a cultural declaration of independence was asserted by a large number of Negro writers, but in numerous ways Sutton E. Griggs demonstrated in the world of fiction his personal freedom from the forces which had hitherto circumvented the art of the Negro storyteller.

In 1899 Griggs' first novel was issued. *Imperium in Imperio* chronicles the story of an imaginary Negro organization which is a national militant group whose central purpose is to take by force enough land in America in order to establish a Negro state. The central characters are Bernard Belgrave, a Harvard graduate, and Belton Piedmont. When Piedmont first asks him to join the Imperium in Imperio, Belgrave is reluctant but he finally relents and is elected as the organization's president. As the story relates the conflicts which arise among the members of the group, Griggs is able to analyze the problems of the "color line" occasioned by miscegenation, the unfairness of the oppressive Jim Crow laws designed to keep the Negro in his "place," and the manipulation of Negroes by existing political organizations. The central action of the novel revolves around Belgrave's recommendation that the Imperium in Imperio declare war on the United States in order to gain the territories of Louisiana and Texas. According to his plan, Texas would become the home for all Negroes in America, and Louisiana would be given to the foreign power who gave the group the most help during the impending "war." Piedmont, recognizing the futility of the proposed "war," suggests instead that all Negroes simply move into Texas and take over the state in a peaceful way. Once there they could then work out a more reasonable means of attack. The unpopularity of his plan causes him to be condemned by his own group, and he is eventually executed as an "enemy of progress." Griggs concludes with the observation that oppression, whether meted out by whites or blacks, is antithetical to the human spirit. And Piedmont's choice of death is a testimony to his refusal to subject himself to black racism anymore than he would submit to white racism. Underlying the entire novel is the subtle suggestion that if Negroes were permitted to assume their rightful political roles in American life such excesses as demonstrated by the Imperium in Imperio, an organization which developed out of the frustrations of a disfranchised people, would not be possible.

Two years after the publication of his first novel Griggs turned his attention from the political sphere of American democracy to the social structure of the United States. *Overshadowed* uses miscegenation as the basis of the ills which are faced by the characters who themselves are so interrelated that the story is difficult to follow; however, the central theme indicates that the sins of the fathers are truly visited upon the sons. As the novel ends Griggs seems more convinced that an American society which is created by lustful white men preying upon defenseless black women can only result in tragedy for both groups. Yet he is also convinced that the patterns established during the days of slavery will not be eradicated in the foreseeable future. The past, in this instance, does not furnish potent messages to the present.

The pessimistic analysis of the social structure of American life which is presented in *Overshadowed* is also continued in *Unfettered* (1902). The novel is also a compilation of one tragic incident after another, most of which are the results of the type of miscegenation which was rampant in the South. The characters are so manipulated by the author that they lose what little reality they might have possessed. But in spite of this the novel adequately surveys the then-current attitudes toward Negro participation in government and concludes that the success of the Negro in America is in a large measure related to the freedom of the darker peoples throughout the world. The novel concludes with the idea that only by unfettering the minds of both Negroes and whites can there be any semblance of racial accord. At one point in the novel Dorlan Warthell, a Negro politician, proposes what he calls "Dorlan's Plan" as a means of achieving a more harmonious life in America. One of the most significant aspects of the novel is the essay which appears at the end of the novel. Entitled "Dorlan's Plan: Sequel to *Unfettered:* A Dissertation on the Race Problem," the essay permits Griggs to present his own views on race relations in America. It begins with the assertion that color is an artificial and untenable means of determining the worth of any individual. Merit, rather than color, would provide a much more equitable means of judgment. He then supports political awareness, education both liberal and technical, friendship with men of goodwill in the North and in the South as some possible means by which true integration can be achieved. The essay itself is a sober, well-reasoned one which simply re-states the central theme of the novel.

The Hindered Hand, or the Reign of the Repressionist (1905) is a detailed attack upon Thomas Dixon's *The Leopard's Spots* which had appeared in 1902. Dixon, one of the most vocal white racists in American literature, continued his anti-Negro writings in *The Clansman* (1905) which, according to James Hart in *The Popular Book in America,* was reported "to have sold 40,000 copies in ten days (p. 204)." Both the influence of *The Clansman* and its popularity are attested by the fact that the well-circulated motion picture *The Birth of the Nation* (1915) was based upon the Dixon novel. Dixon, of course, was not alone in his inflamatory and prejudicial attacks upon Negro Americans; he was joined by such men as Charles Carroll, William P. Calhoun, Thomas Nelson Page, William B. Smith, and Robert W. Shufeldt to name a few. Within a few years at the opening of the present century Carroll wrote two books whose popularity is a further testimony to the general attitudes of the American reading public. In 1900 he issued *The Negro Is a Beast,* and in 1902 his very self-righteous *The Tempter of Eve; or the Criminality of Man's Social, Political, and Religious Equality with the Negro, or The Amalgamation to Which These Crimes Inevitably Lead. Discussed in the Light of the Scriptures, the Sciences, Profane History, Tradition and the Testimony of the Scriptures* appeared. The year 1902 also saw the publication of William P. Calhoun's *The Caucasian and the Negro in the United States* which attempts to prove the inferiority and bestiality of Negroes as well as the need for repressive measures to control them. In 1904 Thomas Nelson Page, whose *Bred in the*

Bone contains his arguments in support of the idea of the innate inferiority of Negroes, joined the growing group of anti-Negro writers. The same year in which *The Clansman* appeared and Griggs' attack saw the publication of William B. Smith's *The Color Line: A Brief in Behalf of the Unborn* which uses miscegenation as the singularly most criminal of all crimes which ultimately would cause the destruction of the "purity" of the Anglo-Saxon strain. By 1907 when Robert Shufeldt wrote *The Negro, A Menace to American Civilization* these racial assaults were becoming more frequent and more vicious. Historians of American culture may never be able to record the extent to which these writers contributed to the tensions between the races, the tensions which led to so many racial skirmishes and conflicts. Neither may they be able to discover how influential were such men as W.S. Armistead, who wrote in answer to Carroll *The Negro Is a Man: A Reply to Professor Charles Carroll's Book The Negro Is a Beast* in 1903, and Sutton E. Griggs in calming the fears in the Negro community by their reasoned approaches to the rantings of the demagogues. Certainly in *The Hindered Hand* there is an awareness of the nature of the literary uses made of bigotry and prejudice. One of the characters is especially concerned about this.

Ensal thought of the odds against the Negro in this literary battle: how that Southern white people, being more extensive purchasers of books than the Negroes, would have the natural bias of the great publishing agencies on their side; how that Northern white people, resident in the South, for social and business reasons, might hesitate to father books not in keeping with the prevailing sentiment of Southern white people; how the residents of the North, who essayed to write in defense of the Negro, were laughed out of school as mere theorists ignorant of actual conditions; and, finally, how that a lack of leisure and the absence of general culture handicapped the Negro in fighting his own battle in this species of warfare (p. 95).

The novel also deals with the psychological aspects of the emphasis upon race. Those who attempt to "pass" are treated with understanding, for their efforts to receive acceptance by the white majority are based solely upon their recognition of a social system which uses color as a standard for judgment. At the same time the character who "passes" is faced with the maintenance of a secret which often becomes such an obsession that he loses all contact with reality. Insanity or death become the results of many of these attempts to find acceptance in another social sphere. If the character survives, he must cope with the all too pressing identification crisis.

By 1908 and the publication of *Pointing the Way* Griggs had become more optimistic about the possibilities of the integration of Negroes into American society. The action of the novel centers around an experiment which occurs in Belrose, a southern city. In a cooperative effort Negroes and whites of goodwill align themselves politically and take control of the city. The Belrose experiment becomes a nationwide example of what can be achieved through mutual trust. And the novel presents Griggs' own answer to the problems of race relations.

Throughout all of his novels Griggs celebrates the blackness of his heroes. While he does concern himself with the problems of the "color line," his characters who pass do so out of their frustrations and their basic sense of inadequacy. Griggs has little respect for them although he realizes that much of what they do is due to their feelings of oppression and that they are overpowered by forces beyond their control. Yet it is his characters of unmixed blood who are the vital ones and the ones for whom the author has profound admiration. Although he touches upon every conceivable problem in the American racial struggle, Griggs never accepts the idea of revolution nor the theory that a return to Africa will provide workable solutions. Instead he finds all necessary answers to rest in America and in the American way of life; specifically through political awareness and its attendant requirements Griggs asserted recognition was to be achieved. All of the faults of the protest novel are present in Griggs' fiction. The characters are frequently stereotyped in order to serve as a vehicle for the author's message. The action is often contrived, and the

elements of propaganda are so obvious that the art of the storyteller is more often than not sacrificed as the novels become
illustrated sermons. Yet Griggs demonstrated the possibilities of
the Negro novel devoted solely to the issues and problems of life
in America, and he further demonstrated that a sizeable Negro
reading public could be created which could respond to this type
of novel. His realistic portrayal of types of characters and situations provided adequate notice that the Negro artist could create
out of purely racial materials a novel which could speak to the
issues of the times and which could become a part of American
protest fiction. But perhaps more important was the fact that by
the time of the Harlem Renaissance the Negro artist in America
had his own audience and did not necessarily have to depend upon
unsympathetic publishers nor an unreceptive public for support.
Griggs had been influential in proving that unpopular subjects
might be handled in fiction without alienating his reading public.
Very much like his characters in *Pointing the Way,* Sutton E.
Griggs pointed the way for the Negro novelist in America.

CHAPTER VII

Another Declaration of Independence: A View of the Harlem Renaissance

THE HARLEM RENAISSANCE was not merely a product of the twenties although the cohesiveness of the period made it a distinct and unique era in American Negro literature. Actually it was the culmination of forces and ideas which had been gathering momentum from the latter part of the eighteenth century to the post-World War I days. From the neoclassical poems of Phillis Wheatley and the earliest prose efforts of Benjamin Banneker to the work of Countee Cullen there is evidence of the Negro writer's awareness of his ambiguous position in American life and the writer's endeavor to prove—through his work—that the charges of his inferiority were false. From the eloquence of the spirituals and slave narratives to the documents of freedom which preceded and followed the Civil War there were innumerable attempts made to give literary form to this ambiguity. And this was done without compromise and with no loss of dignity. Thus what became known as the Harlem Renaissance was rooted in the writings of Afro-Americans as they reacted to the American experience and as they—consciously and unconsciously—recorded it. In varying degrees Negroes have been profoundly aware that their contributions could and would be distinctive elements of American culture. The slave experience, for example, was used as a point of departure for artistic expressions which became perhaps the most "American" literary forms—the spiritual and the slave narrative.

Among the free population in the days before the total end of slavery was apparent there was a concern with giving voice to the American experience. Although many of these men were bitter and although the very contemplation of conditions produced in some a high degree of cynicism, only a few of these men were in favor of any colonization scheme. The tacit agreement, even in those days, seems to have been as James Weldon Johnson was to say later "this land is ours by right of birth/ this land is ours by right of toil." This essential nationalistic spirit was to appear repeatedly. Even during the Renaissance the element of protest was seldom extended to a complete rejection of America. Of course, the Garvey movement was a notable exception. In the 1930's some of the intellectuals considered communism as a solution for the problems of American capitalism. And for a while some of the writers associated with the Harlem Renaissance explored this solution but gave it up for one reason or another. Perhaps the best statement of the disillusionment which he felt is rendered by Richard Wright in *The God That Failed.*

I

The early sense of nationalism in the nineteenth century was matched by a great interest in Africa for historical purposes. The search for an ancestral home had been manifested in the numerous histories which were written in which the Negro was traced—not from his American origins in slavery—but rather from his beginnings in Africa. But even at this point the interest in African culture did not assume the proportions of a universally accepted back-to-Africa movement. But it did include a recognition of the reality of blackness itself in an attempt to counteract the propaganda so often offered by the pro-slavery forces. This attitude continued after the Civil War and served as a deterrent to those forces which emphasized white supremacy and which accepted Jim Crow laws or Black Codes as the only operative precepts.

The solidification of the Negro community became greater during the period which immediately followed the Civil War. In the period which Rayford Logan has called "The Nadir" Negroes were called upon to exercise every bit of their inner strength and creative powers simply in order to survive. At the same time this became a period which saw the growth and development of many Negro institutions. In a very real sense the Harlem Renaissance became in part an answer to "The Nadir," for it served notice to America that Negroes had been to the depths and had been isolated from the so-called American mainstream but had survived.

While the host of Negro writers who preceded the Renaissance contributed a great deal to the ideas and themes of the period, perhaps no one writer better summarized the issues and the theses than W. E. B. DuBois who later became an active participant in the movement. As a forerunner of the Harlem Renaissance, he embodied the spirit and the ideology of the movement itself. In 1899 he published a strangely symbolic poem entitled "The Song of Smoke." Long an advocate of a recognition of African culture and a firm believer that the Negro's salvation in America must first begin with the pride of race, DuBois chants a panegyric to blackness not as a traditional symbol of evil but rather as a positive indication of strength.

> I am the smoke king,
> I am black.
> I am swinging in the sky.
> I am ringing worlds on high:
> I am the thought of the throbbing mills,
> I am the soul of the soul toil kills,
> I am the ripple of trading rills,
>
> Up I'm curling from the sod,
> I am whirling home to God.
> I am the smoke king,
> I am black.
>
> I am the smoke king,
> I am black.
> I am wreathing broken hearts,

I am sheathing devils' darts;
Dark inspiration of iron times,
Wedding the toil of toiling climes
Shedding the blood of bloodless crimes,

Down I lower in the blue,
Up I tower toward the true,
I am the smoke king,
I am black.

I am black.
I am the smoke king,

I am darkening with song,
I am hearkening to wrong;
I will be as black as blackness can,
The blacker the mantle the mightier the man,
My purpl'ing midnights no day dawn may ban.

I am carving God in night,
I am painting hell in white.
I am the smoke king,
I am black.

I am the smoke king,
I am black.

I am cursing ruddy morn,
I am nursing hearts unborn;
Souls unto me are as mists in the night,
I whiten my blackmen, I beckon my white,
What's the hue of a hide to a man in his might!
Hail, then, gritty, grimy hands,
Sweet Christ, pity toiling lands!

Hail to the smoke king,
Hail to the black!

The paradoxical position of the Negro in America also claimed
DuBois' attention in 1903 with the publication of *The Souls of*

Black Folk. In the first chapter DuBois establishes the inevitability of the Negro's ambivalent situation in America by asserting:

Between me and the other world there is an ever unasked question: unasked by some through feelings of delicacy; by others through the difficulty of rightly framing it. All, nevertheless, flutter round it. They approach me in a half-hesitant sort of way, eye me curiously or compassionately, and then, instead of saying directly, How does it feel to be a problem? they say, I know an excellent colored man in my town; or, I fought at Mechanicsville; or, Do not these Southern outrages make your blood boil? At these I smile, or am interested, or reduce the boil to a simmer, as the occasion may require. To the real question, How does it feel to be a problem? I answer seldom a word.

He continues somewhat later in the chapter, after recounting his first experience as a youngster with the question of race, to record his own personal evaluation on the results of the "problem." He then analyzes the ambiguous position of Negroes in American life.

After the Egyptian and Indian, the Greek and the Roman, the Teuton and Mongolian, the Negro is a sort of seventh son, born with a veil, and gifted with second-sight in this American world,—a world which yields him no true self-conscious, but only lets him see himself through the revelation of the other world. It is a peculiar sensation, this double-consciousness, this sense of always looking at one's self through the eyes of others, of measuring one's soul by the tape of a world that looks on in amused contempt and pit. One ever feels his twoness,—an American, a Negro; two souls, two thoughts, two unreconciled strivings; two warring ideals in one dark body, whose dogged strength alone keeps it from being torn asunder.

The history of the American Negro is the history of this strife,—this longing to attain self-conscious manhood, to merge his double self into a better and truer self. In this merging he wishes neither of his older selves to be lost. He would not Africanize America, for America has too much to teach the world and Africa. He would not bleach his Negro soul in a flood of white Americanism, for he knows that Negro blood has a message for the world. He simply wishes to make it possible for a man to be both a Negro and an American, without being cursed and spit upon by his fellows, without having the doors of Opportunity closed roughly in his face.

With his knowledge of the past and his prophetic announcement of future developments within the Harlem Renaissance and in the still later black-is-beautiful movement of the 1960's, DuBois' second chapter of *The Souls of Black Folk* begins by avowing that "the problem of the twentieth is the problem of the color line. . . ." Chesnutt, of course, had recognized this and had become virtually the novelist of "the color line," but DuBois' approach was more realistic than that of Chesnutt who had little knowledge of the hopes and fears of the ordinary man. While *The Souls of Black Folk* is a collection of essays and reminiscences, the work is important as setting forth many of the precepts which were to become operative during the Harlem Renaissance. And just as Alain Locke was to become the period's philosopher so DuBois served as its high priest.

DuBois demonstrated in his poetry and in his fiction that the element of protest could be artistically effective. As a poet he was more interested in innovative forms than with traditional patterns. As a result of the 1906 Atlanta riot he wrote the long prose poem "A Litany of Atlanta" whose subtitle announced "Done at Atlanta, in the Day of Death, 1906." The poem, which is a series of pleas to God, ends:

In yonder East trembles a star.
> *Vengeance is mine; I will repay saith the Lord!*

Thy will, O Lord, be done!
> *Kyrie Eleison!*

Lord, we have done these pleadings, wavering words.
> *We beseech Thee to hear us, good Lord!*

We bow our heads and hearken soft to the sobbing of women and little children.

We beseech Thee to hear us, good Lord!

Our voices sink in silence and in night.
Hear us, good Lord!

In night, O God of a godless land!
Amen!

In silence, O Silent God.
Selah!

Five years later he issued *The Quest of the Silver Fleece* which is a social novel after the manner of Frank Norris in which cotton becomes an overpowering force. Both white and black politicians who succumb to their greed are satirized.

DuBois furnished his great guidance for the approaching Harlem Renaissance while he was the editor of *The Crisis*. Especially significant was his editorial "The Immediate Program of the American Negro" which appeared in the April, 1915, issue. The article asserts:

In art and literature we should try to loose the tremendous emotional wealth of the Negro and the dramatic strength of his problems through writing, the stage, pageantry, and other forms of art. We should resurrect forgotten ancient Negro art and history, and we should set the black man before the world as both a creative artist and a strong subject for artistic treatment.

And this statement unconsciously offered a formula which became the basis for the Harlem Renaissance as the writers of the period did indeed "loose the tremendous emotional wealth of the Negro." There was a renewed interest in African art and culture. Through various media the problems of the American Negro were dramatized, and the Negro emerged not only as a serious creator but also as "a strong subject for artistic treatment."

While the literature of the 1920's did exhibit a great sense of racial pride and racial dignity in perhaps a new and more self-conscious way, the Harlem Renaissance was not merely a period in which there developed a recognizable group of Negro artists who were committed to the articulation of their racial awareness. These artists were joined by a substantial group of white writers who recognized the artistic value of Negro materials. Too frequently, of course, the white writers emphasized the exotic or the primitive, but at least they had recovered from the two-dimensional influence of Joel Chandler Harris and Irwin Russell. Many of these writers were genuinely concerned about attacking racial problems and racial attitudes in America. Furthermore both Eugene O'Neill in *The Emperor Jones* (1920) and in *All God's Chillun Got Wings* (1924) and Paul Green in *Abraham's Bosom* (1926) clearly demonstrated in dramatic literature that Negro actors and materials could be used effectively without resorting to minstrel techniques. In fact for *All God's Chillun Got Wings* Paul Robeson was selected to play the male lead, and the predicted trouble did not result. Victor Calverton, Robert Kerlin, Carl Van Vechten, H. L. Mencken, and Sherwood Anderson did their best to call attention to the Harlem Renaissance as it was evolving in the 1920's. Perhaps for the first time in American literary history there was an appreciable group of writers who were mutually concerned about an adequate usage of Negro materials. Because all of the writers tended to socialize and to interact with one another, the Harlem Renaissance gained a power and a force which it otherwise would not have had.

After the First World War American writers searched for new forms, and the Harlem Renaissance, in its quest for different literary techniques, became a part of the dominant strain of American literature. At the same time the writers of the Renaissance translated their bitterness, their shock at injustice, their desire for a place in the American sun in a number of ways. By artistically using the materials of their unique experiences and position in America they were to create a body of distinctive literature. Nor was this merely the peculiar domain of literature. In painting, music, sculpture, drama, and motion pictures there was the same evident creativity and interest. Dramatic history will not soon forget the outstanding talents of Charles Gilpin who in 1920 took the title role in Eugene O'Neill's *The Emperor Jones* and cemented his reputation as well as that of the playwright. Nor can the work of Paul Robeson be overlooked as he portrayed roles from O'Neill's work to Shapespeare's. *Shuffle Along,* the all-Negro musical revue of 1921, is still considered as one of the most outstanding musicals to have appeared on Broadway. Written and produced by Negroes, it proved that Negroes could take their places in all phases of dramatic life from the serious to the comic, from the dramatic to the musical. After *Shuffle Along* there appeared a series of musicals more or less patterned upon this successful production.

There was a revival of interest in the spiritual and the old work songs. Because outstanding singers such as Paul Robeson and Roland Hayes were re-interpreting these songs, they became musically more respectable than they had been since the early days of the Fisk Jubilee Singers. Outstanding musicians such as J. Rosamond Johnson, Harry T. Burleigh, R. Nathaniel Dett, and Carl Diton not only did much to resurrect these songs through their editions and arrangements of spirituals but also created scores which became outstanding contributions to American music. Perhaps America has not produced a more remarkable composer than William Grant Still. Three of his symphonies *Africa, Afro-American Symphony,* and *Symphony in G Minor: Song of a New Race,* are still being executed by prominent orchestras. The interest in music was coupled with an interest in painting and sculpture. While the Renaissance did not produce an artist as well-known as Henry Owassa Tanner, both Aaron Douglass and Edward A. Harleston achieved a degree of success. By the end of the period Hale Woodruff and Charles Alston had produced outstanding work. And the ability of Meta Warrick Fuller as a sculptor is demonstrated by the power of her figures.

Prior to World War I the realistic movement in American literature seldom included the American Negro. Generally where such realistic portrayals existed they were produced among Negro writers who did not have access to the larger white reading public. In the search for new literary forms and new values after the war, there was the discovery of a large untapped reservoir of material in Negro America. Spurred by the realistic and naturalistic movements, white writers began to look seriously at Negro life in America. This does not mean, of course, that the plantation tradition of Harris, Page, and Russell miraculously disappeared neither does it mean that the racist novels of Dixon no longer had an audience, but there was a growing interest in a more balanced portrait of the Negro in literature.

Many of these portraits obviously failed because the writers were not quite so certain of their subject matter; others placed too great an emphasis upon the primitivism of the race but all provided a forum for the discussion of approaches which had only a few years earlier been taboo. Perhaps the greatest contribution during this period were the dramatic works of O'Neill and Ridgely Torrence. Between 1914 and 1924 they produced a series of plays which utilized Negro characters in a new and different way. In 1922 T. S. Sibling published *Birthright* which was later praised by Sterling Brown in his *The Negro in American Fiction* (Washington, 1937) because the novel "places the Negro at the center of the picture, attempts to show the influence of environment upon character, and attacks injustice (p. 115)." During the same year Clement Wood published *Nigger* and Hubert Shands issued *Black and White*. In the following year Waldo Frank wrote *Holiday* whose symbolic naturalism was to shock many readers as he recounted the love story of a white woman and a Negro in the town of Nazareth, a story which ends with a highly descriptive lynching. Sherwood Anderson's *Dark Laughter* appeared in 1925, and in 1926 Carl Van Vechten's *Nigger Heaven* was the apex of this type of work by white writers. Certainly Van Vechten did much to popularize the life of Harlem and to make the community a tourist attraction. While these as well as the more romantic studies lack a great deal of insight into Negro life, they at least popularized a subject which had previously been employed—in most instances—in a more derogatory manner. Realism and naturalism had freed American literature to probe beneath the genteel veneer of middle class white America, and there were groups of writers who took immediate advantage of this new-found freedom. During the entire period Negro writers were being courted and were being heeded as they provided still a better insight into the lives of their own people.

And when did all of the activity which miraculously had been centered in and around Harlem end? By the beginning of the Depression the concentrated efforts in Harlem had become diffused. Many of the people who had been integral parts of the movement had departed for other places. At the same time the Federal Writers' Project provided employment for a number of artists who had been involved in the movement of the twenties as well as for the new generation of artists.

One of the central problems which had faced Negro writers, and the writers of the Renaissance came to grips with the problem, was the procedure by which a literature with a universal appeal, a literature which was artistically valid, could be created out of the more immediate and specific reactions to American racism. The writers had now discovered that older writers such as Frances E. W. Harper had often forfeited art in favor of a message. Yet at the same time when Dunbar forgot the message and emphasized only the art, he ceased to be a Negro writer in the fullest sense of the term. The dilemma was a real one but was not unique to American Negroes. Other oppressed groups throughout world history had been faced with a similar duality. The problem could be resolved, it was recognized, by taking the rejection of oppression and turning it into a positive statement of racial consciousness, into an affirmation of racial faith. As other writers from oppressed people had attempted to do so the Negro Renaissance attempted to codify subconsciously its principles so that the ultimate result would not be mere protest but would be primarily a product of their inner lives in such a way that their relationship with humanity at large would be evident. At the same time they desired to incorporate their sense of their special past—the African heritage, the American slave experience, and the on-going search for freedom and equality—without giving up their pride of race, a pride which wells up in the DuBois poem in its last line: "Hail to the black!" Hardships, of course, had to be portrayed, but the emphasis upon ethnic dignity demanded that the beauty and the special role of Negroes had to be also considered. For these men groping with the essential problems of artistic creation "black is beautiful" was more than a mere slogan. It was a manifestation of individual worth, a sense of ancestral pride, a sense of belonging which grew out of the American experience and which was illustrated repeatedly in the stories and poems of the period. One needs to look no further than the work of Countee Cullen to discover how thoroughly this personal integration had taken root. This was, in the final analysis, the important legacy of the Harlem Renaissance to a later generation.

From the beginning of Negro literature in America there had been the subtle influence of the culture of America. Disparate though the experience may have been with the American dream, these experiences had to be explained in terms of American dominant culture. This is perhaps best illustrated by a very simple fact— the usage of American English. With the exception of the forays into the use of dialect, the major works are produced in the language of the oppressor not because another language was unavailable but rather because these writers were part of America, and the country's literary heritage as well as its literary forms belonged to the Negro writer. Thus what they had to say really became an integral part of American literature. As more and more work was produced, Whitman's dream of the literature of America, "the nation of nations," was coming closer to fulfillment. As he declared in his "Preface" to the 1855 edition of *Leaves of Grass:*

The American poets are to enclose old and new for America is the race of races. Of them a bard is to be commensurate with a people. To him, the other continents arrive as contributions . . . he gives them reception for their sake and his own sake.

During the Renaissance there was no one single form nor common technique which prevailed. There were those who experimented with poetic structure such as Langston Hughes, others followed the James Weldon Johnson interest and attempted to project a Negro idiom into an artistic vehicle, still others found their heritage in a by-gone literary era such as the combined classicism and romanticism of Countee Cullen. In short, each writer within the framework of the culture which he knew and understood created and worked. Even here, of course, the duality of the Negro American's position became obvious, and the issues raised by W. E. B. DuBois gained relevance. Alain Locke, the philosopher of the Harlem Renaissance who more than any other individual helped to codify the principles of the period and who edited *The New Negro* in 1925—the significant collection of writers and artists of the period—, was aware of this strange ambivalence. He constantly emphasized the fact that the Negro was primarily an American; consequently, anything produced by him would be "American." Yet Locke maintained that the subtle—and sometimes not so subtle—forces which operated on Negroes in America resulted in an artistic expression which was primarily racial. While he was well aware of the fact that every artist ultimately had the power to choose his own subjects as well as his forms, he was convinced that "Negro poetry . . . represents many strains, having only one common factor,—the fact of reflecting some expression of the emotional sense of race or some angle of the peculiar group tradition and experience." Locke continued by asserting: "In the case of the American Negro the sense of race is stronger than that of nationality; and in some form or other is a primary factor in the consciousness of the Negro poet." As he continued to concern himself with the more covert aspects of race and with the psychological effects of race upon creativity—especially that of the poet, Locke declared:

Race has many diverse ways of reflecting itself in the equation of life; each temperament reflects it just a bit differently and reacts to it just a bit differently. We too frequently neglect this important pòint, that the racial factors may reside in the overtones of artistic expression and there is often more of race in its sublimations than in its crude reportorial expression.

Richard Wright felt that as America progressed toward a more objective view of the American Negro, the literature of the nation would reflect this. He associated racial themes with an attempt to indicate the extent to which prejudice, segregation, and all others aspects used by the supremacists were affecting Negroes. While he did acknowledge in "The Literature of the Negro in the United States" which appears in *White Man, Listen!* that a time might come when racial considerations might be totally absent from the work of American Negroes, he sets up certain conditions.

If the expression of the American Negro should take a sharp turn toward strictly racial themes, then you will know by that token that we are suffering our old and ancient agonies at the hands of our white American neighbors. If, however, our expression broadens, assumes the common themes and burdens of literary expression which are the heritage of all men, then by that token you will know that a human attitude prevails in America toward us. And a gain in humaneness in America is a gain in humaneness for us all. When that day comes, there will exist one more proof of the oneness of man, of the basic unity of life on this earth (pp. 104-105).

In spite of the dichotomy which seems to exist between race and art the writers of the Renaissance successfully merged the two. Some writers even demonstrated quite conclusively that mere protest could be developed into aesthetically valid experiences. And the consciousness of race ceased to be a handicap. The consciousness of race, interestingly enough, was a prime factor in the development of the literature in both Africa and the West Indies. This becomes even of greater significance when one considers the usual tendency is to think of influence flowing from Africa to American rather than in the reverse direction. The writers of the Renaissance were translated in the major capitals of the world, and their work was read by all—especially by African students in Europe. In "A Conversation with Leopold Senghor" which appeared in the May (1967) issue of *Negro Digest,* Sènghor referred to Langston Hughes and Sterling Brown as "the most Negro" poets in American literature. He continued his remarks on literature by saying: ". . . we owe a great deal to the United States. Indeed with regard to our Negritude, we have depended largely on the teachings of our professors of ethnology, anthropology on the subjects of Black African civilization." He concluded his remarks:

But, was it not the 'New Negro' movement, the movement of the 'Negro Renaissance," with Alain Locke and the others, was it not they who stimulated us to do as they did, to write poetry! In this way, and at this moment, I want to give to America that which is due to her, that is to say to have been, in a way, the initiator of Negritude.

II

Until the most recent years "The Harlem Renaissance" suffered from the silence of scholarship. Perhaps nowhere else in Negro American literature is the tendency to ignore an event more apparent than in the treatment of a significant literary movement which covered approximately ten years and involved more than a hundred writers and artists, not to mention the untold number of sculptors and actors. From time to time individual Negro writers find their ways into American literary histories, and almost invariably when they do so the author is attempting to point out the uniqueness of the writer so cited. Thus a Phillis Wheatley who, though so thoroughly a product of the neoclassical tradition in American life, becomes unique not upon the basis of her work (which in reality in similar to that of every other American neoclassicist) but upon the fact of her race and her stature as a slave. A Dunbar is mentioned primarily because Howells, long considered the dean of American letters, invited the American reading public to consider him; but once again the emphasis was misplaced, because the dialect poems of Dunbar which were singularly praised by Howells by no means represent the outstanding contribution of Dunbar to American letters. And for years the remainder of his work was left untouched critically and ignored by later readers who hardly knew of its existence. Allusions are made to Chesnutt, Dunbar's contemporary who published in the quality magazines and journals of his day, but too frequently his creativity was dismissed in an effort to ascribe his work to his mixed parentage! The other writers who enjoyed some kind of critical note during the nineteenth century and early twentieth century were Frederick Douglass, Booker T. Washington, and W. E. B. DuBois, but too often they were dismissed by simply a mention of racial identity and titles of their works. The extent to which this silence of scholarship prevailed is most obvious when one peruses the outstanding *Literary History of the United States,* first published in 1948, which purported to survey writing in America but which ignored the major Negro writers.

Difficult though it may appear to be, it is a relatively simple matter to ignore individual writers because the author of a literary history can legitimately plead the necessity of selectivity demanded by his time and space. But to omit a movement such as the Harlem Renaissance becomes a somewhat different matter because the movement itself was so intricately interwoven with the general events of the period and with the direction of American literature itself in those days immediately following the First World War that to omit this movement is to tear at the very fiber and being of American literature as our national literature was in the process of searching for new forms and for a different kind of identity. The study of American literature has suffered from the exclusiveness of its literary histories and anthologies. While there was a tacit recognition that cultural America was to be made up of many races and creeds just as the political America, this composite generally broke down at the point of the consideration of the American Negro.

Eventually American writers were to become victims of a form of cultural racism which, according to Horace M. Kallen in *Cultural Pluralism and the American Idea* (Philadelphia, 1956), resulted in the belief that "the American Idea and the American Way were hereditary to the Anglo-Saxon stock and to that stock only . . . other stocks were incapable of producing them, learning them, and living them (p. 82)."

From one point of view the Harlem Renaissance can be viewed as a part of a general movement in American literature after the First World War whose dominant *raison d'etre* was in its search for a different form for expression and for a more workable set of values. Including Waldo Frank, Sherwood Anderson, and Carl Van Vechten, the post World War I literary movement frequently ended its search for new forms by emphasizing the primitive or the exotic. In order to promote further this primitivism and exoticism white writers "discovered" the Negro community, and once there found a working group of Negro writers who were able to join them. Thus while Van Vechten was repeating Dunbar's theme in *Nigger Heaven* (1926) in his exploration of Harlem, he met a group of writers who were able to view Harlem as insiders rather than as outsiders. Interest in Negro culture became the vogue. From the cabarets of Harlem to the college theater groups of the southern colleges, from the most insignificant and poorly written newspapers to the scholarly manifestoes of W. E. B. DuBois, from the pens of obscure poets and novelists to the recesses of Africa in a search for artifacts, there issued usable material as white America fostered a unique desire to learn about this sub-culture which had existed in America so long. Unfortunately, the period did foster mediocrity as many people attempted to "get into the act." Negroes, of course, took advantage of this interest to produce a multitude of materials since there was the inclination to believe that the more authentic material was to come from the race itself.

From another point of view the Harlem Renaissance can be viewed as a moment of freedom for the Negro writer. The search for new forms in American literature permitted Negro writers to pursue those subjects which heretofore had been cast aside in favor of a more universally accepted manner and method. For the first time there was the incorporation of folk material into the writings of this group. This satisfied the primitive and exotic search on the part of white writers and readers and also furnished Negro writers the chance to view themselves culturally with objectivity. The reality of being a Negro in America was given voice and expression. Although this had been done before, for the first time there existed a group of writers who were committed to the achievement of political and cultural freedom.

At the same time that the Renaissance may be characterized as a period of protest, it can also be described as a period of cultural independence. No longer was there a tendency to overlook differences in order to achieve complete integration into the so-called "mainstream of American culture." Instead the writers and artists now took their differences and developed an artistic creed. Perhaps the best explanation of this attitude was voiced by Langston Hughes in "The Negro Artist and the Racial Mountain" which appeared in *The Nation* (June 23, 1926). Hughes began his article by observing:

One of the most promising of the young Negro poets said to me once, 'I want to be a poet—not a Negro poet,' meaning, I believe, 'I want to write like a white poet'; meaning subconsciously, 'I would like to be a white poet.' And I was sorry the young man said that, for no great poet has ever been afraid of being himself. And I doubted then that, with his desire to run away spiritually from his race, this boy would ever be a great poet. But this is the mountain standing in the way of any true Negro art in America—this urge within the race toward whiteness, the desire to pour racial individuality into the mold of American standardization, and to be as little Negro and as much American as possible (p. 692).

One might disagree with Hughes' analysis of the statement by the young poet, but one is forced to consider the "racial mountain" which more often than not was erected by others for the Negro artist. Hughes ends his article by pronouncing a philosophy of the period:

We younger Negro artists who create now intend to express our individual dark-skinned selves without fear or shame. If white people are pleased we are glad. If they are not, it doesn't matter. We know we are beautiful. And ugly too. The tom-tom cries and the tom-tom laughs. If colored people are pleased we are glad. If they are not, their displeasure doesn't matter either. We build our temples for tomorrow, strong as we know how, and we stand on top of the mountain, free within ourselves (p. 694).

The freedom of expression which was so universally praised and the emphasis upon racial identity which were so characteristic of the period carried the seeds of destruction. But the excitement of the 1920's was never wholly destroyed, the Depression simply carried with it a different sense of urgency which resulted in a new alignment of values as well as of artistic principles. The creative energies of the 1960's and the attitudes so frequently expressed are merely extensions of the complex Harlem Renaissance.

In an optimistic attempt to make America a better place, to make the American dream a reality, a number of white writers attacked social and economic problems with renewed vehemence. Problem or protest fiction had been developed prior to World War 1 but as a by-product of realism and naturalism. Not until after the First World War, after the heyday of popular romanticism, did it gain a more widespread acceptance for disenchantment was more common. In their search for "problems" the writers of America discovered untapped material in the situation of the Negro in this country. Not only did they turn their attention to the so-called "Negro Problem," but they prepared the country for Negro writers. As white readers became aware of the host of Negroes in their midst, they also became more aware that there were Negroes capable of interpreting themselves. And America was now of age, she could hear what these Negro artists had to say. What was said was in a large measure repetitions of eighteenth- and nineteenth-century concerns, but the twentieth-century audience was far more broad.

The Harlem Renaissance proved that artistic principles and racial awareness did not have to be mutually exclusive. One did not rule out the existence of the other. The element of protest, of course, is present in Negro American literature from its very inception. Even such writers as Phillis Wheatley and Jupiter Hammon were aware that a slave should have the right of freedom. Although they were products of their immediate colonial environments, both of them recognized that there was a disparity between the eighteenth-century talk of freedom and their own immediate plights. The element of protest is a dominant characteristic in the literature of a minority ethnic group in this country, and American Negro literature is no exception. From the slave narratives to the present day, the emphasis has been upon freedom, upon the need to be recognized as individuals, upon the desire to achieve a rightful place without the distortions so frequently associated with differences of race, religion, or creed. Because the Harlem Renaissance specifically addressed itself to these problems of artistic productions by Negroes, it may be described as a period of concerted protest. The work of the period was a direct answer to those who had attempted to claim that the Negro's "place" in American culture was to be determined by outside forces. Not only were these artists convinced that their "place" was as co-creators of American culture but also were they convinced that only they could present their stories. Either consciously or unconsciously they agreed with Margaret Fuller, the nineteenth-century Transcendentalist, who had asserted that American literature was to result only when all segments of the population were heard. But Margaret Fuller was not alone in this view. During the mid-years of the nineteenth century writers such as Emerson and Whitman constantly alluded to American literature as a national literature which was to be responsive to all races and creeds. In what Whitman was to call "a teeming nation of nations" the literature was to be distinctive and unique only when it reflected this many-faceted society. By the period of the Harlem Renaissance there was almost a tacit agreement among Negro artists to demand their rightful places in American creative history. Out of this decision one can see some of the more overt characteristics of the period, characteristics which had been present from the beginning of Negro writing in America: emphasis upon racial pride, a search for an ancestral home which led to a renewed interest in African art and history, an optimistic belief that the future would soon bring the fulfillment of the American dream, and an emphasis upon the artistic value and use of race.

Similar to other movements of its scope and dimension, the Harlem Renaissance did not suddenly appear on the American cultural scene. The path had been laid for it in the very earliest awareness on the part of Negro writers and artists that they had something of value to contribute to American civilization. It evolved out of that pride which was evident even before the end of slavery; however, the First World War did much to solidify its principles and to prepare a climate in which these cultural flowers might grow. The days and the years after the Civil War had been trying ones. The defeated South retaliated by its numerous Jim Crow laws and by instilling a fear into the hearts of most of its residents. And so there was substituted simply a different form of slavery to replace the old peculiar institution. In the meantime conditions were not appreciably different in the North. Here the various "Black Codes" restricted movement and education, and the more subtle patterns of segregation were put into operation. Thus throughout the United States there was an unspoken acceptance of the inferiority of the Negro and an insistence that he remain simply a second-class citizen. Perhaps the final blow was dealt by the Supreme Court decision of 1896 that made the doctrine "separate but equal" acceptable throughout the land.

Needless to say, these conditions did not preclude the absolute stifling of any creative ability, but creativity—when it existed— was exercised in a cultural vacuum and in spiritual isolation. Throughout the years from the end of the Civil War to the First

World War the roster of Negro writers grew longer and longer with each passing year. Many of these writers were intent upon exposing what to them seemed unjust conditions in America, but all of them—with the possible exception of Griggs who used his own method for issuing his works—were forced to rely upon white publishers who more frequently than not were uniniterested in certain types of materials. In isolated cases writers were published by reputable journals and houses, but the cultural quarantine of these writers became more and more apparent. This "apartness" was due in part to white America's attitudes. Out of this cultural isolation, however, some notable writers appeared who were intent upon giving voice to that creative urge which existed within their own souls. It is really impossible to categorize those post-Civil War and pre-World War I writers by means of any dominant philosophy, but they all shared in common a desire to be considered as human beings first. There was no real attempt made to deny race, in fact some of them not only made racial considerations and subjects their primary concern but also glorified in the idea of race. Thus out of this racial consciousness, out of this belief that an American artist could be a Negro, the seeds for the Harlem Renaissance were planted.

World War I gave to the average American Negro a new sense of dignity and self-confidence. He gained his new sense of worth because he was in demand as northern industrialists went South in order to recruit workers for the places which had heretofore been held by the immigrants. With the coming of the hostilities, immigration had been seriously curtailed, and their jobs were vacant. Thus wooed by the promise of more money and better lives Negroes made a mass exodus from the South. Once in northern cities these people were generally heartened by a greater sense of freedom. The fact that they were often crowded into the worst sections of the cities and the reality of the inevitable labor problems did not deter this move toward urbanism. At the same time Negro soldiers were being sent to Europe and were meeting—some for the first time—men and women who did not automatically condemn them on the basis of race. On the battlefield there were no Jim-Crow laws nor Black Codes. White America now saw what others had seen during preceding American wars, the Negro soldier handled himself with distinction and with dispatch. Slowly the old attitudes began to crumble.

The war to make the world safe for democracy ended, but there could be no return to the old way of doing things. There were those who desired to return to a pre-war America, but this was impossible. The renewed determination of Negro Americans to receive those promises which had been made after the Civil War, to take a rightful place in the nation whose honor had been defended by Negro soldiers, to share in her bounties as well as in her failures, led to the so-called *New* Negro of the 1920's.

The emphasis upon race which characterized the New Negro in this period was aided by Marcus Garvey and his Universal Negro Improvement Association. What Garvey espoused was not original. Prior to the Civil War Martin Delany and Alexander Crummell had proposed a similar program, and after the war there were echoes of the back-to-Africa movement. So once again there appeared a man so devoted and dedicated to black nationalism that he found the only hope to rest in a return to Africa. Unlike, however, preceding advocates of this idea Garvey immediately struck a responsive chord among the masses as he promoted his "black is beautiful" program. Though he was to fail miserably and was to be convicted for fraud, Marcus Garvey was able to filter to a popular level some of the principles which had been discussed in an earlier day in American culture. Garvey's program was predicated upon the universal kinship of all dark-skinned peoples of the world; and his first principle was to emphasize the beauty, the dignity, and the glory of blackness itself by proposing that American Negroes exert effort not only to "free" all black people throughout the world but also to create a black nation, preferably in Africa. He further emphasized that this could be accomplished if American Negroes went beyond their slave roots and stressed their cultural heritage in Africa as well as Africa's great contribution to world civilization. In their dissatisfaction with American the Garveyites searched for an ancestral home and found it in Africa.

Whatever else one might think of Marcus Garvey today, one must acknowledge that his emphasis upon blackness and his interest upon Africa were to become an important segment of the Harlem Renaissance as well as of the current mood of the 1960's. As Garvey gained more and more adherents among the Harlem masses, he explained all facets of human life and human existence in terms of *blackness*. Even religion was provided with a black Jesus and a black God. There were those among the Negro community who saw the excesses of Garveyism. Charles Johnson, the noted sociologist who was to become president of Fisk University, asserted in an article, "After Garvey—What?" which appeared in the first volume of *Opportunity* (1923) that Garvey was fostering "a black version of that same 100 per cent mania that now afflicts white America . . . (p. 232)."

Garvey's proposal for the establishment of a separate state in Africa was based upon the supposition that Negroes would never be able to achieve equality and fair treatment in the United States. He soon, by various means, interested a large number of people in his colonization scheme. That these same people were eventually to lose a great deal of money which had been invested in the plan is an indictment more of Garvey's inability to manage large sums of money than of the plan itself. He established The Provisional Republic of Africa, an interim government, and a number of corollary offices such as the UNIA and the Black Star Line, the steamship company which was eventually to transport Negroes from the United States to the Republic which was being established. Information concerning the movement was disseminated through the weekly paper *The Negro World*. While Garvey's program certainly attracted large numbers who had little hope of ever achieving complete freedom in this country, it also attracted those who were impressed by the "pomp and circumstance" which Garvey attached to his plan. And as he traveled throughout the country gaining adherents, he conferred titles and gave uniforms to his lieutenants. His militancy provided the last resort for many of the oppressed.

Ultimately it is difficult to assess the extent to which Garvey influenced the Harlem Renaissance. Certainly much of his program had been advocated many years before he came to this country from his native Jamaica, but he did re-echo some of the major themes of the period and illustrated the frustration which accompanied second-class citizenship. By avowing the possibility of union with all of the darker-skinned peoples of the world and by creating a substantial "black-is-beautiful" movement and cult he did much toward creating a desire on the part of the masses to learn more about themselves. Not only was a renewed interest in history a by-product of the black nationalistic spirit but also was there fostered an appreciable audience for the creative efforts of the artists of the period.

The search for an ancestral home naturally led historians and artists to Africa. With perhaps the notable exception of the work of Alexander Crummell, early Negro historians tended to concentrate on the story of the Negro in America although they did not deny the African origins of their subject. This was done in order to stress the dominant idea that Negroes had been in the United States long enough to have forged some kind of life here. However, there were sporadic efforts and instances made to include at least portions of African history in their works. Perhaps the greatest impetus for the study of African life and culture was an outgrowth of the Association for the Study of Negro Life and History founded in 1915 by Carter G. Woodson. In its official publication *The Journal of Negro History* appeared many articles dealing with various aspects of African life as a precursor of the American experience.

When the cohesive force of the Harlem Renaissance had passed, the years which followed were not silent ones. Some of the most outstanding work was produced by Zora Neale Hurston who began her career as an anthropologist and ended as a creative artist of

some magnitude. Emphasizing primarily the folk material of the
United States as well as that of Haiti and Jamaica, the two Carrib-
bean areas about which she wrote most exclusively, she produced
among her major works: *Jonah's Gourd Vine* (1934), *Mules and
Men* (1935), *Their Eyes Were Watching God* (1937), *Tell My
Horse* (1938), and *Moses Man of the Mountain* (1939). Among
the later poets, Melvin Tolson published *Rendezvous with America*
in 1944, but "Dark Symphony," one of the major poems of the
volume, had been issued earlier in *The Atlantic Monthly*. Robert
Hayden published his first book of verse in 1940 entitled *Heart-
Shape in the Dust*. After writing traditional and experimental verse
for several years, Owen Dodson collected his works in a volume
Powerful Long Ladder in 1946. The Negro poet achieved great
recognition in 1940 when Margaret Walker won the Yale Younger
Poet Series Award with *For My People,* and a few years later
Gwendolyn Brooks won the Pulitzer Prize for Poetry, the first
Negro ever so honored. Among the host of novelists who appeared
during and after the Depression were Arna Bontemps, George W.
Henderson, George W. Lee, Walter Turpin, William Attaway,
Chester Himes, Ann Petry, and Richard Wright. Each one used
the themes and motifs which had been expressed during the Harlem
Renaissance and produced works which have become an integral
part of American literature.

III

New York had long been a mecca for American artists when in
the 1920's a group of writers and painters found themselves bound
together by the urban environment. For short-lived periods Boston, Philadelphia, Charleston, and Chicago functioned as the
literary capitals of the United States; however New York became
not only a literary capital and publishing center but also the most
sympathetic urban environment in meeting the demands of the
American artists. From the latter part of the nineteenth century
into the twentieth century artists migrated to New York in search of

an understanding audience as well as success. It was no wonder that Negro artists also cast their lots with New York City.

In addition to providing the necessary urban climate for creativity, New York had long been associated in the minds of many as the one urban area which allowed more freedom to Negroes. And it soon became a haven for Negroes from all parts of the country. Dunbar, of course, had early pointed out some of the social problems and matters of adjustment which had to be met by the migrants in Harlem, but these considerations did not deter the large numbers of southern Negroes who crowded into the city during the First World War. Early in its history New York had faced a racial riot, and this 1900 riot had resulted in a strong Negro community with an equally-strong sense of destiny. Negro newspapers had crusaded for equality of opportunity, and the city became the headquarters of the N.A.A.C.P. with James Weldon Johnson functioning as its field secretary and W.E.B. DuBois as the editor of its journal, *The Crisis.* The native Negro population was joined by the more vocal and militant West Indians who became an integral part of the Negro's move toward equality and greater freedom. Thus the new spirit which prevailed after World War I found a ready-made audience as well as eager participants not only in Harlem but also in New York City. And one by one the Negro artists moved into New York and produced through their concerted efforts "The Harlem Renaissance" which was neither confined to Harlem nor to New York alone.

Washington, D.C., for example, served as the center for several outstanding poets during the Renaissance. Georgia Douglas Johnson (frequently considered to be the immediate successor to Frances E.W. Harper), Angelina Grimké, Waring Cuney, and Sterling Brown formed a quartet that could not have been more effective if they had planned it. Both Johnson and Grimke couched their protests in beautiful lyrics which appeal first as poetry. Following the romantic tradition of Shelley and Keats, they were able to do what Countee Cullen did and artistically weave their racially-conscious poetry into poems of great merit. Of the two, Grimke was perhaps the better poet, but few can forget or overlook the appealing femininity of Johnson's collections *The Heart of A Woman* (1918), *Bronze* (1922), and *An Autumn Love Cycle* (1928).

In 1926 Waring Cuney submitted a short poem "No Images" to the *Opportunity* poetry contest and with the winning of the prize he received instant critical notice. Simple, yet innovative in twelve short lines, Cuney captures one aspect of the Negro woman's experience in America. Several years later Sterling Brown, a young English Instructor at Howard University, demonstrated his ability to use folk materials and the new idiom which had been popularized by James Weldon Johnson. Just as Langston Hughes was successful in doing, so Brown—in a series of tragi-comic and serious poems—was able to point out some of the ridiculous results of the racial situation in America. But perhaps no one did more to synthesize the Harlem Renaissance than Alain Locke also of Washington, D.C. It was he who collected its offerings and gave meaning through *The New Negro* of the period itself. Through Locke the writers better understood the significance of the movement of which they were a part as he simplified and codified its principles. He became the necessary interpreter for an important movement in American culture, a movement whose force might have been lost without Locke's perception.

Many of the writers now associated with the Harlem Renaissance were never residents of Harlem, but in one way of another they demonstrated either an interest in new forms or a sense of artistic race consciousness which was characteristic of the movement. At the same time there was a significant group of writers and artists in Harlem who worked together and who produced— perhaps unwittingly—a major contribution to American culture. For all of these people Harlem was both a symbol and a reality.

Of all of the members of the Harlem Renaissance no one writer was as consistently involved as James Weldon Johnson. As a forerunner of the movement he did as much as any writer to channel its direction. As a writer during the 1920's he put into practice the dominant philosophy of the period. And when the era had spent its force, as its historian he recorded its contributions to American literature for posterity. In 1900 he wrote "Life Every Voice and Sing" which was destined to become known as the Negro national anthem after J. Rosamond Johnson, his brother, composed the music. In 1917 he published *Fifty Years and Other Poems.* The idea expressed in the title poem, "Fifty Years"—a commemorative poem in honor of the fiftieth anniversary of the Emancipation Proclamation—emphasizes that Negroes are as much a part of the American experience as anybody else. As an integral part of the nation, they—according to Johnson—intend to work still harder to make the American dream come true. The poet also answers those critics who insisted that Negroes had a "place" which must be kept.

. . . .

For never let the thought arise
    That we are here on sufferance bare;
Outcasts, asylumed 'neath these skies,
    And aliens without part or share.

This land is ours by right of birth,
    This land is ours by right of toil;
We helped to turn its virgin earth,
    Our sweat is in its fruitful soil.

. . . .

No stand erect and without fear,
    And for our foes let this suffice—
We've bought a rightful sonship here,
    And we have more than paid the price.

. . . .

In 1922 he edited *The Book of American Negro Poetry* a pioneer anthology in a pioneer field. His long prefatory essay demonstrated his critical ability as well as his skill in the interpretation of the work of early Negro poets. By surveying the work of Negro poets from the beginning to the writers of his own day, he made it clear that Negroes had contributed to the growth and development of American literature. With the appearance of *God's Trombones* in 1927 he himself made an outstanding mark in the development of American poetry. Rejecting dialect as too limiting and accepting the role of the Negro preacher as one of the most significant in Negro life, he created seven sermons and a prayer which captured the rhythmic idiomatic sermons of the nineteenth-century preacher. Three years later in *Saint Peter Relates an Incident of the Resurrection Day* he was to demonstrate how American prejudice could be judiciously incorporated into a work of art.

While he is considered to be primarily a poet, Johnson did produce some notable prose. In 1912 he published *The Autobiography of an Ex-Coloured Man.* The novel enjoyed a degree of success. Its concern with the Negro problem served as a source book for later novelists who found in the story ideas for their own work. In many ways the novel seems reminiscent of the work of Chesnutt in its preoccupation with the problem of the "color line." The Harlem Renaissance provided the material for *Black Manhattan,* a novel which appeared in 1930. Even his autobiography *Along This Way* which was issued in 1933 is a significant document. Because of the positions held by Johnson he was in contact with all of the important people of his day. Not only does he record the history of the Harlem Renaissance in his autobiography but also he recounts episodes in the lives of many Negroes who did not themselves write of their experiences. Johnson's autobiography is in actuality the history of an age.

It is ironic that the writer who did more to give immediate voice to the Harlem Renaissance was not an American at all. Both DuBois and Johnson, of course, in one way or another had provided the necessary background to make such a literary movement possible, but it was the young man from Jamaica, Claude McKay, who became—by common critical consent—the first of a long line of distinguished poets of the period. The defiant pride which was to characterize much of the protest literature of the Harlem Renaissance is an important aspect of his work. Before coming to this country to study agriculture at Tuskegee Institute and at the University of Kansas, McKay had achieved a degree of success in Jamaica as a poet. *Songs of Jamaica,* a series of militant poems, had appeared in 1911, and the following year *Constab Ballads* appeared in London. Fascinated by the United States and by the possibility of a literary life, McKay soon forsook agriculture and moved to New York City. There he became associated with the literati of the period. After the war he journeyed to Europe, and during his year in London he published a small volume of poems entitled *Spring in New Hampshire* (1920). The lyrics of this volume were immediately successful, and when he returned to the United States, he became the associate editor of Max Eastman's *Liberator.* Clearly devoted and committed to the underprivileged Negro in this country, McKay used the pen to rail against prevailing social and economic conditions. In 1922 he published *Harlem Shadows,* and his poetic reputation was secure.

The ability of McKay to handle the language with insight and with poignancy is evident in all of his poems but most especially is this seen in "The Harlem Dancer." Here in a few masterful strokes McKay is able to develop the character of a single person by penetrating the brittle surface of an exterior hardened by circumstances.

> Applauding youths laughed with young prostitutes
> And watched her perfect, half-clothed body sway;
> Her voice was like the sound of blended flutes
> Blown by black players upon a picnic day.
> She sang and danced on gracefully and calm,
> The light gauze hanging loose about her form;
> To me she seemed a proudly-swaying palm
> Grown lovelier for passing through a storm.
> Upon her swarthy neck, black shiny curls
> Profusely fell; and, tossing coins in praise,

> The wine-flushed, bold-eyed boys, and even girls,
> Devoured her with their eager, passionate gaze;
> But looking at her falsely-smiling face,
> I knew her self was not in that strange place.

"If We Must Die" was written as an aftermath of the race riot of 1919 in Chicago. Although the casualty figures of the riot vary, it is generally agreed that the toll was large not only in terms of the more than thirty-eight killed or the six hundred injured or the more than 2,000 left homeless but also in terms of attitudes and the hardening of old-line prejudices. Perhaps this is one of the most artistically conceived protests of the Renaissance.

> If we must die—let it not be like hogs
> Hunted and penned in an inglorious spot,
> While round us bark the mad and hungry dogs,
> Making their mock at our accursed lot.
> If we must die—oh, let us nobly die,
> So that our precious blood may not be shed
> In vain; then even the monsters we defy
> Shall be constrained to honor us though dead!
> Oh, Kinsmen! We must meet the common foe;
> Though far outnumbered, let us show us brave,
> And for their thousand blows deal one death-blow!
> What though before us lies the open grave?
> Like men we'll face the murderous, cowardly pack,
> Pressed to the wall, dying, but fighting back!

Only occasionally did he write poetry after 1922 but rather turned his creative energies to prose. In 1928 he wrote *Home to Harlem,* a novel of Negro life in New York, and in 1929 *Banjo,* a novel set in France, was published. The same year saw the publication of *A Long Way from Home,* his autobiography, and *Harlem: Negro Metropolis,* a panoramic view of New York life in the Negro community. Five years after his death, there appeared his *Selected Poems,* a volume which includes some of his later work.

Literary experimentation was one of the dominant characteristics of the period which included the Harlem Renaissance, and among the innovators was Jean Toomer. In 1923 he published *Cane* and became a member of the Harlem group. *Cane* consists of a series of prose studies of Negro life executed realistically and a group of intricate lyrics. The combination of poetry and prose within a single volume gave the work a distinction which marked its author as one of the outstanding contributors to the era. The air of quiet dignity which pervades his work further heightened the sense of race-consciousness which is embodied in it.

With the publication of Countee Cullen's *Color* in 1925 there was the completion of the merger of the poetic protest movement with the lyric tradition. Nowhere did Americans read such excellent lyrics which sometimes were so subtle that the element of protest was lost on all but the most perceptive. While McKay used the sonnet form to great advantage, the anger of McKay was never in doubt. In the case of Cullen, however, his message is so finely-wrought that he emerged as one of the outstanding lyricists of the period. As a student at New York University where he was inducted into Phi Beta Kappa before receiving his baccalaureate degree in 1925 and then later at Harvard University where he received a master's degree in 1926, Cullen was primarily fascinated by the poetry of Shelley and Keats. And this romantic classicism is evident in all of his poetry as he used the traditional poetic forms in order to express his ideas. In an age devoted to literary innovation and experimentation, Cullen seems particularly staid, but in this same age through the use of old, established forms Cullen was able to give voice to the strivings and aspirations, the hopes and the fears, of the "New Negro."

In 1927 two other volumes of verse appeared: *The Ballad of the Brown Girl* and *Copper Sun*. During the same year he edited an anthology of Negro poetry entitled *Caroling Dusk*. Two years later he published *The Black Christ* whose title poem is the first and perhaps only attempt on the part of a Negro poet to produce an epic. Although "The Black Christ" is little more than a long narrative poem, Cullen interestingly used a lynching as the background of his action around which he introduced the type of characters which conceivably could be found in an epic. Although the language is stately and dignified as befits the language of an epic, the stateliness of the language seems strangely incongruous with the central action which tends to be associated with those who would be completely incapable of using such diction. The hero is a young Negro who has just returned from participation in World War I to his home in an unidentified section of the South. Ironically the man who has dodged bullets and mortar fire on the European front is incapable of escaping the inevitable lynchers' mob when he attempts to assert his rights as an American citizen, a citizen who has assumed his role in helping to make the "world safe for democracy." It is significant that Cullen, a sheltered young man who had been brought up in a Methodist parsonage, should have had the sensitivity to feel the fatalistic pull of human existence. In spite of his social and economic well-being Cullen demonstrates an awareness of the facets of life which is a more perceptive awareness than that of Claude McKay or Langston Hughes both of whom were far more "experienced" than Cullen.

Oftentimes Cullen is referred to as a classicist; he most certainly was knowledgeable about English poetic forms. *Copper Sun,* for example, contains the ballad stanza, heroic couplets, four-stress couplets, blank verse, and Spenserian stanzas; and he was probably the first American poet to use the rime royal made famous by Chaucer. On the other hand, Cullen might have become the outstanding romantic poet in America without any indication of race because he certainly had the disposition for romanticism. His tendency toward it was not the sentimental didactic variety, for he did not believe that poetry should preach—yet at the same time he was capable of merging profound messages in perfectly constructed art forms. At one point in his life he is reported to have said: "In spite of myself . . . I find that I am actuated by a strong sense of race consciousness. This grows upon me, I find, as I grow older, and although I struggle against it, it colors my writing, I fear, in spite of everything I can do (Bronz, *The Roots of Negro Racial Consciousness—the 1920's: Three Harlem Authors,* p. 68)."

The extent of artistic discipline during the Harlem Renaissance is evidenced by the fact that many poets took the greatly formalized sonnet and used it with great skill to produce protest poetry. This fact proves rather conclusively that an artistic form and a technique devoted to protest are not mutually exclusive. One has merely to note Cullen's "The Dark Tower" and Yet Do I Marvel" or McKay's "If We Must Die," "The White House," or "The Harlem Dancer" in order to see how well protest poetry could be finely wrought. And out of the merger of form and subject there developed a poetry which was rooted specifically to Negro oppression in this country but which went beyond the confines of a single racial protest in a single country to become applicable to all types of oppression everywhere. When Winston Churchill declared during the Second World War "Like men we'll face the murderous cowardly pack, Pressed to the wall, dying but fighting back," the Harlem Renaissance had indeed become a universal movement.

Langston Hughes was far more versatile than any other poet of the Harlem Renaissance, and his versatility became more and more obvious as he continued to produced in the years following the heyday of the Renaissance. Angry young man though he was in the 1920's, he had developed even then an ability to laugh at incidents and situations that had hitherto been subject for only the most serious kinds of discussions. Through his laughter he was able to evoke similar responses from his readers. In his more serious poetry this tendency produced a rather sardonic quality. Hughes refused to be circumscribed by existing poetic patterns. He maintained that poetic forms and traditions were meaningless. The subject of the poem was, according to Hughes, the only determining factors relative to establishing its form. Furthermore, he refused to accept the theory that only certain subjects were the fit area for the poet. He widened his range of subject possibilities and freed himself to look at anything. He is realistic in the sense that he reports life exactly as he sees it. Seldom does he adopt the pattern of Cullen and limit himself to a description of his feelings about life. Yet, Hughes could write outstanding lyrics which never sank to the mawkishly sentimental. And perhaps nowhere is his ability more graphically displayed than in "The Negro Speaks of Rivers," one of his early poems and one which demonstrates the degree to which he was influenced by the search for an ancestral home. At the same time he surveys the history of the Negro from Africa to America in a few short lines.

> I've known rivers:
> I've known rivers ancient as the world and older
>   than the flow of human blood in human veins.
>
> My soul has grown deep like the rivers.
>
> I bathed in the Euphrates when dawns were young.
> I built my hut near the Congo and it lulled me to sleep.
> I looked at the Nile and raised the pyramids above it.
> I heard the singing of the Mississippi when Abe Lincoln
>   went down to New Orleans, and I've seen its
>   muddy bosom turn all golden in the sunset.
>
> I've known rivers:
> Ancient dusky rivers.
> My soul has grown deep like rivers.

Just as James Weldom Johnson had done, Hughes also experimented with the Negro idiom in an attempt to capture a more authentic racial portrait. Instead, however, of using the nineteenth-century preacher Hughes turned his attention to the "blues" as a poetic pattern. His success might well be measured by the number of imitators who have attempted to use the blues form in poetry.

While she was interested in the poetry of the West Indies to the extent that she translated much of it from French into English and while she tried to write poetry, it is as the novelist of the growing Negro middle class that Jessie Redmond Fauset is best remembered. Through the use of rather typical characters in typical situations reacting in typical ways, she did a great deal toward showing that these characters were not substantially different from the average American. Through her novels she counteracted the idea that Negroes and Negro life had to be exotic in order to form the rationale for creativity. Although her novels are similar to a host of domestic novels which have been popular in this country, her essential racial pride is evident in all of her work.

In both *There Is Confusion* (1924) and *Plum Bun* (1929) she presents characters who "pass" because they cannot cope with the problems of American life, but in all cases she shows these characters in a greater state of confusion as these essential conflicts revolve around whether their choice has been a correct one. In her analysis of prejudice she includes not only the prejudice of the white man as it is directed against Negroes but she also includes the more deadly and more provoking prejudice of Negroes against Negroes. In *The Chinaberry Tree* (1931) and *Comedy: American Style* (1933) she continues to analyze the problem of race as it affects above-average families and as it becomes realized in their own preoccupations with matters of color. Tragic though these situations are, Fauset ultimately does not blame her characters for their own weaknesses rather she blames American society which so emphasizes the differences between the two races that these characters become victimized by it. Especially does she demonstrate in *Comedy: American Style* the tragic implications which arise when even a single member of the family becomes so engrossed with the idea of "color" that every other member is not permitted to live wholesome normal lives. Fauset appears to hold a mirror to these people in an attempt to portray what America has done to otherwise average people.

As the first modern Negro female novelist to achieve a degree of success, Jessie Fauset does not allow for the free will nor independent actions of her characters. With few exceptions they are caught within the maelstrom of American prejudice and react by attempting to join rather than battle their oppressors and oppressions. And she demonstrated how many of the condemned tactics employed by the white majority toward the Negro community are also used by light-skinned Negroes as they deal with their darker-skinned brothers. But all of this is a result not of inherent evil but rather of the system of American society which looks at the color of a man before it looks at his worth. In her portrayal of an educated, highly cultured group of the eastern seaboard, Fauset has presented some excellent case studies and brilliant characterizations. She did for the Negro novel what Howells had earlier done for the domestic novel in America. By using middle-class characters and by concerning herself with the commonplace and the ordinary she demonstrated that her characters were thoroughly American and that they were not different from any other character in a similar situation.

Walter White, who as a light-skinned Negro collected data in the South concerning lynchings and other atrocities committed against Negroes, also contributed to the realm of fiction of the Harlem Renaissance. Like Fauset, White used the rising middle-class to serve as his fictional vehicle, but he was probably more influenced by Chesnutt. Negro writers were fond of using the physician as the epitome of their social and professional worlds. Often these men had been educated in Europe as well as in America and had a great deal of appeal for women who were trying to gain status. There is a great similarity between Dr. Miller in Chesnutt's *The Marrow of Tradition* (1901) and Dr. Kenneth Harper in White's *Fire in the Flint* (1924). White's characters, like those of Jessie Fauset, "pass" not so much because they truly believe to live as a white man is better, but because they recognize they can avoid the problems of race in America.

Not only does *Fire in the Flint* present the catastrophic life among Negroes in the South but also *Flight* (1926) deals with the same theme. *Flight* is an excellent study of a young woman who is forced to flee Atlanta and its society because of an unwanted pregnancy. Once in New York and "passing" she is able to marry a distinguished white stockbroker, yet her entire life is made miserable by her longing for her own people. On the other hand, *Fire in the Flint* presents one of the ablest studies of the professional Negro in a hate-ridden small southern town and the ease with which lynchings take place. It characterizes fully the poor white into whose hands the fates and lives of so many Negroes fall.

Nella Larsen focuses her attention primarily upon the effects of "passing" upon female characters who—for a variety of reasons— are more apt to get caught up in this extremely ambivalent position. In both *Quicksand* (1928) and *Passing* (1929) she notes that the personal unhappiness of her characters who "pass" is not worth the sacrifice which they make when they leave their own people. Too frequently they are plagued by tremendous guilt feelings which make satisfactory adjustments impossible. And what do they really gain? As Fauset and White had made clear so Larsen also reveals that the gains are little in relationship to the losses. The tragedy of the mulatto who is a member of neither race and who can identify with neither is perhaps more clearly stated in the protagonist of *Quicksand,* Helga Crane, who spends a great deal of her time running from one group to another and eventually from one country to another. The protagonist of *Passing* successfully goes from one race to another, but once firmly established as the wife of a wealthy man she cannot stay away from her former associates and friends. Her desire to be a part of her race eventually leads to her loss of everything she had gained. The problems of "passing," primarily those of detection, are handled realistically and sympathetically.

The characters of Fauset, White, and Larsen who "pass" enjoy their new white world only briefly. In spite of the problems of Negro life, they do not hate their race and are miserable until they can get back to their own people. Often the characters became aware that the psychological problems which result from the possibility of "being found out" are not really worth the few moments in the white world where they really are not free from intensive fear of discovery.

Operating in the Van Vechten tradition with an emphasis upon the exotic and the primitive was Wallace Thurman whose descrip-

tions of Harlem portray the night life and gay parties so reminiscent of Van Vechten. In *The Blacker the Berry* (1929) he
demonstrates the effects of Negro prejudice upon other Negroes
and concludes that the darker the skin the greater is the need to
excel if one is to be accepted. Light-skinned Negroes, according to
Thurman, demand the same type of excellence from their darker
brothers as white people demand of Negroes in general.

In *Infants of the Spring* (1932) there is a full-length critical
study of the Harlem Renaissance. Because Thurman himself was
so personally involved, his satiric portraits are weakened by his
own obvious likes and dislikes. But in spite of these apparent flaws
he presents quite clearly the argument which raged during the
Renaissance and which is once again—in a large measure—applicable today. Should the Negro emphasize his continuity with
African culture and tradition or should he function totally within
the framework of American culture and institutions? If these fail,
should he then join forces with those dedicated to the defiance of
America by advocating peaceful—or violent if necessary—overthrow of the government? Or, ultimately should he attempt to live
the fullest life independent of all of these limiting concerns? From
all indications it is apparent that Thurman was not as enthusiastic
about the future of Negro literature neither was he too impressed
with the results of the writers of the Harlem Renaissance except
for the work of Jean Toomer who, it is claimed in *Infants of Spring,*
has "the elements of greatness." Writing in later years about the
movement Langston Hughes in his autobiography *The Big Sea* recounted the attitude of Wallace Thurman who felt that "the Negro
vogue had made all of us too conscious of ourselves, had flattered
and spoiled us, and had provided too many easy opportunities for
some of us to drink gin (p. 238)."

One of the outstanding naturalists of the Renaissance was Eric
Walrond who, like Claude McKay, used his native land as a basis
for some of his fiction. Walrond's major contribution to the fiction
of the period was *Tropic Death* (1926) which realistically portrays
the brutal forces which can operate against man. *Tropic Death*

consists of ten short narratives all of which deal with Negro life in the Carribean and all of which are related through their portrayal of some aspect of death. Throughout all of the stories the reader sees the natives being victimized either by each other but more often than not by overpowering physical and social forces. Interestingly enough, the stories gain power and force because of the objective portrayals of the author. While the volume might be considered a tremendous document of protest, Walrond himself does not voice a single protest; but by picturing a world where human life is almost worthless, he presents an eloquent statement on the types of situations which even permit this type of behavior. His volume further aided American Negroes in recognizing that their drive for justice and equality was not unique. By color and by deprivations resulting from color, they are associated with other darker peoples of the world. Unlike most of the writers of the period—with the exception of Jean Toomer and Claude McKay—who used urban settings, Walrond presented stories which were far removed from Harlem or from any other large urban center.

Rudolph Fisher wrote about the ordinary lives of ordinary people in Harlem. He was not concerned about the exotic nor the primitive. In *The Walls of Jericho* (1928) and in *The Conjure Man Dies* (1932) he describes realistically the host of respectable inhabitants of Harlem. He was very much convinced that those writers who described Harlem as one big cabaret party were as guilty of stereotyping as the white writers who were accused of racism. *The Conjure Man Dies* has the distinction of being the first Negro detective story; and while it is historically interesting, it is in his first novel that Fisher displays to great advantage his knowledge of the various social classes and types which abound in the Negro community.

When it was published in 1931, *Black No More* became one of the few full length satires in American Negro literature. Its author, George S. Schuyler, had developed the all too rare ability to poke fun not only at whites but also at blacks who took themselves seriously. The novel is dedicated "to all Caucasians in the great republic who can trace their ancestry back ten generations and confidently assert that there are no black leaves, twigs, limbs, or branches on their family trees." The discomfort occasioned by the improbability of the dedicatory statement is only heightened throughout the novel which is based on the story of "Black-No-More," a treatment whereby Negroes can be turned white. Its discover, Dr. Junius Crookman, is confident that he has found the real answer to the racial problems in America. The thousands of Negroes who travel to New York to receive Dr. Crookman's treatment look upon it as a means by which they can gain whatever personal desires can be achieved through skin whiteness. "Black-No-More" causes an instant withdrawal of members from racial organizations for the promise of being white eliminates the need to support such groups as the National Social Equality League, the Negro Data League, and the Back to Africa Society. These organizations are thinly disguised replicas of the Urban League, the N.A.A.C.P., and the Garvey movement. (Without exception Schuyler suggests that these organizations are more interested in promoting certain of its members but never the masses.) As the novel progresses, the South becomes totally frightened because the Negro exodus is proving to be disastrous to the economy and does all that it can to prevent Negroes from leaving to receive Dr. Crookman's "cure." But the South is practically abandoned. After a series of incidents and episodes which include the births of a number of dark-skinned babies to some outstanding southern whites, Dr. Samuel Buggerie, a renowned scientist, announces that more than fifty million white Americans have Negro blood. As this announcement is being understood, an even greater number of black babies are being born. Eventually Dr. Crookman claims—as a result of his own experimentation—that the real Caucasian is much darker than the pseudo ones who have been treated with "Black-No-More." His announcement leads people to suntanning and to any other activity which will bring out skin coloring. Throughout the entire work Schuyler points out the gross humor of a situation based solely upon color, and both races must share the blame for the stupidity of American society. The author pessimistically concludes that people, however, are basically mean, opportunistic, and hypocritical regardless of race.

Obviously there were both whites and Negroes who did not fully comprehend the significance of the Harlem Renaissance while it was in progress. There were those who looked upon the efforts of the white writers as being merely another example of the patronizing attitude which was so very often offensive. There were those who condemned the Negro writers as being mediocre and seizing any opportunity to get before an audience. Others looked upon all of these productions of the period as being unfortunate displays of the more dismal side of Negro life in America. Certainly, they claimed, the primitive elements nor the exotic elements should be dramatized. There should be more attempts made, these critics asserted, to portray the more ordinary and the more usual aspects of Negro life. While many of these critics were basing their objections on a subconscious denial of race, many were genuinely concerned lest that a false picture of Negro life enter into American culture. Stereotyping of any sort was not to be condoned. Many of these objections were answered by Hughes in his essay "The Negro Artist and the Racial Mountain," and the spirit of optimism which pervades the Hughes' article is representative of the period. There was a feeling that all things were indeed possible. And even though much of the work was a tacit protest against social, economic, and cultural ideas, the protest seldom was a pessimistic recognition that life in America was essentially hopeless. The millenium had not arrived, but there was a general feeling that its coming was imminent.

Although they seldom tend to discredit the movement, American literary histories have tended to ignore the Harlem Renaissance. Negro writers and artists, on the other hand, have obviously been more aware of its significance since much of what has been produced in later years has its immediate roots in some aspect of the movement. A study of Negro literature in America will reveal that the Renaissance represented more than a few years of intensified artistic activity, rather it summarized the activity which had its beginning in the first crude poems of Lucy Terry, Phillis Wheatley, and Jupiter Hammon and moved through the slave narratives and the spirituals, through the search for a distinctive form of expression in the nineteenth century, through the work of Douglass, Chesnutt, and Dunbar, and culminated in the novelists of the pre-World War I days. At the same time the Renaissance announced the themes and concerns which were to claim the attention of Richard Wright, Margaret Walker, Gwendolyn Brooks, Ralph Ellison, James Baldwin, and the host of men and women who are currently writing. So it was not a completely isolated age with its own peculiar form, with its own predetermined rationale. It was simply one stage in the developing continuum of the Negro artist in America or of the American artist who happened to be a Negro. True, it did gain a certain impetus from the post-war conditions, but these alone are nor sufficiently great or strong to explain the entire movement.

Sterling Brown recognized the scope of the period. In his address entitled "The New Negro in Literature (1925-1955)" which was subsequently published in *The New Negro Thirty Years Afterward* (Washington, D.C., 1955), he asserted:

I have hesitated to use the term Negro Renaissance for several reasons: one is that the five or six years generally allotted are short for the life-span of any 'renaissance.' The New Negro is not to me a group of writers centered in Harlem during the second half of the twenties. Most of the writers were not Harlemites; much of the best writing was not about Harlem, which was the show-window, the cashier's till but no more Negro American than New York is America. The New Negro had temporal roots in the past and spatial roots elsewhere in America, and the term has validity, it seems to me, only when considered to be a continuing tradition.

Ralph Ellison, on the other hand, did not view the Harlem Renaissance as a "continuing tradition" in spite of the fact that his work is spiritually related to that of this earlier period, neither did he find in it an element of success. Attacking the movement from the standpoint of its exoticism and emphasis upon the primitive, he declared in an interview which appeared in the March (1967) issue of *Harper's Magazine:*

The Negro writers who appeared during the 1920's wished to protest discrimination; some wished to show off their high regard for respectability; they wished to express their new awareness of the African background, and, as Americans trying to win a place as writers, they were drawn to the going style of literary decadence represented by Carl Van Vechten's work. This was an extremely ironic development for a group whose written literature was still in its infancy—as incongruous as the notion of a decadent baby. . . . So during the twenties we had wanted to be fashionable and this insured, even more effectively than the approaching Depression, the failure of the 'New Negro' movement.

Somewhere between the evaluations of Brown and Ellison rests the final judgment of the Harlem Renaissance which ultimately must be viewed in terms of events in American literature rather than as a separate phenomenon.

So much, of course, has been made of the period's exoticism and primitivism that it is frequently forgotten that the racial consciousness of the Harlem Renaissance did not artistically produce an "either/or" situation. The writers were able to begin at the points of their own experiences and to transcend those experiences to produce, in some cases, works of universal appeal. There really is no dichotomy for Negro poetry is in many ways the *most American* of all poetry in this country for it stresses the ideals and the dreams of America. Much of the poetry of the Renaissance is an affirmation of faith in the potential of the nation.

The Harlem Renaissance parallels in some ways the events of the 1960's in that as a collective movement of creative energy it did a great deal to make white America conscious of the contributions of American Negroes to the cultural life of the United States and at the same time it broke down many of the barriers which had earlier prevented publishers from accepting the work of Negro writers. Numerous magazines and journals devoted their pages to providing a forum for these new Negro voices. The spirit of the Harlem Renaissance addressed itself to the soul of the Negro in American life and was not a rebirth in the technical sense of the term but rather a synthesis of the various motifs which had existed earlier. Through the collective spirit engendered by the Renaissance there emerged a desire to be viewed as creators of at least a significant portion of American culture and a flat refusal to accept any racial stigma whether delivered by the well-meaning liberal or the white racist. The unscrupulous in both races did use the movement for selfish gains, but out of the collective positive approach there emerged what Alain Locke called "the New Negro" who was no longer culturally isolated. With the concerted effort made to study American Negro life objectively and to dispel old stereotypes, there was a more realistic portrayal of life in America. That the myths were difficult to eradicate is evidenced by the lack of recognition given to the movement among American literary historians and by the need in the 1960's to go over much the same material as was treated in the 1920's. But the movement did achieve an integrity of its own, an integrity which is now becoming apparent in the study of American culture.

Bibliographical Notes

In spite of the number of works dealing with the Negro in American life, the attempts to illustrate the Negro's role in American literature have been more limited than his contributions would warrant. These notes, which are suggestive rather than exhaustive, are intended for both the general reader as well as the scholar who might wish to do further research.

There are several bibliographies which are designed to aid the person interested in Negro life in America; among the most useful are:

Dumond, Dwight L. *A Bibliography of Antislavery in America.* Ann Arbor: University of Michigan Press, 1961.

Fuller, Juanita B. "An Annotated Bibliography of Biographies and Autobiographies of Negroes, 1839-1961." ACRL Microcard. Rochester, N.Y.: University of Rochester Press for the Association of College and Research Libraries, 1964.

Harlan, Louis R. *The Negro in American History.* Service Center for Teachers of History, Publication #61. Washington: American Historical Association, 1965.

Kessler, S. H. "American Negro Literature: A Bibliographical Guide." *Bulletin of Bibliography,* XXI (1955), 181-185.

Lash, John H. "The American Negro and American Literature: A Checklist of Significant Commentaries." *Bulletin* of Bibliography, XIX (1946-47), 12-15; 33-36.

Lewinson, Paul. *A Guide to Documents in the National Archives for Negro Studies.* Washington: American Council of Learned Societies Committee on Negro Studies, 1947.

Negro Bibliographic and Research Center, Inc. *Bibliographic Survey: The Negro in Print.* Washington: The Center, 1965-

New York Public Library. *The Negro in the United States: A List of Significant Books.* 9th rev. ed. New York: The Library, 1965.

Porter, Dorothy B. "Early American Negro Writings: A Biblio-
    graphical Study." *The Papers of the Bibliographical Society of
    America,* XXXIX (1945), 192-268.
————. *North American Negro Poets: A Bibliographical Check
    List of Their Writings (1760-1944).* Hattiesburg, Miss.: The Book
    Farm, 1945.
Welsch, Erwin K. *The Negro in the United States.* Bloomington:
    Indiana University Press, 1965.
Whiteman, Maxwell. *A Century of Fiction by American Negroes,
    1853-1952: A Descriptive Bibliography.* Philadelphia: Saifer, 1955.
Work, Monroe N. *A Bibliography of the Negro in Africa and
    America.* New York: Wilson, 1928.

Additional significant bibliographical materials can be found in
the issues of *The Journal of Negro History, The Negro History
Bulletin,* and *Phylon.* Most of the histories of Negro life contain
adequate bibliographical information, but the historian who presents the most exhaustive bibliography is John Hope Franklin
whose *From Slavery to Freedom* (New York, 1947), which has
gone through a series of editions since it was first published, is still
one of the best histories of Negro life in America.

I. A New Home in a New Land

There are many sources for materials dealing with the slave
trade. The following are well-written and provide objective, al-
though varying, studies of the period: Frederic Bancroft, *Slave-
Trading in the Old South* (Baltimore, 1931); Elizabeth Donnan,
*Documents Illustrative of the History of the Slave Trade to Amer-
ica,* 4 volumes (Washington, 1930-1935); W.E.B. DuBois, *The
Suppression of the African Slave-Trade to the United States of
America, 1638-1870* (New York, 1896); Melville J. Herskovits,
The Myth of the Negro Past (New York, 1941); Warren S. How-
ard, *American Slavers and the Federal Law, 1837-1862* (Berkeley,
1963); Daniel P. Mannix and Malcolm Cowley, *Black Cargoes:
A History of the Atlantic Slave Trade, 1518-1865* (New York,

1962); and Willis D. Weatherford, *The Negro from Africa to America* (New York, 1924).

One of the invaluable but little-used sources for early Negro history is the work of the Negro historian himself. An attempt was made by Earl Thorpe to survey Negro historiography in *Negro Historians in the United States* (Baton Rouge, 1958), but the deficiencies of his work become apparent as one reads the early historical works. Among the first Negro historians who were committed to telling the story of their own race, the following—while not easily accessible—made significant contributions to the study of Negro life in America. It should be noted, however, that there is now a growing tendency to reissue a number of the nineteenth-century documents pertaining to Negro life in America. Some of these have been republished by the Arno Press (New York) in *The American Negro: His History and Literature,* Series I (1968), Series II (1969), and Series III (1970). Many of these early recorders of life in America not only wrote history but also helped to make it: William G. Allen, *The American Prejudice Against Color: An Authentic Narrative, Showing How Easily the Nation Got into an Uproar* (London, 1853); William Wells Brown, *The Black Man: His Antecedents, His Genius, and His Achievements* (New York, 1863); Martin R. Delany, *The Condition, Elevation, Emigration, and Destiny of the Colored People of the United States,* Politically (Philadelphia, 1852); Edward Augustus Johnson, *History of Negro Soldiers in the Spanish American War and Other Items of Interest* (Raleigh, 1899) and *A School History of the Negro Race in America, from 1619 to 1890; with a Short Introduction as to the Origin of the Race; also a Short Sketch of Liberia* (Raleigh, 1891); William Cooper Nell, *The Colored Patriots of the American Revolution, with Sketches of Several Distinguished Colored Persons: to which is added a Brief Survey of the Condition and Prospects of Colored Americans* (Boston, 1855); William Still, *The Underground Railroad. A Record of Facts, Authentic Narratives, Letters, Etc., Narrating the Hardships, Hair-Breadth Escapes and Death Struggles of the Slaves in*

Their Efforts for Freedom, as Related by Themselves, and Others, or Witnessed by the Author; Together with Sketches of Some of the Largest Stockholders and Most Liberal Aiders and Advisers of the Road (Philadelphia, 1872); Booker T. Washington, *The Story of the Negro: The Rise of the Race From Slavery* in two volumes (New York, 1909); George Washington Williams, *History of the Negro Race in America, from 1619 to 1880* in two volumes (New York, 1883) and *A History of the Negro Troops in the War of the Rebellion, 1861-1865, Preceded by a Review of the Military Services of Negroes in Ancient and Modern Times* (New York, 1888); and Joseph Thomas Wilson, *Black Phalanx: A History of the Negro Soldiers of the United States in the Wars of 1776-1812, 1861-65* (Hartford, 1888).

Perhaps the evolution of Negro historiography can best be seen by comparing James W. C. Pennington's *Textbook of the Origin and History of the Colored People* (Hartford, 1841), one of the earliest historic efforts, with the twentieth-century historians whose work is more readily available. In addition to the work already cited by John Hope Franklin, other highly readable general accounts are provided by Benjamin Brawley, *A Short History of the American Negro* (New York, 1913); Merle R. Eppse, *The Negro, Too, in American History* (Chicago, 1939); Rayford Logan, *The Negro in the United States: A Brief History* (Princeton, 1957); and Carter G. Woodson and Charles H. Wesley, *The Negro in Our History*, tenth edition (Washington, 1962). Representative of the work of the younger historians is Lerone Bennett's *Before the Mayflower: A History of the Negro in America, 1619-1964* (Chicago, 1964).

Of the many existing specialized historical studies the general reader will probably find the following most useful: Philip Durham and Everett L. Jones, *The Negro Cowboys* (New York, 1965); John Hope Franklin, *The Militant South, 1800-1861* (Cambridge, 1956); Lorenzo J. Greene, *The Negro in Colonial New England, 1620-1776* (New York, 1942), Leon F. Litwack, *North of Slavery: The Negro in the Free States, 1790-1860* (Chicago, 1961);

Rayford Logan, *The Negro in American Life and Thought: The Nadir, 1877-1901* (New York, 1954) which appears in a Collier paperback as *The Betrayal of the Negro: From Rutherford B. Hayes to Woodrow Wilson* (1965); Benjamin Quarles, *The Negro in the American Revolution* (Chapel Hill, 1961); Kenneth Stampp, *The Peculiar Institution: Slavery in the Ante-Bellum South* (New York, 1956); and Richard C. Wade, *Slavery in the Cities: The South, 1820-1860* (New York, 1944).

During the nineteenth century there were many attempts made to record the histories of the growth of the Negro church and to assess the role of religion among both the enslaved and the free. Some of these studies are even more important today due to a general lack of information on the development of the church as a religious as well as a social and cultural force. In addition to the multitude of printed sermons of the period which frequently give some indication concerning the origin of the church and in addition to the printed works of Richard Allen and Absalom Jones, both the Methodist and Baptist churches hold significant repositories of documents dealing with the evolution of each denomination. Although there have been numerous twentieth-century studies of the role of the church such as E. Franklin Frazier's *The Negro Church in America* (New York, 1964), Benjamin Mays and Joseph W. Nicholson's *The Negro's Church* (New York, 1933), Willis D. Weatherford's *American Churches and the Negro: An Historical Study from Early Slave Days to the Present* (Boston, 1957), and Carter G. Woodson's *The History of the Negro Church* (Washington, 1945), there still seems to be a need for further research by scholars who have access to all of the church records and documents and who understand the polemics of the church itself. Before, of course, such research could be undertaken there would have to be a massive cataloging of the existing documents and papers which are currently being held by individual churches.

Specific efforts to study the beginning years of Negro American writing have been extremely limited. Much of the material dealing with American literature tends to overlook Negro writers or, when they are included, to restrict any analysis to a few names and dates. To gain any adequate knowledge of what occurred during the eighteenth and nineteenth centuries demands that even the general reader turn to the original sources. There have, however, been some general studies which are of value. Both Benjamin Brawley in his *The Negro Genius: A New Appraisal of the Achievement of the American Negro in Literature and the Fine Arts* (New York, 1937) and the later work by Margaret Just Butcher, *The Negro in American Culture* (New York, 1956) are concerned with the varying influences which affected the Negro creative artist in America. Less sympathetic and more given to the expression of personal prejudices is Vernon Loggin's *The Negro Author in America* (New York, 1931).

Not enough is known about the life and works of Jupiter Hammon. In addition to his works cited in the text the 1915 study entitled *Jupiter Hammon* by Oscar Wegelin might prove helpful as well as the article by Arthur A. Schomburg, "Jupiter Hammon before the New York African Society," *Amsterdam News,* January 22, 1930. Far more is known about Phillis Wheatley. For years she was considered the first Negro author in America until Oscar Wegelin cited Hammon's work in "Was Phillis Wheatley America's First Negro Poet?" in the August (1904) issue of *The Literary Collector.* Wheatley was the subject for numerous nineteenth-century studies, and her name appears in the outstanding literary histories of that period. Much of this nineteenth-century scholarship has been summarized in Julian Mason's edition of *The Poems of Phillis Wheatley* (Chapel Hill, 1966), but for the best early study of her work see B. B. Thatcher, *Memoir of Phillis Wheatley, a Native African and a Slave* (1834). Benjamin Banneker, whose relation to literature is tangential, has been the subject of several studies; however, a thorough comparative study of his almanacs with those of the period has not as yet been made. The following works are valuable background information for a study of Banneker: Will W. Allen, *Banneker, the Afro-American*

Astronomer (1921); Henry E. Baker, "Benjamin Banneker, the Negro Mathematician and Astronomer," *Journal of Negro History,* III (April, 1918), 99-119; M. D. Conway, "Benjamin Banneker," *Atlantic Monthly,* XI (January, 1863), 79-84; and Martha E. Tyson, *Banneker, the Afric-American Astronomer* (1884).

David Walker's short life is presented by Henry Highland Garnet in his 1848 edition of *The Appeal . . .* , but no study has been made of the possible influence of David Walker upon the various protest movements of the nineteenth century. The writings of such men as Paul Cuffee, Prince Saunders, and James Forten were purely utilitarian as each tried to convince audiences of the efficacy of a specific cause. Their biographies and work are best treated by Richard Bardolph, *The Negro Vanguard* (New York, 1959), pp. 31-51 *passim;* Vernon Loggins, *The Negro Author* (New York, 1931), and Dorothy B. Porter, "Early American Negro Writings: A Bibliographical Study," *The Papers of the Bibliographical Society of America,* XXXIX (1945), 212-214 *passim.*

Still further research is needed on the growth and development of Negro newspapers and magazines. While Negro journalism is primarily associated with the protest movements of various periods, even such early journals as *Freedom's Journal* and Douglass' *North Star* furnished an outlet for the works of writers who did not appear in the white journals of the day. Throughout the history of the Negro press there has been some concern with the presentation of the Negro as a creative artist. While it is true that these journals and papers were often short-lived, they served a useful purpose as the means by which ideas were communicated within a rather restricted community. At the same time many of the poets and writers of fiction who appeared in these ephemeral publications demonstrated talent and ability. Ultimately no story of Negro writing in America can be completed without delving into the pages of these nineteenth-century publications. Still one of the best analyses of the Negro press is the work by Frederick G. Detweiler, *The Negro Press in the United States* (Chicago, 1922).

II. *The Spiritual and Its Poetic Tradition*

While the spiritual was apparently an early nineteenth-century development, few references appear concerning them outside of the slave narratives and the travel books which often mention the music of the slaves. The first attempts to collect or to analyze them appear in the 1860's. *Slave Songs of the United States* (New York, 1867), compiled by William F. Allen, Charles P. Ware, and Lucy McKim Garrison, is highly significant. The book contains a limited number of songs, but in a well-developed prefatory essay the musical elements of the spirituals and the language of them are analyzed. In spite of the fact that the compilers were primarily interested in the Port Royal area (since South Carolina was thought to be the locale of the origin of many of the spirituals), there is an analysis of the dialect of the songs which furnishes a pattern by which dialect can generally be studied. Perhaps the most outstanding collections of spirituals were edited by James Weldon Johnson and his brother, J. Rosamond Johnson. *The Book of American Negro Spirituals* first appeared in 1925, and *The Second Book of Negro Spirituals* appeared in 1926. There have been other collections, editions, and songbooks, but the introductory essays by the Johnsons remain classic statements of the role of the spiritual not only in American music but also in Negro life in this country. These books edited by the Johnsons were subsequently issued by the Viking Press in 1940 as *The Books of American Negro Spirituals,* a paperback version of which was issued in 1969.

After the spirituals were introduced on a national and international scale by the Jubilee Singers of Fisk University, there were a series of arguments which developed concerning their creation and their significance. Various aspects of the arguments can be found in the works of Richard Wallaschek, W.E.B. DuBois, Henry E. Krehbiel, Guy B. Johnson, Newman White, and George Pullen Jackson. The African elements of the spirituals have been lucidly presented by Miles Mark Fisher in his *The Slave Songs in the United States* first published in 1953. Fisher also deals with the spirituals as coded messages. The creation of the spirituals cannot be reduced in simplistic terms to either a carry-over of an African tradition or an imitation of white spirituals. Needless to say, one of the difficulties in the interpretation of them rests upon the fact that few of them exist in their first forms. The study of the poetic elements of the spirituals has not as yet received the attention which it merits. Frequently an editor or a critic might make a passing reference to the use of a given symbol within a single song, but the idea of the spirituals as examples of primitive poetry needs further study and amplification. The essential religious tradition of the spirituals is carried over into much of the poetry written by American Negroes. And this area, also, needs further analysis.

III. *"We Hold These Truths to be Self-Evident . . .":*
The Prose of Freedom

The dates given for the selected slave narratives in the chapter represent the edition used and not necessarily the first edition of the work. Neither does the discussion in the text indicate the extensiveness of the form. Out of the hundreds of extant narratives the chapter merely notes a few which are intended to give the general reader an idea about this type of American writing.

There have been two excellent doctoral dissertations which deal with the subject of the slave narratives. Charles H. Nichols' "A Study of the Slave Narrative" was done at Brown University, 1948. Since that time he has published *Many Thousand Gone: The Ex-Slaves' Account of their Bondage and Freedom* (Leyden, 1963) and which appeared as a paperback from Indiana University Press in 1969. The other dissertation was completed at Cornell University by Margaret Young Jackson in 1954. Entitled "An Investigation of Biographies and Autobiographies of American Slaves Published Between 1840 and 1860: Based Upon the Cornell Special Slavery Collection," the work demonstrates the great frequency with which these works appeared.

The Schomburg Collection of the New York Public Library

contains the largest single collection of slave narratives; however, there are some existing in university libraries as well as in state historical societies. Another large collection is to be found in the seventeen-volume typescript compilation, "Slave Narratives: A Folk History of Slavery in the United States from Interviews with Former Slaves," completed by the Federal Writers' Project in 1941. Benjamin A. Botkin's *Lay My Burden Down: A Folk History of Slavery* (Chicago, 1945) also contains some short narratives. The antislavery journals of the nineteenth century published accounts of ex-slaves' escapes from bondage, but the book-length narratives are far more revealing in terms of style and technique.

In the last few years interest has been rekindled in the slave narrative, and there have appeared several interesting works relative to it such as: Solomon Northrup's *Twelve Years A Slave* first published in 1853 and now edited by Sue Eakin and Joseph Logsdon (Baton Rouge, 1968); Gilbert Osofsky's *Puttin' On Ole Massa* (New York, 1969) which contains the narratives of Henry Bibb, William Wells Brown, and Solomon Northup; and Robin W. Winks' *Four Fugitive Slave Narratives* (Reading, Mass., 1969) which contains the work of Josiah Henson, William Wells Brown, Austin Steward as well as Benjamin Drew's *The Refugee: A North-Side View of Slavery*. Each work is prefaced by an excellent introduction. The Arno Press' presentation of Series I, II, and III of *The American Negro: His History and Literature* has issued the narratives of William and Ellen Craft, Elizabeth Keckley, John Mercer Langston, Daniel A. Payne, and Samuel Ringgold Ward as well as Theodore Dwight Weld's 1839 volume *American Slavery As It Is: Testimony of a Thousand Witnesses* which contains several slave narratives.

The slave narrative was not the only prose form to gain a high degree of circulation during the nineteenth century. That much of the prose was occasional is evidenced by the concern with immediate problems and situations. But out of this utilitarian writing one can draw some conclusions about the nature of the works as well as the commitment of the writers. For the reader who is interested in the work of free Negroes in the early years of the nineteenth century, the minutes, proceedings, and records of the various conventions which were called provide excellent repositories of the essays and orations of the leading thinkers of the day. These annual conventions were prompted by different groups in order to effect not only the end of slavery in the South but also the cessation of the flagrant discriminatory practices of the North. The coldly logical aproach of these black men to their own problems is often in direct contrast to the emotionalism of many of the white abolitionists of the same period. A comparative approach to these two groups might yield congent analyses of the general abolition movement in the United States. Howard H. Bell has edited *The Minutes of the Proceedings of the National Negro Conventions: 1830-1864* (New York, 1969); however, various church organizations might reveal holdings larger than any which even Bell has imagined.

IV. And the Poets Came Forth: Tendencies in Nineteenth-Century Negro Poetry

Very little research has been done on the poets of the period, and few full-length studies exist. Much of the poetry appeared in such journals as *The Liberator*. Perhaps the most extensive survey of nineteenth-century poetry has been done by Vernon Loggins.

The story of George Moses Horton, for example, has to be put together from a variety of sources, the most notable being his own introductions to his published works. In addition valuable information is to be gained from Stephen B. Weeks, "George Moses Horton: Slave Poet," *Southern Workman*, XLIII (October, 1914), 571-577. Horton's life on the campus of the University of North Carolina is described by Kemp B. Battle in the first volume of *The History of the University of North Carolina* (1901). Generally speaking, the dearth of materials on the poets of the nineteenth century might lead one to imagine that there was little or no poetic activity. But such was not the case. The work of Negro poets appeared frequently in the press and periodicals of the day. Of the poets cited in this chapter much information can be gained from their own prefatory statements to their works. In the twentieth century still the best source of the works of many of these poets is *The Negro Caravan,* edited by Sterling A. Brown, Arthur P. Davis, and Ulysses Lee, which was first published in 1941; however, a reprint of the edition appeared in 1969. Other adequate anthologies are Victor F. Calverton, ed., *Anthology of American Negro Literature* (New York, 1929); Herman Dreer, *American Literature by Negro Authors* (New York, 1950); and Sylvester C. Watkins, ed., *Anthology of American Negro Literature* (New York, 1944).

V. The Masking of the Poet

The tragedy of Paul Laurence Dunbar is in a large measure the tragedy of the Negro writer in America. Up to the time of Dunbar there had been—relatively speaking—greater integration of the Negro writer in the so-called "mainstream" of American literature. This is borne out by the number of Negro writers who appear in nineteenth-century anthologies and critical studies but who are absent from the twentieth-century counterparts of these works. When Dunbar appeared, the Civil War was over, America was going through the period which Rayford Logan calls "The Nadir," and a new attitude emerged concerning Negro creativity, an attitude destined to penalize the writer and frustrate the artist, an attitude against which the writers of the Harlem Renaissance revolted. Some of these problems are treated by J. Saunders Redding in *To Make a Poet Black* (Chapel Hill, 1939).

The existing Dunbar scholarship usually emphasizes the poet's contribution to dialect studies and almost uniformly neglects his work in standard English. Much needs to be done with his non-dialect poems as well as with his fiction which, while not always great, is cast in the mold of the sentimental fiction which was so popular in the closing years of the nineteenth century. Furthermore, *The Sport of the Gods* (1902) needs to be re-interpreted in light of the naturalistic tendencies which Dunbar used. It may well be that had Dunbar lived longer he would have adopted naturalism as his *modus operandi*. One of the earliest attempts to assess his value was done by Lida Keck Wiggins in *Life and Works* which includes Dunbar's complete poetical works, his best short stories, numerous testimonies from those who knew him, and a complete biography (Naperville, Ill., 1907). Still a classic of Dunbar criticism is Benjamin Brawley's *Paul Laurence Dunbar* (Chapel Hill, 1936). A cursory knowledge of Dunbar has been more widespread than that of many of his predecessors, but even here there have been serious restrictions.

Not only does Dunbar's fiction need additional investigation in order to establish his relationship to American romanticism, realism, and naturalism, but also needing further study is the plantation tradition in American literature as it relates directly to Negro writers. The white writers who used this technique re-enforced a popular post-Civil War attitude concerning the relationship of slave to master. From 1876 to 1900 Joel Chandler Harris was associated with the Atlanta *Constitution*. The Uncle Remus stories were first published in this newspaper and later in a collected edition (1880). *Uncle Remus, his Songs and Sayings* was hailed throughout the nation as the "true" picture of plantation life. In a large measure the plantation tradition in American literature was perpetuated by the work of Harris whose career has been analyzed by Stella Brewer Brooke, *Joel Chandler Harris: Folklorist* (Athens, Ga., 1950). In view of the fact, however, that the writers of many of the early slave narratives used the animal stories Harris' works need to be re-evaluated. Furthermore, Harris' emphasis upon the docile happy slave does much to foster a false image of plantation life. Yet the popularity of Harris is attested to by the number of editions of his works which appeared during his lifetime and the frequency with which reprints have been issued since his death. Much of the work of George William Bagby has been lost; however, his daughter did edit *The Old Virginia Gentle-man, and Other Sketches.* He too was instrumental in fostering the portrait of the plantation tradition and presented romantic views of life in Virginia prior to the Civil War as well as pictures of happy contented slaves. The bulk of Bagby's work, which appeared in Virginia newspapers, was published originally between 1854 and 1882. As a southerner Thomas Nelson Page felt it necessary to defend the South and to recapture what he thought were the glorious days before the Civil War. Unlike Sidney Lanier, who had been a Confederate soldier and who had also used dialect in some of his poems dealing with Georgia, Page emphasized the contentment of plantation life. Lanier, on the other hand, became committed after the war to healing the wounds of war by stressing the need for *one* nation rather than two sections. In both *In Ole Virginia* (1887), a group of short stories and sketches, and in *The Old South: Essays Social and Political* (1892) Page presented the South as the aggrieved party and the Negro as being far happier while in slavery. Because Page had the ability to write well and to convince through his use of logical reasoning, his books were extremely popular in the North as well as in the South. Despite his well-known biases Page became an "authority" on race relations in America. His work is another illustration of the methodology employed by the practitioners of the plantation tradition. Irwin Russell's major place in American literature is as the poet of "Christmas Night in the Quarters." Of all of the writers within the plantation tradition Russell perhaps demonstrates the greatest personal sympathy with his characters, but his use of dialect and "Negro" subjects did much to degrade the people about whom he wrote. Although he must be considered among the minor writers in American literature, he was among the first to use this type of dialect in poetry. Born in Mississippi, Russell did not portray the "elegance" associated with plantation life of Virginia. His collected works appeared after his death which occurred in 1879.

While these white writers were becoming popular with the plantation tradition, there developed a barrier to the communication of ideas by Negro poets and writers of fiction. And the career of Dunbar was caught in the vise of this developing negativism.

V. The Art of the Storyteller

Still the most objective and lucid full-length study of the Negro writers of fiction is Hugh Gloster's *Negro Voices in American Fiction* (Chapel Hill, 1948). The more recent study by Robert Bone, *The Negro Novel in America* (New Haven, 1958), lacks the perception necessary to understand the role of the Negro storyteller in his community. Both works furnish excellent bibliographies for further reading. Among the many evaluations of the Negro novel are Eugene Arden, "The Early Harlem Novel," *Phylon,* XX (1959), 25-31; T. C. Cochran, "White Stereotypes in Fiction by Negroes," *Phylon,* XI (1950), 252-256; Nick A. Ford, *The Contemporary Negro Novel: A Study in Race Relations* (Boston, 1936); and Charles I. Glicksberg, "Negro Fiction in America," *South Atlantic Quarterly,* XLV (1946), 477-488.

There is also a need to study further the short fiction of the nineteenth century and early years of the twentieth. As in the case of poetry one of the best sources for the works are the many journals of the period where these stories often appeared. John H. Clarke in "Transition in the American Negro Short Story," *Phylon,* XXI (1960), 360-366, does attempt briefly to survey some dominant trends discernible in the shorter works.

VII. Another Declaration of Independence: A View of the Harlem Renaissance

The most fertile sources of information on this highly significant movement of the 1920's come from the writers and artists who were intricately involved in the productivity of the period. Such men as James Weldon Johnson, George Schuyler, and Wallace Thurman were highly perceptive and were gifted with the ability of self-criticism. But nowhere does the period receive greater articulation than in the work of Alain Locke. His edition of *The New*

Negro (New York, 1925) set forth the creative principles of the period. Few full-length studies have been done on the individuals closely associated with the movement. A notable exception is Blanche E. Ferguson's *Countee Cullen and the Negro Renaissance* (New York, 1966).

The perusal of such journals as *Opportunity* and *Crisis* will reveal the productivity of the writers during this period. Ultimately the history of the Harlem Renaissance must rest with the scholars who have the resources to examine carefully the magazines of the period. While the role of Marcus Garvey has been the subject of numerous essays and of Edmund Cronon's *Black Moses: The Story of Marcus Garvey and the Universal Negro Improvement Association* (Madison, 1955), there still needs to be a study made of his relationship to the Renaissance itself. The similarity between the Harlem Renaissance and the "Black Is Beautiful" movement of the 1960's is singularly striking. And in time a series, no doubt, of worthwhile comparative studies of the two periods can be written.

Illustrations

Job, Son of Solliman Dgiallo, High Priest
of Bonda in the Country of Foota, Africa.

ILLUSTRATION 1.—Title page of the 1734 edition of *Some Memoirs of the Life of Job,* one of the earliest biographies of its type (from the Collection of The Library Company of Philadelphia)

THE

INTERESTING NARRATIVE

OF

THE LIFE

OF

OLAUDAH EQUIANO,

OR

GUSTAVUS VASSA,

THE AFRICAN.

WRITTEN BY HIMSELF.

VOL I.

Behold, God is my salvation; I will trust and not be afraid, for the Lord Jehovah is my strength and my song; he also is become my salvation.
And in that day shall ye say, Praise the Lord, call upon his name, declare his doings among the people. Isaiah xii. 2, 4.

LONDON:

Printed for and sold by the AUTHOR, No. 10, Union-Street, Middlesex Hospital;

Sold also by Mr. Johnson, St. Paul's Church-Yard; Mr. Murray, Fleet-Street; Messrs. Robson and Clark, Bond-Street; Mr. Davis, opposite Gray's Inn, Holborn; Messrs. Shepperson and Reynolds, and Mr. Jackson, Oxford-Street; Mr. Lackington, Chiswell-Street; Mr. Mathews, Strand; Mr. Murray, Prince's-Street, Soho; Mess. Taylor and Co. South Arch, Royal Exchange; Mr. Button, Newington-Causeway; Mr. Parsons, Paternoster-Row; and may be had of all the Booksellers in Town and Country.

[Entered at Stationer's Hall.]

ILLUSTRATION 2.—Title page of Vassa's autobiography, an early slave narrative (from the Historical Society of Pennsylvania) This work is significant in part because it indicates the evolving spirit of independence which was evident among many slaves by the end of the eighteenth century. The work was first published in 1789 and by 1794 at least eight other editions had been circulated.

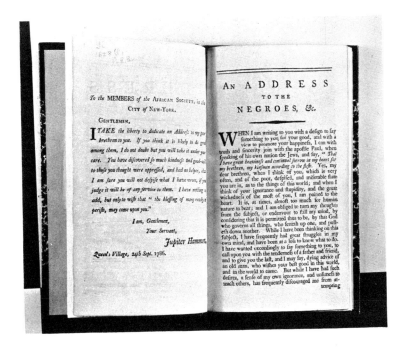

ILLUSTRATION 3.—Jupiter Hammon's *An Address to the Negroes in the State of New York* is frequently used to indicate Hammon's satisfaction with his slave condition because in this speech he sets up the obligations of the slaves to obey their masters. At the same time the work echoes his own belief in the futility of seeking freedom without the preparation for it. His awareness of the inconsistency of bondage with the principles of Christianity is subtly presented. (from the Collection of The Library Company of Philadelphia)

PHOTO-ILLUSTRATORS OF PHILADELPHIA, PENNSYLVANIA

ILLUSTRATION 4.—1770 broadside printing of Phillis Wheatley's poem in memory of George Whitefield (from the Collection of The Library Company of Philadelphia)

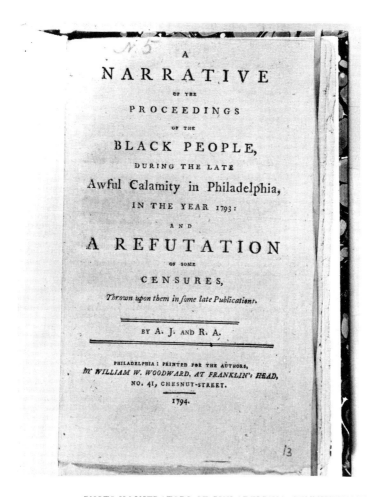

ILLUSTRATION 5.—Title page of an early historical work by Absalom Jones and Richard Allen in which they refute the charges made by Mathew Carey that Negroes did nothing to aid in the 1793 yellow fever epidemic in Philadelphia. *A Narrative of the Proceedings of the Black People . . .* recounts the horrendous, and often thankless, tasks performed by Negroes in Philadelphia during the disaster. Jones and Allen used this experience to substantiate their belief that Negroes were ready for total freedom in both the South and in the North. (from the Collection of The Library Company of Philadelphia)

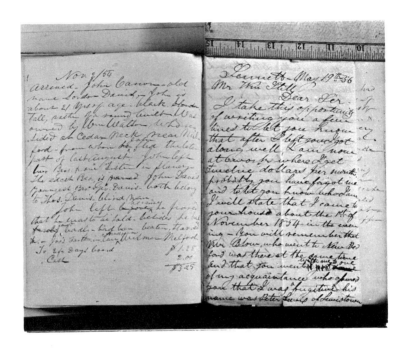

PHOTO-ILLUSTRATORS OF PHILADELPHIA, PENNSYLVANIA

ILLUSTRATION 6.—Entries from the Manuscript Journal of Fugitive Slaves maintained by William Still (from the Historical Society of Pennsylvania) The Entry of November 2, 1854 and a portion of a letter dated May 19, 1856 indicate the care with which William Still, an important figure in the Underground Railroad, kept a record of the slaves with whom he had contact. Eventually much of this information was used in his *The Underground Railroad . . .* (1872).

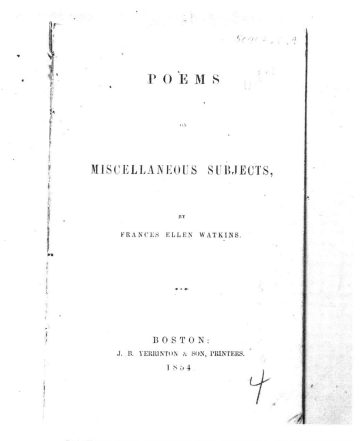

ILLUSTRATION 7.—Title page of the 1854 volume by Frances Ellen Watkins Harper (from the Collection of The Library Company of Philadelphia)

During the nineteenth century Mrs. Harper was considered to be one of the outstanding poets. Her *Poems on Miscellaneous Subjects,* which went through a series of editions, included not only anti-slavery verse but also religious poetry. Before the Civil War she was an ardent abolitionist who spent a great deal of time traveling in northern communities as a lecturer. After the war she turned her attention to a number of other "causes." Although much of her poetry is reminiscent of the work of Longfellow, she did make a contribution to the development of Negro poetry.

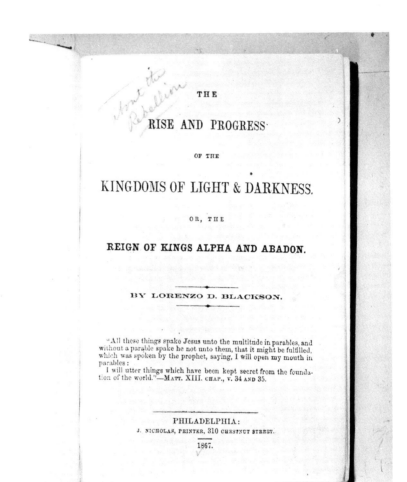

THE

RISE AND PROGRESS·

OF THE

KINGDOMS OF LIGHT & DARKNESS.

OR, THE

REIGN OF KINGS ALPHA AND ABADON.

BY LORENZO D. BLACKSON.

"All these things spake Jesus unto the multitude in parables, and without a parable spake he not unto them, that it might be fulfilled, which was spoken by the prophet, saying, I will open my mouth in parables:
I will utter things which have been kept secret from the foundation of the world."—MATT. XIII. CHAP., v. 34 AND 35.

PHILADELPHIA:
J. NICHOLAS, PRINTER, 310 CHESTNUT STREET.

1867.

ILLUSTRATION 8.—Title page of Blackson's long allegorical work which is a combination of poetry and prose. In style and scope the work is similar to Bunyan's *Pilgrim's Progress.* (from the Collection of The Library Company of Philadelphia)

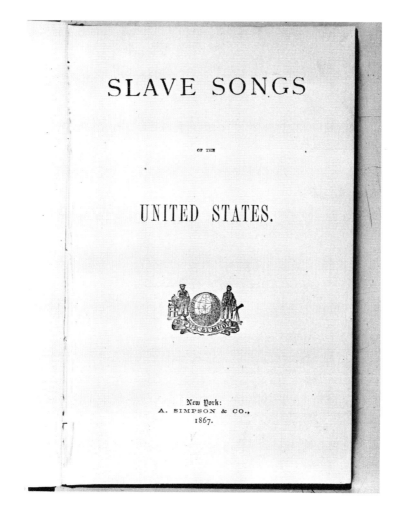

SLAVE SONGS

OF THE

UNITED STATES.

New York:
A. SIMPSON & CO.,
1867.

ILLUSTRATION 9.—Title page of the Allen, McKim, and Garrison 1867 edition of the spirituals, the first such collection of slave songs to be made (from the Collection of The Library Company of Philadelphia)

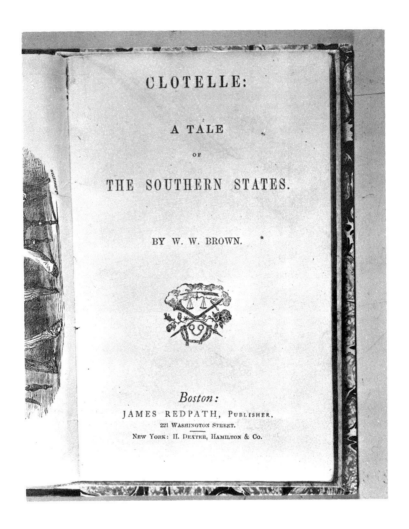

ILLUSTRATION 10.—The title page of the American edition (1864) of the first novel by an American Negro (from the Collection of The Library Company of Philadelphia)
Clotelle . . . was first published in England (1853) as *Clotel: Or, The President's Daughter* and gained notoriety for its use of Thomas Jefferson as the father of Clotel by his slave mistress. In the American editions Jefferson was replaced by an unnamed U.S. Senator.

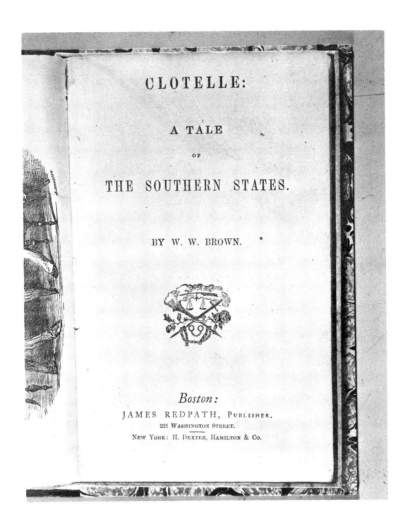

CLOTELLE:

A TALE

OF

THE SOUTHERN STATES.

BY W. W. BROWN.

Boston:
JAMES REDPATH, Publisher.
221 Washington Street.
New York: H. Dexter, Hamilton & Co.

PHOTO-ILLUSTRATORS OF PHILADELPHIA, PENNSYLVANIA

ILLUSTRATION 10.—The title page of the American edition (1864) of the first novel by an American Negro (from the Collection of The Library Company of Philadelphia)
Clotelle . . . was first published in England (1853) as *Clotel: Or, The President's Daughter* and gained notoriety for its use of Thomas Jefferson as the father of Clotel by his slave mistress. In the American editions Jefferson was replaced by an unnamed U.S. Senator.

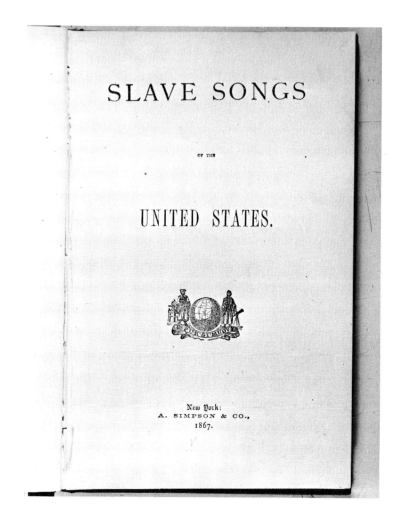

SLAVE SONGS

OF THE

UNITED STATES.

New York:
A. SIMPSON & CO.,
1867.

PHOTO-ILLUSTRATORS OF PHILADELPHIA, PENNSYLVANIA

ILLUSTRATION 9.—Title page of the Allen, McKim, and Garrison 1867 edition of the spirituals, the first such collection of slave songs to be made (from the Collection of The Library Company of Philadelphia)

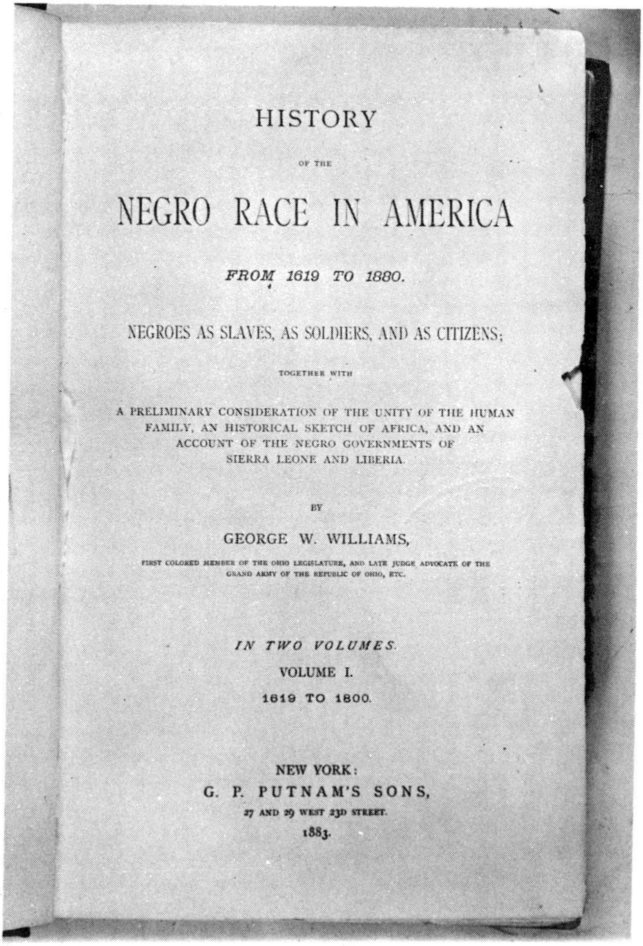

HISTORY

OF THE

NEGRO RACE IN AMERICA

FROM 1619 TO 1880.

NEGROES AS SLAVES, AS SOLDIERS, AND AS CITIZENS;

TOGETHER WITH

A PRELIMINARY CONSIDERATION OF THE UNITY OF THE HUMAN FAMILY, AN HISTORICAL SKETCH OF AFRICA, AND AN ACCOUNT OF THE NEGRO GOVERNMENTS OF SIERRA LEONE AND LIBERIA.

BY

GEORGE W. WILLIAMS,

FIRST COLORED MEMBER OF THE OHIO LEGISLATURE, AND LATE JUDGE ADVOCATE OF THE GRAND ARMY OF THE REPUBLIC OF OHIO, ETC.

IN TWO VOLUMES.

VOLUME I.

1619 TO 1800.

NEW YORK:
G. P. PUTNAM'S SONS,
27 AND 29 WEST 23D STREET.
1883.

PHOTO-ILLUSTRATORS OF PHILADELPHIA, PENNSYLVANIA

ILLUSTRATION 11.—Title page of Volume I of George Williams' significant nineteenth-century history (from the Collection of The Library Company of Philadelphia)

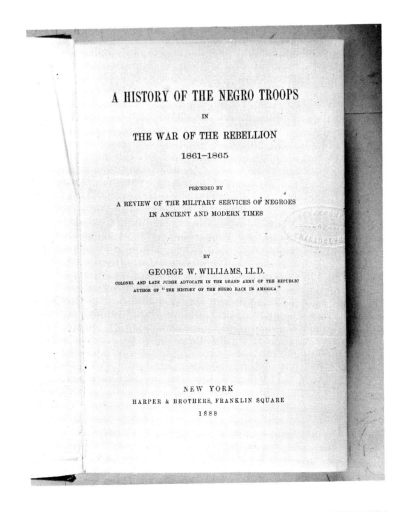

A HISTORY OF THE NEGRO TROOPS

IN

THE WAR OF THE REBELLION

1861–1865

PRECEDED BY

A REVIEW OF THE MILITARY SERVICES OF NEGROES
IN ANCIENT AND MODERN TIMES

BY

GEORGE W. WILLIAMS, LL.D.

COLONEL AND LATE JUDGE ADVOCATE IN THE GRAND ARMY OF THE REPUBLIC
AUTHOR OF "THE HISTORY OF THE NEGRO RACE IN AMERICA"

NEW YORK
HARPER & BROTHERS, FRANKLIN SQUARE
1888

PHOTO-ILLUSTRATORS OF PHILADELPHIA, PENNSYLVANIA

ILLUSTRATION 12.—Title page of George Williams' military history which emphasizes the role of the Negro soldier during the Civil War Although not permitted in the Union Army initially, Negroes sought the right to enlist. Frederick Douglass was one of the outstanding recruiters. Williams, who wrote his history from the available documents of the period, stressed the participation of the Negro troops in more than 250 encounters and the extensive losses which they suffered. (from the Collection of The Library Company of Philadelphia)

INDEX